W9-CLE-280

Advance Praise for *So Much to Do*

"Dick Ravitch has been making impossible dreams come true for millions of Americans for over half a century. His book is a riveting trip through the bone-crushing political and fiscal crises he's handled, and a refreshing reminder that—with dedicated and street smart leadership—politics and government can work for all the people."

—Joseph A. Califano Jr., top domestic aide to President Lyndon B. Johnson and former US secretary of health, education, and welfare

"In schools of business, government, and politics, *So Much to Do* should be required reading. It is a textbook for everyone interested in leading a full, purposeful life: A primer and testament to how one can do well while doing good. And given what it has to say about the fiscal challenges to cities, states, and the federal government, it couldn't be more timely."

—Dan Rather, journalist

"How does government actually get things done—when it does? How do fiscal crises get resolved? How do subway systems get fixed? How do dreams of urban development turn into new centers of civic vitality? Dick Ravitch knows, not just because he has seen it happen, but because he has made it happen. Anyone who wants to know how public servants really serve will enjoy the ride with this amazing entrepreneur."

—Richard Tofel, president, *ProPublica*

SO MUCH TO DO

A Full Life of Business, Politics, and Confronting Fiscal Crises

Richard Ravitch

PublicAffairs
New York

Published in the United States by PublicAffairs™, a Member of the
Perseus Books Group

Printed in the United States of America.

PublicAffairs books are available at special discounts for bulk purchases in the US
by corporations, institutions, and other organizations. For more information, please
contact the Special Markets Department at the Perseus Books Group, 2300
Chestnut Street, Suite 200, Philadelphia, PA 19103, call (800) 810-4145, ext. 5000,
or e-mail special.markets@perseusbooks.com.

Library of Congress Cataloging-in-Publication Data

Ravitch, Richard, 1933-
    So much to do : a full life of business, politics, and confronting fiscal crises /
Richard Ravitch.
        pages cm
    Includes index.
    ISBN 978-1-61039-091-0 (hardback)—ISBN 978-1-61039-092-7 (e-book)
1. Ravitch, Richard, 1933- 2. Lieutenant governors—New York (State)—New
York—Biography. 3. New York (State)—Politics and government—1951–
4. Businessmen—New York (State)—New York—Biography. 5. Political
consultants—New York (State)—New York—Biography. 6. Finance, Public—
New York (State)—History. 7. New York (State)—Economic policy. 8. New York
(N.Y.)—Economic policy. 9. U.S. states—Economic policy. I. Title.

F125.3.R38A3 2014
974.7'043092—dc23
[B]
                                                                  2013043888

First Edition

10 9 8 7 6 5 4 3 2 1

*For Kathy, without whose love and patience
this book would not have been written.*

"One of the penalties of good men's refusing to participate in politics is that they end up being governed by their inferiors."

—PLATO

"A democracy can exist only until the majority discovers that it can vote itself largess out of the public treasury."

—ATTRIBUTED TO
ALEXANDER FRASER TYTLER

"Democracy is the worst form of government, except for all those other forms that have been tried from time to time."

—WINSTON CHURCHILL

Contents

PROLOGUE

IN THE SUMMER OF 2009, New York State was in what could only be called a horrible mess. In March of that year, Eliot Spitzer, the state's highly intelligent and highly aggressive governor, had been forced to resign in the midst of a prostitution scandal. Spitzer's lieutenant governor, David Paterson, succeeded him and got off to a shaky start. Having served in the New York State Senate, Paterson understood state politics, but he lacked executive experience and faced formidable problems. Democrats and Republicans each held thirty-one seats in the state Senate. The chamber was deadlocked, its leadership was in dispute, and the self-seeking horse-trading that resulted was of the kind that gives politics a bad name. The country faced economic collapse, and the State of New York had a rapidly growing budget deficit. The deepening political and economic morass presented the most serious mix of challenges that the state had faced since its economic capital, New York City, almost went bankrupt in the mid-1970s.

In July, with the post of lieutenant governor vacant, Paterson asked me to accept the job. If he became unable to serve, he said, the issue of succession was critical. He could not risk the claim that he should be succeeded by the Senate majority leader, at a time when the Senate was bitterly divided over the question of just who the majority leader was. He wanted me, in particular, to be his lieutenant governor because I had experience relevant to what he called a "staggering" and "unprecedented" fiscal crisis. He thought that my knowledge of government and capital markets would be valuable and that I could be, as he later put it, a "credible bridge to the financial, business, and labor communities" in the state.

The post of lieutenant governor offered neither power nor glamour. In fact, as I understood it, New York's lieutenant governors had very little power to do anything at all. So, if New York's government was in such an abysmal state and the job was so thankless, why did I take it? And when my term was over, why, instead of returning to the pleasant dilemma of cabinet-making versus golf, did I prevail on my friend Paul Volcker to join me in a three-year study to explain many of the reasons for the chronic fiscal dysfunction in New York and other states?

The answers to these questions are embedded in this book. During a career that stretched from my volunteering in Adlai Stevenson's 1952 presidential campaign to the day when my term as lieutenant governor ended, I was consistently drawn to public service and periodically engaged in it, sometimes in just an advisory role and at other times seven days a week. When I was asked by a governor or a mayor to undertake a public task, I rarely said no.

In the past sixty years, I have done many things and found that I had the temperament to enjoy many different worlds—law, construction, real estate, labor, politics, and government. I loved crunching the numbers that held the key to the financial condition of public and private organizations. I relished negotiations, in labor or politics, that lasted late into the night. And, in truth, I was competitive and easily bored. Public life offered contests and excitement on a scale the private sector could rarely match. Above all, it offered a real sense of purpose.

There have been constants in my career: an interest in politics, the values instilled in me by my parents, and a love of learning. It amazes me that seemingly disconnected experiences and relationships have

so often converged in ways that helped me address the public challenges described in this book. Sadly, it also amazes me that the public problems I encountered in New York thirty and forty years ago
are so similar to those faced by cities and states today. The stories I
recount here are not just episodes in New York history. These past
crises taught fundamental lessons about the consequences of under-
estimating the costs of providing public benefits, failing to balance
recurring expenditures with recurring revenues, and failing to invest
sufficiently in education and the public infrastructure. Our present
crisis could have been avoided if those lessons had been learned.

Still more striking, however, is the extent to which the experience of the public challenges I have faced has reinforced my faith in
democratic politics and my belief that politics, the art and science of
government, is to be respected, not demeaned. In a democracy, if you
insist on being above politics, you cannot govern well.

The American democracy has overcome many problems and difficulties, by and large without sacrificing democratic principles and
processes. But our current fiscal crisis, in the states as well as the federal government, poses a fundamental challenge to those principles
and processes. The nation and its states have made social commitments that are admirable but exceed government's current financial
resources. The media focus on national budget issues, but it is the
states and their local governments that bear most of the responsibility for delivering essential services to our citizens. Thus, a major
challenge to our democracy, in state capitals at least as much as in
Washington, is the question of how a free society can reduce benefits
for some and increase burdens for others without tearing unaccept-
ably at the social fabric. Recent events—the bankruptcy of Detroit,
the Philadelphia school district's having to borrow in order to open
its schools for the year, the acknowledgment that there is no way for
a state like Illinois to make its promised pension payments to its retirees—demonstrate with increasing drama that the absence of fiscal
sustainability among state and local governments is an unaddressed
problem of growing seriousness.

The things I've seen and the lessons I've learned may bear on this question. There is little gossip in this book, but I do offer a candid insider's account. The book is one part personal memoir, one part a dissection of the reasons why we seem unable to be honest with ourselves about the gap between the government services we demand and the taxes we are willing to pay, and one part an account of how democracy works, and that it has worked, does work, and must work. If half of my sixty years' worth of lessons concerns the existential seriousness of the fiscal problems that now face the American democracy, the other half offers the conclusion that individuals can make a difference in the way democracy copes with the challenge. This is not just a feel-good exhortation to be an upstanding citizen but something much more specific, drawn from the lessons of a lifetime.

Anyone reading this book is likely to have skills that can contribute to the process of addressing public problems. But many such readers may have developed a certain amount of contempt for the political process. In a city like New York, this contempt is the default attitude among the professional classes.

When business or financial leaders gather, their frustrations with government, whether federal, state, or local, are almost invariably high on the list of topics of conversation. And people involved in commerce are not the only complainers. Doctors complain about the dealings that medical professionals are required to have with government. Architects complain about the need to deal with the legislation and regulations produced by their states and localities and the officials who enforce them. Lawyers who are paid to mediate their clients' problems with government are well acquainted with its operations and ready to describe its irrationalities in detail.

Particular complaints may or may not be justified. As a whole, however, they are made in a tone—resigned, condescending, dismissive, or outraged—that would be more appropriate from the resentful subjects of an authoritarian regime than from citizens of a democracy, who have it within our power to ameliorate whatever ticks us off.

The amelioration begins with a respect for the political process, despite its frustrations and occasional corruptions, and a willingness to participate in it. I hope that what is written here will convince some that this participation is not just an obligation but in many instances a source of immense satisfaction. And it is the only way democracy can work.

1

Beginnings

IN THE SPRING OF 1951, I staged what passed in my family for a rebellion. Having just graduated from high school in New York City, I was supposed to be headed for the Ivy League, or at least one of the big state universities. Instead, I chose Oberlin College, thirty-five miles southwest of Cleveland, Ohio. I thought I was going to rural America, where I would meet real people. I wanted to transcend my New York roots.

I should have known they couldn't be shed so easily. They were planted too deep.

&

IN 1885 MY GRANDFATHER, Joseph Ravitch, emigrated from Russia at the age of seventeen to escape the pogroms and went into the business of making sidewalk gratings and manhole covers. He prospered in the 1920s, and in 1925 he founded a small-time contracting business for his son, nephew, and son-in-law. It became the HRH Construction Corporation. When the Great Depression came, my grandfather went bankrupt and never fully recovered, financially or emotionally. But he left a durable legacy for the family and New York City. One day in the 1960s, I was walking on Allen Street in Lower Manhattan when I came across a sidewalk grating inscribed

"Ravitch Brothers, 17 Mangin Street." I had it removed and installed at Waterside, a project I built in Manhattan almost fifty years later.

My father, Saul, built some of the landmarks on Central Park West, including the famous double-towered Beresford and San Remo apartment buildings. Many of his projects were owned by the Bank of United States, a bank founded in 1913 by Jewish immigrants that served many newcomers to the country. Its customers may have thought that the name signified government backing, but in fact the bank lacked not only the backing of the US government but also the support of the rest of the banking industry. When the bank crashed at the beginning of the Depression, Wall Street's other bankers refused to bail it out.

When it failed, the bank owed HRH thousands of dollars, which the bank didn't have. In place of the funds, our family was granted four apartments at 15 West 81st Street, where we never had to pay rent. I spent my childhood there, on the broad street overlooking the American Museum of Natural History, in the block where they still inflate the balloons for the Macy's Thanksgiving Day Parade. One street west on Columbus Avenue, the El, one of four New York pre-subway elevated trains, rumbled its way from Lower Manhattan to Harlem.

We kids had the neighborhood wired. We knew the Good Humor man, the cops, the guy who sold newspapers and comics, the deli man, the candy man, and everyone else of critical value to a child in the streets of New York.

More than a half-century after playing in those streets, I climbed into a rented limousine at 6:00 one morning on my way to a board meeting in Princeton, New Jersey. The driver took a look at me and yelled, "Dickie! Don't you remember me?"

I didn't.

"It's Ziggy! Alan Ziegenfeld, Dickie! We played stoop ball on 82nd Street!"

Now I remembered. Ziggy and Dickie reminisced all the way to

Princeton. There are a lot of Ziggies in my life. As I write this, I am eighty years old; I know a lot of New Yorkers.

My mother, Sylvia Lerner, grew up in Dodgers territory— Flatbush, Brooklyn. We visited her family on weekends. My grandfather Samuel Lerner took me to Coney Island on Sundays. He was a gregarious man with many friends to show for it. He began his career as a postman and was promoted to the cavernous US Post Office on Eighth Avenue and 34th Street. On the late shift one night, he got a phone call from a man who introduced himself as Otto Abraham. He was a stockbroker, Abraham said. His firm had mistakenly put an envelope of bonds in the US Mail. They were bearer bonds. They could be turned into cash by anyone who laid hands on them. Could my grandfather find the envelope?

He found it, hand-delivered it to Abraham, and ended up moonlighting in Abraham's office as a stockbroker. My grandfather turned out to be a great customer's man and started working for Abraham & Co. full time. He and grandma moved to a nice apartment on the Upper West Side.

My mother lived several generations before her time. She got her BA from Hunter College, then a master's degree, writing her thesis on Geoffrey Chaucer. She was a beautiful woman who played the cello and sculpted. My father was different; he loved his building business, his golf, and his family. After a hard day at the office, he wanted nothing more than to relax in the living room with us. He came to my high school baseball and basketball games and took me to see the Yankees and Dodgers play. He occasionally brought me along when he played golf with his buddies, though the game would hold no interest for me until sixty years later.

On December 7, 1941, a cold Sunday when I was eight years old, Dad took me to a Giants football game at the Polo Grounds. As the game went on, the Giants fell further behind the Brooklyn Dodgers—yes, there were football Dodgers back then—and a kind of murmuring swept through the stands. The radio reports had leaked into the stadium, and by halftime most of the 55,000 people in attendance had a lot more than football on their minds. The announcer began calling for generals and admirals to contact their offices, but many had already heard the news: just before the kickoff, at dawn in the central Pacific, Japan had launched its raid on Pearl Harbor.

My father, who was then forty-one, volunteered. He was commissioned as a Navy officer and assigned to the 55th Naval Construction Battalion, the newly formed Seabees. Across the Pacific, this new force of engineers and builders landed right behind the Marines to construct runways, roads, bridges, and other infrastructure needed by the invading US troops.

While Dad and his comrades worked their way toward Japan, we waited at home. My mother found a job at a news magazine. I was attending the Lincoln School, a progressive educational experiment in Harlem run by Columbia University Teachers College and funded by the Rockefellers, who enrolled several of their children in the school. My parents sent me to Lincoln from kindergarten through my freshman year in high school. My classmates were a socioeconomic cross section of New Yorkers—rich and poor, black and white. Lincoln's was an "experience" curriculum. To study botany, we grew flowers. To study math, we made grocery budgets. I thrived, making a diverse group of friends for life.

But Nicholas Murray Butler, then president of Columbia, wanted the school's endowment. Accordingly, Columbia claimed that the school had fulfilled its original purpose and closed it, not without incurring years of litigation. With my father home from the war, I finished high school at Ethical Culture Fieldston in the Bronx, still liberal but much more traditional. Then, in the fall of 1951, I set out for the wilds of Oberlin, Ohio.

જ્જ

OBERLIN COLLEGE wasn't what I had expected. For one thing, it turned out that most of the students were Republicans. Every four years, the college held a mock presidential convention, and prominent politicians paid visits. Early in 1952, the students nom-inated Earl Warren, then Republican governor of California, for president. We few Democrats rallied around Wayne Morse—still a Republican, albeit one who had begun his idiosyncratic shift toward the Democratic Party.

Oberlin wasn't all I had hoped for academically, either. I was in-creasingly interested in American history and government, and there were stronger programs at other schools. My rebellion at an end, I applied for a transfer to Harvard.

Personal circumstances made a different decision for me. During my freshman year, when I arrived home for Christmas vacation, my father was looking thinner and weaker. He was often fatigued. My mother told me not to worry. She said he was just getting over mononucleosis.

She was trying to protect me from the truth, but she didn't suc-ceed very well. Two months later, back at Oberlin, I was sitting in class when I saw my father's best friend walk into the room. I knew instantly what had happened. My father had died of what turned out to be a virulent form of lymphoma. I thought my mother would need me. I went home to New York and spent the last three years of my undergraduate life at Columbia College.

It was an immensely fortunate change for my intellectual devel-opment. In the aftermath of World War II, young people my age had grown up with an increasing awareness of the war itself and the un-folding horrors of the Holocaust. The early Cold War years were the heyday of Senator Joseph McCarthy and his attacks on Communists, real and imagined, in the ranks of the US government and public life. We were fully aware that politics was a serious business.

In that climate, I studied with the country's greatest scholars and exponents of Western liberal democracy. Their ideas inspired much of what I would do in my life.

The course in intellectual history was taught jointly by Jacques Barzun and Lionel Trilling. Like others in the class, I was inspired by Trilling's 1952 introduction to the first American edition of George

Orwell's memoir *Homage to Catalonia*, an account of his experience in the Spanish Civil War. In the 1930s, Western intellectuals were enamored of the socialist ideals of the Spanish Republic and its fight against right-wing fascism. Orwell had joined the war and discovered how readily those ideals could be corrupted by an equally totalitarian fascism of the left. His book was the era's great caution against the notion that high ideals of the left or right could save people from having to engage in the messy work of coming to grips with opposing points of view in a democracy.

Trilling, like Orwell, had a clear view of the incompatibility between democracy and political absolutism. Trilling loved the ambiguities of democratic politics; he gloried in its quotidian and commonplace aspects, antidotes to the pernicious effects of unfettered ideas.

In addition to Trilling and Barzun, the list of critics, historians, and political scientists with whom I studied at Columbia—including Richard Hofstadter, William Leuchtenberg, Henry Steele Commager, and David Truman, a theorist of political pluralism—was a roster of the best in American academe of that or any other time, made up of great teachers with an extraordinary depth of knowledge. Each in his way, taught a profound and lasting engagement with American political life. I was and have remained very much their student.

When I transferred to Columbia in the fall of 1952, the US presidential race was nearing its climax. The Republican candidate was Columbia University's own president, the former general and war hero Dwight D. Eisenhower. Most Columbia people liked Ike, but I came from a family of Democrats. I stayed true to our tradition and worked for the about-to-be-trounced Democratic presidential nominee, Illinois Governor Adlai Stevenson.

Wanting to campaign for Stevenson, I joined the local Tammany Hall club, part of the New York State Democratic political machine. But despite the campaign's slogan—"Madly for Adlai"—I couldn't find anyone in the organization actively working for Stevenson, madly or otherwise. The Tammany club leader, Dennis "Denny"

Mahon, held court once a week. Ordinary club members could see him then, if they lined up. I joined the queue.

When my turn for an audience came, I asked Mahon why I couldn't find an organized Stevenson campaign to join. He looked at me with bemusement but then decided to give me my first lesson in local politics. If too many Democrats voted in the 1952 presidential election, he said cryptically, too many Democrats might vote in the 1953 primary.

Dismissed, I was left to figure out Mahon's delphic utterance, which I finally did. If a lot of strangers—Democrats who weren't controlled by Mahon's machine—registered to vote for Stevenson in 1952, the same non-machine voters might show up the next year to vote in a contest Mahon considered much more important, the New York City mayoral primary race. From Tammany's point of view, they would inject much too much unpredictability into the proceedings.

This was my introduction to the reality that politics is complicated and that campaigns, for better or worse, are not necessarily driven by idealistic fervor or loyalty. The revelation did not discourage me. I became cochairman of Columbia's Students for Stevenson.

Our group had the nerve to write a letter to President Franklin D. Roosevelt's widow, Eleanor Roosevelt, then living in New York on East 62nd Street, to invite her to speak at one of our rallies. About a week later, Mrs. Roosevelt's secretary wrote to ask that I call to work out a convenient date and time. I was thrilled. We scheduled a 2:00 P.M. appearance for her on campus.

With the chutzpah of youth, I told the secretary that it would be an honor for me to take Mrs. Roosevelt to lunch before the rally. The secretary thought that was a delightful idea. She suggested that I call for Mrs. Roosevelt at noon. I asked my mother to recommend a convenient restaurant, and she suggested a little French place on East 60th Street.

But how would I get Mrs. Roosevelt to the restaurant and then to the Columbia campus on the Upper West Side? I couldn't see myself hailing a taxi with a former First Lady in tow. So I borrowed my mother's car, an old Buick, and called for Mrs. Roosevelt at her home. She strode out of her building precisely on time, the familiar proper lady in a sensible dress, and greeted me warmly. I drove us to the restaurant in something of a daze, realizing as we approached that I had no idea what I would do with the car. I couldn't drive around with her, looking for a garage.

I decided I had to double-park, notwithstanding the ticket I was bound to get. But I had some luck. A doorman at a nearby building recognized Mrs. Roosevelt and, I'm sure, saw my awkward discomfort. He gave me a wink and said he'd keep an eye on the car.

It was an unforgettable lunch. Mrs. Roosevelt spoke graciously and directly, telling me why it was so important that Stevenson be elected. She described her work as a US delegate to the United Nations, where she was promoting global human rights and her commitment to racial equality in America.

We left the restaurant, found the car unticketed, and drove to Columbia, where, once again, I parked illegally. Students for Stevenson had managed to turn out fewer than a hundred students for our rally. I was embarrassed, but Mrs. Roosevelt seemed indifferent to the size of her audience, her behavior an object lesson in political grace. As she spoke, she inspired us to further efforts to make Stevenson president. We held enthusiastic rallies. We enjoyed the sense of acting on our convictions. We had absolutely no impact on the 1952 election.

Things look different from today's perspective. In the culture I came from, Stevenson was a hero. He was an eloquent speaker and writer, an agent of change who evoked a liberal, progressive future beyond the stolid years that Eisenhower seemed to promise. Unfortunately for us Stevenson partisans, postwar Americans were not about to gamble on Stevenson's kind of change at a time of prosperity at home and a growing Soviet threat abroad.

Stevenson once said, "All progress has resulted from people who took unpopular positions." In his case, unpopularity trumped the promise of progress. Today, I understand that Eisenhower—a Rock of Gibraltar, derided by intellectuals but a consummate practitioner of what the political scientist Fred Greenstein would later call the "hidden hand presidency," who played with an astuteness that outsiders could not see—may well have proved to be the better leader for the America of that era.

The subject of the senior year thesis I wrote in 1955 was the New York State Progressive Party of 1912. Its leaders were frightened by what they saw as the threat of vast immigrations from Italy and Eastern Europe. They opposed the growth of unions and collective bargaining. In the name of reform, they worked hard to limit access to political power by those whose views they saw as too radical.

They failed, of course, in their bid to halt history. Some of them ended up in the Liberty League, an organization that tried to stop Franklin Roosevelt's New Deal reforms in the 1930s. Once again, they failed. "Their Armageddon," my thesis concluded, "was never reached. Industry, labor unions, and political machines grew as the twentieth century swept on. The Progressive Party failed to solve the conflict with which we are struggling today—how to make Democracy work in an industrial society."

The thesis bore the hallmarks of its time, including the idea that industrialism, with the increasing scale of the business and labor enterprises it required, would be the great historical force with which democracy had to contend. The postindustrial society was not even a glimmer on my—or anyone else's—intellectual horizon. But the thesis did recognize the limitations of a Progressive ethos unwilling to accommodate democratic change.

That was more or less the end of my academic career. Professor David Truman thought I should stay at Columbia and get a PhD in American history and politics. But the civil rights movement was building in the South, the fear of nuclear weapons was troubling our sleep, and anyone who could sense the pulse of the times knew that the quiet of the Eisenhower years would soon give way to something more dramatic. History was again picking up speed and momentum. I wanted to be an actor, not an observer.

I ENROLLED IN Yale Law School. I didn't know exactly what I wanted
to do with a law degree, but I knew Yale was the law school for people interested in public service. It had faculty members committed
to the idea of law as a tool for change, not just an instrument for
resolving disputes or a process for setting limits on human behavior.
It seemed like my kind of place.

But even law school, valuable as it proved to be, was too cloistered
for me. I was a middle-of-the-class student. When I fantasized about
my future, I saw a cabinet room, not a courtroom. One summer I
interned at a Wall Street law firm; another summer I was a construction laborer at the Albert Einstein School of Medicine, then being
built in the Bronx. I stripped forms. More experienced men made
the forms and poured the concrete into them, and after it dried my
job was to tear the wood away. It was backbreaking work.

I commuted from Manhattan in my mother's Buick—that same
Buick. At first I was worried about what would happen if my fellow
workers saw me, a common laborer, showing up each day in a fussy
sedan. But when I graduated to having beers with the guys, I learned
that the Buick was nothing compared to the Cadillacs and other
fancy cars that some of my fellow workers drove. Thus, I was introduced to another fundamental principle of modern political and
economic reality: Karl Marx, with his theories of the immiseration
of the working class, was thoroughly useless if you wanted to understand labor and the labor movement in America.

In the spring of 1958, about to graduate from law school, I had to
decide where I wanted to go next; and in those days before the vol-
unteer army, I had to decide what to do about military service. The
"where" was clear: I wanted to go to Washington. Having been taught
the paramount importance of making democracy work, I needed to
understand just how democracy did work. I wasn't much attracted to
New York politics; Denny Mahon of Tammany had put a chill on that
idea. Instead, I would explore national politics and government.

This plan, in turn, dictated my military career choice. I joined
the Army reserve, which required six months of active duty. I spent

those six months at Fort Dix, southeast of Trenton, New Jersey. During the first three months of service, you couldn't leave the Army base. After that, I started visiting Washington every time I got a weekend pass.

I had no contacts and no introductions that could help me get a job. Friends who had graduated from law school a year ahead of me said the best thing to do would be to date Washington secretaries, because they were the best available source of information about job openings. I did just that. Eventually one of those secretaries introduced me to Representative Chet Holifield, a Democrat representing Pasadena, California.

When I met him, Holifield was fifty-five years old and had represented his congressional district for fifteen years. He chaired both the Subcommittee on Military Operations of the House Committee on Government Operations and the Joint Committee on Atomic Energy. Amused that I had negotiated my way into his office by way of his secretary, he began by asking me a question: What did I think of Franklin Roosevelt?

I gave the right answers.

Chet was born in Kentucky and lived in Arkansas before moving to California, where he worked in the dry-cleaning business and sold men's clothing until his enthusiasm for Roosevelt drew him into politics. After we established our common ground, he offered me a job as assistant counsel to the military operations subcommittee. I accepted the offer on the spot. Two weeks after I was released from active duty, I drove down to Washington to begin my new life.

❧

I DIDN'T KNOW much about the nation's capital but quickly discovered that I was making a home in what amounted to a small southern town with an overlay of government and politics. There were only two good restaurants, both on Connecticut Avenue. Arbaugh's, my favorite, offered a rack of ribs and a big beer for eight or nine bucks. Duke Zeibert's, four blocks from the White House, attracted more of the political class, from presidents on down, for its steaks and good deli food. After dinner you could take your date to concerts like the Budapest String Quartet playing at the Library of Congress.

Famous performers would occasionally pass through—Ella Fitzgerald singing on a barge in the Potomac near the Lincoln Memorial, Edith Piaf appearing at the Shoreham Hotel. We junior staffers used to scan the *Washington Post* for the list of embassy receptions and crash them for free food and drink. It was not exactly cutting-edge entertainment.

The military operations subcommittee occupied a walk-up office in the Washington Arms, a rickety structure southwest of the Capitol that would eventually be demolished to make way for today's Rayburn House Office Building. Our little office—a few researchers working in dingy quarters without air-conditioning, sometimes in the swampy heat of a Washington summer—bore no resemblance to the massive congressional staff operations of today. Still, we were part of the action; that was the lure of Washington. During my last year of law school, in October 1957, the Soviet Union had launched Sputnik, the little beep-beep of a satellite that shattered American complacency about its scientific and military superiority. Now, in my first year out of school, I was a tiny part of one of the many teams that were gearing up the nation's readiness for a more competitive stage in the Cold War.

Americans immediately understood the challenge of Sputnik. As a 1959 congressional report later put it, "A space vehicle with enough propulsion to carry a large payload into orbit for science might also be able to deliver a payload of death and destruction to America's heartland." I had a small part in producing that report. My job was to help the subcommittee's general counsel prepare for congressional hearings on the separate ballistic missile programs then being pursued separately by the Army, Navy, and Air Force.

The hearings were organized to pose fundamental questions about the extensive changes under way in our national defense. With

Sputnik, Washington started to make huge investments in scientific education and research and space exploration. The Army, Navy, and Air Force began to build their separate programs to develop and deploy missiles, launching an arms race with one another as well as the Soviet Union. Their plans for missile systems demanded enormous spending on technologies that would cover everything from guidance systems to launch sites and a defense reorganization that would speed up the capacity to make space-age command decisions. Beyond these interservice questions lay a still larger issue: was the rush into missile technology a case of overkill, leaching funds from other important defense needs?

The number of dollars involved was staggering, as were the stakes for national security. I got a taste of lobbying at its most intense. After receiving a top secret clearance, I was escorted by high-level military personnel to many of the major US military installations involved in the missile programs, including the new North American Air Defense Command, NORAD, in Colorado (now known as the Aerospace Defense Command) and the Strategic Air Command headquarters outside Omaha, Nebraska. Fresh out of boot camp, having crawled through the mud for drill sergeants, I found it more than a little ironic to be wined and dined by all those generals and admirals. At dinner one night, the general beside me very politely expressed curiosity about my background. I told him that six months earlier I had been peeling potatoes at Fort Dix. He went silent. I'm sure he spent the rest of the meal figuring out how to get even with whoever had seated him next to a buck private.

The report we produced, *Organization and Management of Missile Programs*, called for cutting back on the armed services' duplication, waste, and jealous rivalries. The Army and Air Force had to merge their missile development efforts; indeed, perhaps the only way to accomplish this job was to merge the two services altogether. "No amount of effort spent in 'clarifying' roles and missions," we stated, "can overcome the ruthless logic of weapon technology. Whereas in the past, weapons could be adapted reasonably well to service missions, now missions must be adapted to weapon systems."

Our report generated a great deal of press coverage. But in retrospect, its invocation of the "ruthless logic of weapon technology" sounds naïve: ruthless logic or no, the Army and the Air Force still compete, not just on the football field but in the Pentagon budget wars as well. The report may have gathered dust, but I didn't. In the manner of congressional staffers, I soon moved on to another project, one that spoke more directly to my interest in domestic politics.

Holifield had joined a small group of House members who were unhappy with the coalition of Republicans and southern Democrats that was then preventing civil rights legislation from reaching the House floor. Democratic Minnesota Congressman Eugene McCarthy had put the group together. In addition to Holifield, it included Lee Metcalf of Montana, Frank Thompson of New Jersey, and George Rhodes of Pennsylvania. I gave the group some informal staff assistance. They had won a major victory in the passage of the Civil Rights Act of 1957, which strengthened voting rights protections.

Eugene McCarthy moved on to the Senate in 1958, but the liberal coalition he left behind became the Democratic Study Group, a sub-caucus within the Democratic caucus. The DSG hired its own staff, met regularly to set legislative strategy, and assigned whips to manage tactics and keep members in line. It would soon spearhead the internal congressional reforms that made it possible to pass the liberal domestic legislation of the mid-1960s.

*

BUT, AS THIS influential political force took shape, the personal thrill of Washington was wearing off.

My time in Congress had given me nothing to complain about. I had worked on one of the most dangerous issues in the world, the future of nuclear missiles. I had been involved in the early skirmishes of what would be one of the great legislative battles of the century, the fight over civil rights. I was still in my twenties.

But I had begun to see what a future as a congressional staffer looked like. Staffers rose up a professional ladder that was too slow for my tastes and, more important, were always in an advisory position. No matter how brilliantly they performed or how much power they seemed to have at a given moment, they were fundamentally dependent on the contingencies of other people's political fortunes. At any time, the congressman to whom they were attached could resign, retire, change committee assignments, or even lose an election, leaving them in the lurch. And anyone looking beyond the excitement of the next congressional hearing or markup could see that the pay was lousy.

When I talked to Holifield and McCarthy about my uncertainties, their reactions were surprising. It was a fine idea for me to make some money; I could always go back to public service later on. They knew what I didn't—that the financial circumstances of an honest public life can be punishing, and that it is not a bad idea to have something in the bank before embarking on such a career. I decided to leave government.

When I first moved to Washington I was dating a young woman who was a student at Wellesley College, a few miles outside Boston. She asked me to look after one of her classmates, Diane Silvers, who was coming to town for a summer internship at the *Washington Post*. When Diane arrived, I introduced her to my friend Milt Gwirtzman, a shy kid from Rochester with degrees from Harvard College and Yale Law School. Milt, then working for Missouri Senator Stuart Symington, would soon join Senator John F. Kennedy's campaign. He would go on to work for John, Robert, and Edward Kennedy as a speechwriter and policy adviser for nearly a half century.

I was a failure as a matchmaker; Milt and Diane didn't work out. But I discovered that I liked showing Diane around the Hill and the local hangouts. She was a newcomer to the East Coast establishment.

She had grown up in Houston, one of eight children. Her father ran a liquor store. Most of her siblings got married and stayed close to home. A local rabbi recognized something different in Diane and helped her get a scholarship to Wellesley. There she became editor of the student newspaper and discovered the passion for journalism that would take her to the *Washington Post*. And now here she was in my company, an attractive, liberal southern woman about to turn twenty-one who had little experience but enormous talent and ambition. The outcome was foreordained.

I started thinking more seriously about what I was going to do if I intended to leave government. My father had left me part ownership of the family's building business, HRH Construction, which two of my cousins were running. When I was in college, I had told the family I had no interest in joining the business, but the invitation was still open. I was also starting to think it was unfair to keep sharing in the profits without making any contribution of my own.

Diane and I decided, at least for the time being, that we would make our life in New York and that I would give the construction business a real try. If it didn't work, I was young enough to pursue something else. At the age of twenty-seven, it is almost impossible to make an irreparably bad career mistake.

We were married on June 26, 1960. We had a honeymoon in Europe. A month later, we settled into an apartment on East 35th Street and Second Avenue with a view of the blank wall of an adjoining building. Diane took a job at the *New Leader*, a magazine edited by Sol Levitas that was read by anticommunists and social democrats all over the world. I began working at HRH Construction.

જા

I NEVER REALLY left politics, of course. Among other things, I remained friendly with Gene McCarthy. In 1964, with President Kennedy just assassinated and President Lyndon Johnson making his first independent run for the office, McCarthy told me he wanted to be Johnson's running mate. He had to make his pitch to an audience of just one, Johnson himself, but McCarthy couldn't seek the job publicly and directly. He thought it would help if his friends and admirers organized a quiet effort to impress upon the White House the reasons why McCarthy would be an ideal vice presidential pick.

We set up a Washington office in the Capitol Park apartment complex that HRH Construction had built. A network of people around the country began talking to the press and Democratic Party officials about McCarthy. A New York congressman got the state's party chairman to appoint me a delegate to the 1964 Democratic national convention in Atlantic City.

This was my first convention. The hall was overhung with bunting—and with the sadness of President Kennedy's death just six months before. But even that didn't fully dampen the convention's excitement, born of a deep desire to elect Johnson and defeat the Republican, Barry Goldwater. National conventions had still not made the transition to their modern-day status as staged television productions. As late as the day before the president and vice president were to be nominated, a Tuesday, no one at the convention knew whom Johnson would choose.

McCarthy's main rival for the vice presidential nomination was his fellow Minnesota Senator Hubert Humphrey. If McCarthy wasn't chosen as Johnson's running mate, he would have to run for reelection to the Senate that year, so he didn't want to pick a fight with Humphrey, who was much more popular than McCarthy with certain Minnesota politicians.

McCarthy and his staff were staying at a motel just outside Atlantic City. On Tuesday McCarthy told his staff he was going to send a message to Johnson urging him to make Humphrey the vice presidential nominee. His staff told him not to do it, arguing that the message might push Johnson toward Humphrey. But McCarthy had what he thought was a more sophisticated calculation: if Johnson meant to choose McCarthy, the message would make no difference. But if Johnson picked Humphrey, and it became publicly known that McCarthy had sent the message, it would make for good feelings back in Minnesota. So McCarthy sent the message, leaked it to the Minnesota press, and went to bed.

Wednesday morning I was swimming in the motel pool with McCarthy and his son Michael when someone ran out to tell the senator that the president was on the phone. We ran back to McCarthy's room, dripping wet, and he picked up the phone, only to hear Johnson tell him bluntly that he was choosing Humphrey. Johnson then handed the phone to Arthur Goldberg, at the time still an associate justice of the Supreme Court, to finish the conversation. Many years later, Goldberg told me he never understood why he had been invited to be in the room with Johnson, the only one there, as the president made his calls to all the unsuccessful candidates for the vice presidential nomination.

An hour after Johnson's call, McCarthy was sitting with his family and close friends when he got another phone call—from Walter Jenkins, Johnson's chief aide. Jenkins asked McCarthy whether he would do what the president had asked. McCarthy answered that the president had not asked him to do anything. Jenkins said the president wanted McCarthy to nominate Humphrey for vice president that night at the convention. McCarthy, still hurt by his rejection, recognized that he had no choice.

Several hours later, we heard on the radio that the president had asked Humphrey and Senator Thomas Dodd of Connecticut to helicopter from the convention to Washington, then back with him to Atlantic City for the evening session. Dodd was not a serious candidate for the vice presidential pick, so everyone knew the nominee would be Humphrey. By the time McCarthy nominated Humphrey that night, the event was an anticlimax.

Insult was about to be added to injury. In Atlantic City the next morning, McCarthy and his friends were having breakfast at the Shelburne hotel when Walter Jenkins approached us. The president, Jenkins announced, had been unhappy with McCarthy's message urging him to choose Humphrey. Johnson had planned to have both Humphrey and McCarthy helicopter with him from the White House to the convention. That way he could maintain suspense until the last moment about which one he was going to pick. McCarthy's leaked message had spoiled Johnson's piece of stage management.

As Jenkins left, McCarthy mused, referring to Johnson's big ranch on the Pedernales River in Texas, that in his second term the president would probably change the national anthem to "Pedernales Uber Alles."

In 1967 McCarthy asked me whether I would help him in his effort to challenge Johnson for the 1968 presidential nomination. I gave it serious thought. But I admired what Johnson had accomplished with the Great Society legislation. More than that, remembering 1964, I sensed that McCarthy was motivated in significant part by his bitterness over what had happened to him in Atlantic City. I told him I was going to have to turn him down. I mentioned Johnson's legislative achievements; I didn't mention "Pedernales Uber Alles." But the thought crossed my mind that Denny Mahon of Tammany Hall wasn't the only politician for whom great political decisions were inextricably bound with calculations of personal advantage and memories of personal slights.

All of that, however, happened later. In 1960, when I left Washington for New York, I had no clear sense of the extent to which the people I had met in Washington would continue to populate my life and that politics and government would continue to occupy my time. I knew only that I was embarking on an adventure in the construction business.

2

One Brick at a Time

So I BECAME A BUILDER; and everything I later accomplished in my career, public and private, was shaped by the concrete (in both senses) facts of the building business. People may think they have acute insights into politics and public issues, but they don't really understand what shapes civic life unless they know how land is allocated and the homes and commercial structures on them are built and financed. I got a quick and deep education in both disciplines.

When I joined HRH in 1960, two of my cousins were already partners there. One of them opened a branch office of the company in Los Angeles. He lost money on his first contracts and left the firm almost bankrupt. The other cousin, Saul Horowitz Jr., more than made up for the losses.

Saul and I grew up in the same Manhattan apartment house; he was eight years older than I, so we didn't know each other well. Saul graduated from West Point, became an Army engineer, and won a Bronze Star in Korea. In 1954, after ten years in the military, he joined the family business. Never losing his military bearing or his well-deserved reputation for integrity, he greatly enhanced the standing of HRH in New York's commercial world.

We were as compatible as partners could be, with complementary interests and skills. Saul had mastered the institutional side of the building business—schools, hospitals, museums—while I began to concentrate on housing. We trusted each other completely. Eventually we tore down the wall between our offices and operated out of a single space. At the end of the workday we would often stay late, open a bottle of Scotch, and make sure each of us knew everything about what the other was up to.

It is hard to think of another line of work more engrossing than the building business. On any given day, you can find yourself meeting architects, engineers, lawyers, bureaucrats, politicians, union leaders, construction workers, bankers, or tenants. If you have a competitive streak, you can exercise it in getting business. You can pursue a project from beginning to end and actually see what you have built.

You can also have the satisfaction of providing people with better housing.

Soon after joining HRH, I met a developer named James H. Scheuer, later a congressman from New York. Jim was older than I but, like me, had gone to high school at Fieldston. We would talk about not just the mechanics of the building business but the need to improve housing in the slums of major American cities.

One of the worst of those slums was in southwest Washington, DC. In the 1950s, the *Soviet Encyclopedia* featured a photograph of it set against the background of the US Capitol, meant to be a symbol of the inequities and poverty produced by modern capitalism. Jim was chosen by the District of Columbia to develop more than 1,700 apartments in the area, and he asked HRH to be his partner.

The development was named Capitol Park Apartments, a well-landscaped array of apartment buildings, row houses, and walk-ups. It made Washington history because it was the city's first desegregated housing complex. It became a showcase. The very first tenant in the development was the African American housing expert Robert Weaver. In 1965, when President Lyndon Johnson created the cabinet-level Department of Housing and Urban Development (HUD), Weaver would become its first secretary.

Jim Scheuer and Capitol Park were part of my introduction to the vast field of government housing policy, an interconnected web of programs, incentives, and subsidies from federal, state, and local governments. If you mastered the details, you could assemble the financing to support housing that was both profitable and socially useful.

These programs were created in stages after World War II, when the American housing landscape underwent a seismic shift. The war accelerated a migration to the country's central cities from the American South and Puerto Rico. At the same time, as the war ended, the GI bill made relatively inexpensive mortgage financing available to veterans. Soon afterward, in the 1950s, the construction of the nation's interstate highway system began. More white Americans could now leave central cities for private homes in the suburbs—and they did. The term "white flight" entered the country's political lexicon.

Housing policy experts sought ways to stem the exodus. They also wanted to house the poor, but the politics of the time made it increasingly difficult to provide housing benefits to the poor without helping the middle class as well. So governments tried to do both.

Cities and states began to enact programs to make it possible to buy or rent urban housing at below-market prices. Cities reduced real estate taxes. States, by issuing tax-exempt bonds, raised funds that allowed them to make mortgage loans at low interest rates. The federal government provided subsidies, in the form of generous mortgage terms from the Federal Housing Administration, to cities that wanted to clear slums by acquiring real estate through their powers of eminent domain, as well as to developers willing to build for the poor and middle class. Eventually some of these programs put limits on developer profits to ensure that the tenants in these developments, not the owners, would benefit from the subsidies.

Many of HRH's competitors in the building industry wanted nothing to do with this type of enterprise. They did not want government looking over their shoulders to limit their profits or dictate the characteristics of the tenants they had to allow into the housing they built. Some of them were also unwilling to bear the burdens and risks of the public disclosure that was part of doing business with the government.

But these programs presented big opportunities to make money and fulfill important social objectives—to do well and do good—at the same time. HRH continued to build hospitals, museums, and office buildings; we built the Whitney Museum, the Gulf and Western Building, NYU Hospital, Citicorp Center, and headquarters for the New York Telephone Companies. But we also became major players in the housing field. We were partners in urban renewal projects in San Juan, Puerto Rico; Brookline, Massachusetts; and New York City. We also built for private developers who were not themselves in the construction business. We built more than 30,000 apartments, including, in addition to apartments in Washington, the apartments that span the Cross-Bronx Expressway approach to the George Washington Bridge, the apartments that replaced Ebbets Field when the Dodgers—sadly—left New York for Los Angeles in 1957, and Trump Village, which adjoins Coney Island in Brooklyn.

Many of our clients were nonprofit organizations that developed housing in close cooperation with government. We knew the lawyers in the field and the professionals in the relevant government agencies; we helped guide these nonprofits through the approval process and, once the developments were approved, earned our fees by constructing the buildings. The Archdiocese of New York was one of our biggest clients.

࿐

I HAD BARELY joined HRH, however, when my career as a builder was briefly but significantly interrupted.

On August 13, 1961, the Soviets raised the stakes in the Cold War by closing the border between East and West Berlin and starting construction of the Berlin Wall, which turned West Berlin into a geographically isolated outpost within East Germany. President John F. Kennedy responded by mobilizing 100,000 Army reservists, and I was one of them. I reported to Fort Gordon in Augusta, Georgia, bringing along my pregnant wife. The Berlin crisis passed after a few weeks, but my call-up lasted ten months.

Once the Army had us, it decided to use the opportunity to get us ready for the next crisis, which, some already saw, would be in the unfamiliar territory of Vietnam. Accordingly, the Army began teaching me to speak Vietnamese.

But I was an enlisted man with a law degree and membership in the New York State bar. A fellow reservist, who was a Port Authority cop in civilian life, had been court-martialed, accused of assaulting the company's first sergeant. The reservist asked me to defend him, and I managed to get him acquitted. In the process, I made an enemy of the first sergeant, who began to assign me to KP with some regularity. But other reservists started coming to me with their legal problems. I served as defense counsel in a number of courts-martial of reservists, and while I did, I was exempt from other duties, including KP.

One of those cases involved a company clerk, in civilian life a photographer for the *Buffalo Evening News*, who was charged with committing an act of sodomy with another soldier. He asked me to represent him. I informed the company commander, Major Weber, in civilian life a butcher. Major Weber, so informed, responded that homosexuality was the equivalent of treason and he would see to it that this young man spent years in the stockade.

It turned out that the soldier who had led my young client into their encounter had done the same with other servicemen and turned them in as well. My client had been entrapped. But entrapment is not a defense under the Uniform Code of Military Justice. Therefore, our case would have to be built not on military law but on the long line of precedents establishing that entrapment is a violation of the privilege against self-incrimination provided by the US Constitution.

Fort Gordon's tiny law library was not equipped for constitutional research. So I called Joseph A. Califano, general counsel of the Army, whom I had met in 1960 during the Kennedy presidential campaign. He was then a young lawyer practicing in New York who hoped for a job in Washington if Kennedy was elected. We had become close friends and have remained so ever since. In 1961 he went to the Defense Department. His talents soon made him Army general counsel, then President Johnson's chief of staff, and President Jimmy Carter's secretary of Health, Education, and Welfare.

When Joe heard what was happening to my client, he reacted, as I knew he would, by offering to help. Soon a brief arrived in the mail, prepared by the Army General Counsel's office on a no-names basis, arguing the constitutional issues in the case. I got ready to drive to the nearest federal courthouse, in Columbia, South Carolina, to file for a writ of habeas corpus that would get my client out of the stockade.

But on the night before I was set to leave for Columbia, a fortuitous event occurred: a visit from the company's supply sergeant. My client was popular with the company, and the supply sergeant said everyone was outraged about what had happened. He told me that Major Weber had stolen a pistol from the company's weapons room, and he provided me with the serial number.

I don't know how I summoned up the nerve to do it, but I decided that before making the trip to the courthouse I would try to scare Major Weber into dropping the court-martial altogether. The next morning I walked into his office, saluted, and asked him what had happened to a certain pistol whose serial number I was able to recite. Major Weber cursed at me and threw me out of his office. But he dropped the case that day.

My client eventually went back to the *Buffalo Evening News*. I heard from him every Christmas for thirty years, then lost contact. In 2010, when I had become New York lieutenant governor, I visited the *News* and asked about him. They told me he had recently died after decades as a respected and, indeed, beloved colleague.

Life in New York City hadn't provided me with much preparation for the raw injustice faced by that company clerk—or the larger injustices I saw in Georgia. I had never been to the South before, not even a vacation in Florida. My only knowledge of racism was intellectual. Now, Diane and I lived just outside Augusta in a little house on Tobacco Road, the setting for Erskine Caldwell's Depression-era novel about the bleak lives of the sharecroppers whose houses lined the dusty byway linking barren tobacco fields to a dying market town. Blacks rode in the back of the bus. When our first son, Joseph, was born in the local hospital in 1962, we had the shock of seeing segregated conditions even in a place built to tend to the most common of human needs. That shock would have a long-term impact on my career.

⁂

WHEN THE PRESIDENT finally released the Army reservists, I was simply happy to head home, especially as there was a lot of activity on the housing front. But I stayed active in politics. In 1963 I volunteered to help, in a very minor way, in the organization of the March on Washington. I had the thrill of standing in front of the Lincoln Memorial and hearing Martin Luther King Jr. declare, "I have a dream." I also became friendly with the civil rights giant Bayard Rustin and his indefatigable assistant, Rachelle Horowitz.

There had never been a figure like Rustin in American politics and never would be again. When I met him, he was fifty. Throughout his adult life, he was a pacifist, gay, and a seminal leader in the movement for black civil rights—indeed, for human rights of every variety. His trajectory remained constant, no matter what the direction of the political winds around him.

He had moved from West Chester, Pennsylvania, to Harlem in 1937 and studied at City College. While there, he joined the Young Communist League, but he left it in 1941 and began working with civil rights leaders such as A. Philip Randolph, president of the Brotherhood of Sleeping Car Porters, a man who had persuaded President Franklin Roosevelt to end discrimination in the US armed services.

Rustin was an early member of the Congress of Racial Equality. In 1947 he organized the first Freedom Ride, designed to test the recent US Supreme Court decision declaring racial discrimination in interstate travel unconstitutional. He was arrested and served a sentence on a North Carolina chain gang. In 1956 he went to work for Martin Luther King Jr., then planning the Montgomery, Alabama, bus boycott, and advised him on the strategy and tactics of nonviolence. The next year, with King, he began organizing the Southern Christian Leadership Conference. At the urging of Randolph and King, Rustin became the chief organizer of the March on Washington.

Because of my association with Bayard, my career as a builder and my passion for politics began to converge. Some months after the March on Washington, he asked me to meet with Randolph. The two of them knew I was in the building business, and they wanted to discuss the fact that many of the building trade unions were exclusively white. It was extremely difficult for young blacks to get union cards, and without union cards it was hard for them to get jobs in the construction business.

Randolph and Rustin had created an organization—the Recruitment and Training Program (RTP), operating primarily in New York City but also in Mississippi and, eventually, other cities around the country—to train young black kids to take the unions' apprenticeship tests so that union leaders would have no excuse to keep them out. At their request, I became active on the board. We recruited Ernest Green, the first black to enter Little Rock High School after the 1954 Supreme Court decision in *Brown v. Board of Education*, to become RTP's president.

RTP was housed in the headquarters of the United Federation of Teachers (UFT), and through the program I met Albert Shanker, who had just become the union's president. Shanker was a product of New York City and contributed to its fabric in many ways. He was the son of Russian-Jewish immigrants; his mother had worked seventy hours a week in a knitting factory. He headed the debate team at Stuyvesant, one of New York's premier public high schools. He joined the Young People's Socialist League and picketed segregated restaurants and movie theaters with the Congress of Racial Equality. After graduating from college, he taught math in East Harlem, then became a union organizer. His election as UFT president threw the Communists out of control of the union.

Shanker was a large part of the reason why RTP succeeded, as was Lane Kirkland, then executive assistant to George Meany of the AFL-CIO, whom I had met through Shanker and who would later become the AFL-CIO's president. Both men stayed my friends until they died and played significant roles in what I was able to accomplish in public life.

✦

I WAS ALSO active in the National Committee against Discrimination in Housing, through which I had met Robert Weaver. When Weaver became secretary of HUD, he and New York's mayor, Robert F. Wagner Jr., asked HRH to build a project to rehabilitate an entire block of tenements in Harlem. Six million dollars for this experiment came from the city, private foundations, and the federal Office of Economic Opportunity.

The work entailed gutting the tenements and renovating the interiors to provide larger rooms and new plumbing and kitchens. We would accomplish the renovation by transforming three tenements at a time. Tenants of the first three tenements would move into temporary housing. When their apartments were done, they would move back, and tenants of the next three tenements would move into the temporary housing so that renovation of the next three apartments could start.

Financing for this type of project could not be put together without low-cost mortgage insurance from the Federal Housing Administration. But in order to get the insurance, a contractor not only had to give the government a fixed price but was also required to post a bond to guarantee the performance. Since it was impossible to know the interior structural conditions in these tenements until the project started and walls were opened, it was impossible to know exactly what the renovations would cost. There weren't many contractors willing to post the bond.

Wagner and Weaver knew that HRH was sympathetic to the project and would post the bond, which we did. But we lost a significant amount of money. Then, adding insult to injury, Representative Adam Clayton Powell held a congressional hearing on the very 114th Street block in which we were working to ask why the city had given a no-bid contract to a white contractor. In short, it was a risky and complicated political climate in which HRH had chosen to build. But sometimes, with difficulty, we were able to make it work for us.

Through the reform Democratic politics that had introduced me to Califano, I also met the architect Lewis Davis. Lew was cofounder of the architectural firm that would become Davis Brody Bond. He would go on to design iconic projects for New York institutions, including the New York Public Library expansion. One of those institutions was Mount Sinai Hospital, where he died in 2006.

In the early 1960s, Lew's firm was known for its fine design of single-family homes, churches, schools, and academic buildings. The firm had never designed an apartment building. But Lew and I agreed on many things about housing policy, including the view that the cookie-cutter publicly subsidized housing produced in New York for the past thirty years, sterile bordering on outright ugly, was unnecessarily awful. We thought we could do better, building architecturally distinguished housing even within the requirements and cost constraints imposed by state and local governments. This was the shared view that started us planning for the Riverbend apartments in Harlem, a dress rehearsal for what would become the Waterside apartments on the East River in Manhattan.

Lew and I decided to develop Riverbend as a co-op, selling the apartments to tenant-owners, rather than as rental apartments. The reason was a combination of government regulations and HRH's economic situation. If the project had been a rental development, the government would have required us to invest several million dollars of equity in it. During those years, when some HRH projects were more profitable and some less so, we did not have that kind of money.

But the government did not require the same kind of equity investment for building a co-op. Moreover, if the apartments sold briskly,
HRH could surely use the cash.

We chose land for the project on East 138th Street between Fifth
Avenue and the Harlem River. The spot was occupied by a sanitation
garage that the city intended to close, but it had several advantages.
First, the neighborhood desperately needed housing. Moreover, although HRH did not have the money to purchase the land in advance, the project would be city-financed, and we would not have
to pay for the land until we secured the city's mortgage loan. Finally,
there were no tenants to relocate.

Sam Ratensky, a senior official at the city's Housing and Redevel-
opment Board had once worked for the famed architect Frank Lloyd
Wright. Ratensky prided himself on his architectural expertise; he,
too, had dreamed of a city-financed housing project that was architecturally excellent. He took a look at Lew Davis's stunning designs,
promised his support, and delivered. He and the city's housing agencies helped us get the project approved by all the necessary government bodies, including the City Planning Commission.

At that time, I was thoroughly naïve about New York City politics.
As I later learned, people in city government were amazed that we
got Riverbend approved without the involvement of a single Harlem
politician. I'm still not sure why they were so amazed; but my guess is
that everyone, including the politicians, kind of admired two young,
idealistic people trying to build in a troubled neighborhood. Maybe
they figured that if we succeeded, they could take the credit.

It took another year to arrange all the financing for Riverbend
and two more years to build it. All the apartments sold. HRH made
the most money it would ever earn as a builder on a single project.
Lew won awards for its design. But Riverbend was simplicity itself in
comparison with Waterside, which would change the face of Manhattan's waterfront. It took ten years.

◊

Getting Permission to Start Getting Permission

On a spring afternoon not long after I returned from Georgia, Lew Davis and I shared a brown-bag lunch on an old wooden pier jutting out into the East River at 25th Street, near Lew's office on Second Avenue. The site around the pier was an old, dirty eyesore, familiar to motorists on the FDR Drive. In my pocket, I was carrying a form letter that the US ambassador to the United Nations, Adlai Stevenson, had sent to everyone in the New York real estate business, asking us to help him find housing for UN personnel.

Lew and I looked north toward the UN complex, less than a mile up the East River, and in one of those epiphanic moments that sometimes shapes a city's history, realized that on the site where we were sitting we could build into and over the river. We rushed back to Lew's office to look at a map of New York City. We quickly figured that on the basis of the pier head line—which determined how far into the river we could build—we had, in theory, five acres.

Over the following weeks, we came up with a brochure describing the plan for the project we had named Waterside. It drew on the history of the New York waterfront and quoted liberally from *Moby-Dick*; Herman Melville, a customs inspector in New York, had lived on East 26th Street. The brochure featured beautiful renderings of four apartment towers and included a well-argued explanation of how the project would both aid the UN in its critical mission and provide housing for thousands of New Yorkers.

But when, after several attempts, I got my chance to present the brochure to James Felt, chairman of the City Planning Commission, it didn't do much for him. "Good work, young man," he said coolly. "You have a great future in the housing business. But don't waste your time on *this* project; it's totally unrealistic."

One morning a couple of years later, when my family and I were visiting Lew Davis and his family on Martha's Vineyard, I opened the *New York Times* and saw a story announcing that the City Planning Commission had a new chairman, William Ballard, an architect, who was lamenting the fact that the highway system around the perimeter of Manhattan prevented the people of New York from enjoying the city's waterfront. I promptly called Ballard's office, and a few days later Lew and I flew to New York to meet the new chairman. Ballard, as warm as Felt had been cool, encouraged us to pursue our plans.

Getting the Land—in Concept

The process of securing city support for the idea of our leasing the Waterside property was a microcosm of the complexity of New York politics. All it took was redefining the navigable status of the East River, fighting off Laurance Rockefeller, and negotiating the politics of race and ethnicity.

We began a closer examination of the legal issues involved in the project and were dismayed. A federal statute dating back to the War of 1812 gave the federal government the right to expropriate, without compensation to the owner, any obstruction to a "navigable waterway," which the East River unmistakably was. The statute had probably been enacted to ensure that the river could be used against a British invasion. The threat was gone, but the law remained. Because of the statute, we couldn't get title insurance for the property. Therefore, we wouldn't be able to get mortgage financing.

Again I called Califano. He produced a letter from the Army Corps of Engineers stating that it had no intention of expropriating property on the East River for the defense of the nation. But intentions are not legal realities, and the letter did not satisfy the title company. In the end, it took an act of Congress to solve the problem—specifically, an amendment to the Rivers and Harbors Act of 1965, introduced in the House of Representatives by New York Congressman Emanuel Celler at Mayor Wagner's instance. The amendment declared the East River between 17th and 30th Streets from the shore out to the pier head line non-navigable for purposes of federal law.

We also had to keep our project from being killed in its cradle

by the self-confident and well-connected philanthropist Laurance
Rockefeller. In 1963 Eleanor Clark French, then New York City's
Commissioner to the United Nations, told me that Rockefeller was
trying to find a place to build a school for the children of UN del-
egates. In response, I told her about our plan for the East River site.
Sensing synergy, she set up a meeting for us with Rockefeller. We
happily described our plan to him in some detail. He was cordial but
noncommittal.

Then, in 1965, Bill Ballard of the City Planning Commission
called to ask what had become of our plan. A resolution to lease
those five acres on the East River to the UN school was pending before the city's Board of Estimate, the final authority at the time on all
matters involving the disposition of city property. Indeed, the board
was meeting at that very moment at City Hall to make the decision.

Laurance Rockefeller had stolen our idea.

I jumped on the subway—then, as now, the fastest way to travel in
the city—and found Ballard at City Hall. He pulled Mayor Wagner
out of the Board of Estimate meeting so that I could tell him my
story. Wagner saw that something fundamentally unfair was going on.
He went back into the meeting and struck the UN school resolution
from the agenda.

Afterward, Wagner had his staff divide the original five-acre property. Part of it could be used for the UN school; the rest was earmarked for Waterside.

Getting the Lease in Reality—
Engineers, Politicians, and the *New York Times*

Having the property earmarked for us was not the same thing as actually getting the city to lease it to us. The latter process began with
the 1965 election of the Republican John V. Lindsay as mayor. He
invited me to Gracie Mansion to ask whether I'd consider becoming
his Commissioner of Public Works. I said no but managed to slip in a
few words about our plan for housing on the East River. Lindsay was

normally not the most demonstrative of men, but the idea excited him. On the spot, he asked the city's Corporation Counsel to figure out how the city could legally enter into a long-term lease with a private developer to build the kind of housing I described.

This, too, was merely preliminary; we couldn't actually begin negotiating the lease until we had a sense of the costs of the project. But the city's tentative commitment enabled us to raise the money to do the engineering studies we needed to estimate those costs. It took six months of testing to answer our questions. What was the condition of the riverbed? How far down did the rock extend? What was its bearing capacity? Could it support the four towers we planned, with 1,470 apartments plus a 700-car garage, a four-acre public plaza, a health club, and miscellaneous office and retail space? But the tests established that the idea could work. The engineering and architectural plans advanced far enough to allow us to make our cost estimates and begin lease negotiations. Mayor Lindsay's office approved a lease agreement in the fall of 1966.

This was not the end of the uncertainties. The project would have to be approved by the Board of Estimate, and the board's procedures called for public hearings in which all interested citizens could voice their support, concerns, or dissent. To our surprise—we were still naïve—there was opposition. Community organizations objected that the Waterside buildings would obstruct traffic and block views of the river for existing residents along the waterfront. Some groups wanted the apartments exclusively for the poor, with no middle-income tenants. Others, including the city comptroller, wanted the apartments to be built for the rich so that they would generate more in property tax revenues for the city.

In early December 1966, Mayor Lindsay told me he had not been able to secure a majority in the Board of Estimate. Professionally, it was a bad time; HRH had lost a lot of money. Personally, it was the worst year of my life. In the spring, my second son, Steven, age two-and-a-half, had been diagnosed with leukemia. He was treated throughout the year at the Children's Blood Center at New York

Hospital and died in December. My office was near St. Patrick's Cathedral, and when I was overwhelmed with anxiety and sadness, I would retreat there to grieve until I could face the jobs that had to be done.

Mayor Lindsay said I should try to win the votes for Waterside by myself. So I did, over several intense weeks. We got decisive help from two lead editorials on two successive days in the *New York Times*— written, I later learned, by Ada Louise Huxtable—saying that because of the quality of Waterside's design and the role it would play in opening the waterfront to New York's citizens, the city would be crazy not to approve the project. As I had hoped, but not fully expected, the project's design turned out to be a political asset.

There followed two weeks of negotiation with the borough presidents of the Bronx and Manhattan, Herman Badillo and Percy Sutton. We finally came to a compromise under which one of the Waterside towers would be reserved for federally subsidized low-income residents. The Board of Estimate finally approved the project. At last, a proud mayor and an excited developer executed the lease.

Getting the Money

The financing was most complicated of all. Some of the details of the complexity need to be understood, because the financing of government-assisted housing in the postwar era was one of the chief expressions of the politics and policies of the time.

At first we thought we could raise the money for Waterside privately. We hoped to take advantage of state legislation that provided real estate tax exemptions to developers who agreed to limit their profits. This was the law that had enabled the Metropolitan Life Insurance Company to build the huge Stuyvesant Town and Peter Cooper Village developments after World War II. We visited commercial banks, savings banks, insurance companies but were turned down by all of them. Financial institutions are not renowned for their sympathy to social betterment, and the idea that limits would be placed on the developer's profits severely reduced the amount of money they were willing to lend against Waterside's future value. I became inured to hearing the word "no." It was a lesson that would later prove valuable in public life.

With Waterside in trouble, we turned to the city's Mitchell-Lama program. The Mitchell-Lama law was enacted in 1955, when it became clear that more powerful incentives were needed to produce middle-income housing. The law not only offered real estate tax abatements but also authorized the state and the city to issue bonds—that is, agreements to repay loans—in order to finance housing. The benefit provided by the bonds works this way: interest on bonds that state and local governments issue for public purposes is exempt from federal income tax. In addition, governments, because of their power to tax their citizens, are viewed as excellent credit risks. Therefore, governments can borrow funds at low interest rates. Governments can then pass on the savings when they lend the funds to developers of middle-income housing who agree to limit their profits. The developers can pass the savings on to their tenants.

We painstakingly negotiated a mortgage loan with the city. Our decision to use Mitchell-Lama financing, however, meant not just limiting our profits but also giving city government substantial authority over the design of Waterside's buildings and the characteristics of the tenants who would live in them. We would have to redesign the project to comply with the city's rules and specifications. The redesign took us until 1969.

The exercise would turn out to be a constructive one; but by the time it was done, New York City had reached the limits of its borrowing capacity. In the Mitchell-Lama program as it was originally designed, the state or city issued housing bonds and obligated itself—pledged its "full faith and credit"—to the repayment of the debt. Then, in 1960, the state established a separate state entity, the Housing Finance Agency, which expanded the state's capacity to borrow for housing by issuing what were called "moral obligation" bonds, which were backed by something a little bit less than state government's full faith and credit. But at the time we were financing Waterside, New York City had no such mechanism, and the city itself was no longer able to raise the money on its own credit to make our mortgage loan.

With little hope, I asked Ray O'Keefe, head of the real estate department at Chase Manhattan Bank, whether Chase would make a construction loan for Waterside if the city would make a commitment to repay the loan as soon as it was able to borrow more funds. Chase agreed to do so if all ten of the other major banks in New York would do the same. I began the grind of making the rounds of every major commercial bank in the city, toting models of our Waterside plans. The banks finally agreed, and the mayor made the commitment. The deal involved city officials, officers of eleven banks, and, of course, eleven law firms. It was the most complicated business transaction I had ever seen, let alone negotiated.

The documents were signed on New Year's Eve, 1970. Construction finally began in February 1971, ten years after my first visit to the City Planning Commission, with the driving of more than 1,700 steel piles, each encased in concrete, into a riverbed already populated by massive amounts of scrap metal and masonry junk.

The Last Crisis

Then came the final obstacle—and the means I devised for overcoming it. As the construction of Waterside neared completion, the banks began to press us and Mayor Lindsay to honor the city's commitment to repay their construction loans. But the city's borrowing capacity remained exhausted. I suggested that Mayor Lindsay ask the governor and state legislature to establish a new city financing agency that could issue bonds like those issued by the state's Housing Finance Agency, and I worked with the mayor's staff to draft the legislation that created the New York City Housing Development Corporation. The agency raised the money that enabled the city to make a mortgage loan to Waterside, so that Waterside could redeem the banks' construction loans and enjoy a stable, long-term source of financing.

In 1971, after we began the construction of Waterside and started tearing down the old wooden piers at the site, we uncovered a bronze plaque dedicated by Great Britain to the American people. Quoting Winston Churchill, it described the dark days early in World War II when a flotilla of American ships brought food and supplies to the people of England and, on the return voyage, carried ballast made up of rubble from the bombed-out cities of Britain's coast. The rubble was deposited just north of 23rd Street. We delivered the plaque to the English Speaking Union in New York.

After Waterside was completed, a ceremony celebrated the reinstallation of the plaque. The main speaker was Cary Grant, born in England as Archibald Leach. His parents were killed in one of those German bombings. It was possible that their remains lay under his feet.

Some thirteen years after Lew Davis and I had that brown-bag lunch on the East 25th Street pier, the first tenant moved into Waterside. Lew won design awards for the project. The rest of us were praised for clearing the financial hurdles in its way. The development was essentially completed in 1974, renting apartments to UN personnel and people who worked in the area's medical facilities. We negotiated federal subsidies that allowed us to keep our promise to devote one of the buildings exclusively to moderate-income tenants. In the years since Waterside's success, similar federal legislation on building in navigable waterways has made it possible to develop waterfront projects in other communities. The idea of having mixed-income families living in a single development has become commonplace. The Housing Development Corporation became the city's chief financing arm in the construction of affordable housing. By now it is the leading local housing agency in the nation, issuing more bonds to finance more housing than any other comparable agency.

WHILE WATERSIDE WAS being built, unrest increased in the nation's cities. The mid-1960s saw a series of riots: in the Watts area of Los Angeles, in the Hough area of Cleveland, Ohio, and in Omaha, Nebraska. In December 1966, President Johnson created both the National Advisory Commission on Civil Disorders, known as the Kerner Commission, and the National Commission on Urban Problems. The latter, headed by former Senator Paul Douglas of Illinois, focused mainly on the housing issues that many believed were an underlying source of the discontent manifested by the riots. I was appointed to the commission, doubtless on the recommendation of Joe Califano, by then Johnson's chief of staff.

The commission held hearings in most of the country's major cities. We heard countless hours of testimony about the need for affordable housing, examined the obstacles posed by local zoning ordinances and building codes, and learned about the effects of racial anxieties on the politics of housing decisions. The staff was first-rate and the members diligent, although they included only one mayor, from Arlington, Texas, halfway between Dallas and Fort Worth, who boasted that almost no one was on welfare in *his* town. Our report to the president noted that the country's accomplishments in subsidized housing had been small and concluded that tax incentives were inadequate to solve the substandard housing problem. We called for modernization of property taxation, zoning, and building codes, along with many other recommendations. The report remains on library shelves. No one paid much attention to it.

✑

MEANWHILE, HRH kept building, adapting to continued changes in housing policy. One day in the summer of 1971, a real estate broker came to HRH's offices and asked whether we would be interested in buying the entire Manhattan square block bounded by East 43rd and East 42nd Streets on the north and south and Ninth and Tenth Avenues on the east and west. It was not prime real estate. In the late 1960s and early 1970s, Times Square and the adjacent Hell's

Kitchen neighborhood, where the block was situated, were home to New York's theater district as well as an urban mess of pawnbrokers, prostitutes, and drug dealers. But a few days after the broker's visit, when I was on my way to an Italian restaurant on Ninth Avenue, it occurred to me that this part of the city could be transformed into a residential area.

Our architects designed Manhattan Plaza with two towers, one with forty-five stories and one with forty-six stories, to take account of the slope of the land. The buildings would include 1,688 apartments, a thousand-car garage, an elevated plaza with an outdoor café, and extensive recreational facilities. Once again we turned to New York City's Mitchell-Lama program for financing.

People thought we were insane to be developing such a good building in such a bad neighborhood, and they were almost right. The year after we got all the governmental approvals, including the mortgage loan that enabled us to start construction, the City of New York almost went bankrupt. Once again, especially in light of the questions about the marketability of the development, the city could no longer fund the mortgage advances it had committed itself to make under the Mitchell-Lama program.

By that time, however, there had been three presidential administrations' worth of changes in federal policy toward housing subsidies, from mortgage insurance to mortgage subsidy programs to, beginning in 1974, subsidies provided through vouchers given to tenants under Section 8 of the Housing Act. It was Section 8 that enabled Manhattan Plaza to survive.

Though many people have claimed authorship of the plan that was finally developed for Manhattan Plaza, it was Gerry Schoenfeld, then head of the Shubert Organization of theaters, who was primarily responsible for the idea of using Section 8 to save the project. Manhattan Plaza would take 70 percent of its tenants from the world of the performing arts. The other 30 percent would be people from the surrounding neighborhood who were eligible for Section 8 subsidies. Manhattan Plaza entered into a contract with HUD under which the agency would provide Section 8 subsidies to the tenants. The question of the marketability of the development was answered. Over time, the complex became the center of a vibrant residential neighborhood. It helped cement New York's preeminence in the arts and anchored an urban transformation still spreading throughout the West Side.

That is the way it is with cities—one layer upon another, each structure representing a moment's accretion of public policies, private visions, and a seemingly endless process of adjusting the conflicting demands of money and politics. There was no general answer to the puzzle of housing in America's cities, but there were pieces of an answer that a willing builder, with government support, could assemble, one by one.

⊘⟋

THERE IS A POSTSCRIPT: a story about a great urban achievement turning into a more or less ordinary landlord–tenant dispute. Twenty years after the completion of a Mitchell-Lama project, a developer is allowed to repay the city's mortgage loan, end the project's tax abatement, and start charging the higher rents that prevail in the competitive private market. To repay the city's mortgage loan, the developer generally has to use conventional mortgage loans, which the developer can get because the higher rents will support the payment of the higher interest rates.

But under the law, if the project was completed before 1974, the developer cannot begin charging market rental rates. Instead, the apartments become rent-stabilized, with rent increases limited by state and city regulations. Because the rents can't be raised to market levels, the developer may be unable to get the conventional financing to repay the city. It can be an endless loop, in which the return of the apartments to the private market is, as they say, indefinitely delayed.

The time had arrived when Waterside could leave the Mitchell-Lama program—if it could repay the city's mortgage loan from conventional sources. But Waterside couldn't get the conventional financing unless it could raise the rents to market levels, and it couldn't raise the rents to market levels if its apartments were finished before 1974. Some Waterside tenants had moved in before 1974, but most had moved in later. Did Waterside have to stay rent-stabilized or not?

Litigation with the Waterside tenants ensued. It took no time at all for Waterside's developers, who had won accolades for pioneering mixed-income housing, to be attacked as greedy landlords. Elected officials were passionately—not to say self-interestedly—on the side of the tenants. Not until 2001 did we reach a compromise: rent increases for the existing tenants would be limited, but apartments that became vacant could be rented at market rates.

That was enough to allow Waterside to raise the funds it needed to repay the city mortgage and exit Mitchell-Lama. In accordance with yet another city political tradition, the baby had been successfully split in two.

3

Governor Rockefeller's Xanadu

I N EARLY JANUARY 1975, I got a phone call from New York's new Democratic governor, Hugh Carey, who had been in office for less than two weeks. I had never met him, hadn't supported his candidacy, and was taken by surprise.

The previous August, Richard Nixon had resigned the presidency rather than face impeachment. Vice President Gerald Ford became president and appointed New York's governor, Nelson Rockefeller, as the new vice president. Rockefeller's lieutenant governor, Malcolm Wilson, became the state's governor until the next gubernatorial election in November 1974, but it was clearly going to be a banner year for Democrats running for office.

One day that summer, Hugh Carey, then a congressman from Brooklyn, called me to say he was running in the Democratic gubernatorial primary against Howard Samuels, a businessman and civil rights activist who was the choice of the Democratic State Committee. Carey asked to visit me; he wanted my support. But Samuels was a friend, and I had made a small contribution to his campaign. I never gave to two candidates in the same race. In fact, because HRH did business with the government, I rarely contributed to any New York state or local candidates. I told Carey apologetically that his visit would be a waste of time. Carey went on to win the primary and the governorship without my help. I didn't hear from him until his phone call the following January.

By the time of the call, Carey had delivered his inaugural address to the state legislature, declaring that the "days of wine and roses are over." The country was in recession, and New York's budget was suffering accordingly. But the governor was facing a more acute emergency. A huge state authority, the New York State Urban Development Corporation (UDC), was on the verge of bankruptcy. The major banks had just informed Carey that they would no longer lend the UDC money or underwrite its bonds. Carey had been told I was an expert on housing finance, so he was calling to ask for help.

⁂

THE RISE AND FALL of UDC reflected years of major developments in American politics and housing finance: growth in the sophistication of municipal financing, expanded confidence in the nation's capacity to solve its economic and social problems, confusion amid the social unrest that followed, and shock at Watergate and its aftermath. The crisis finally came to a head on Carey's watch, but it began with Rockefeller—and John Mitchell.

Rockefeller was the state's governor for fifteen years, from 1959 until he resigned in 1973 to focus on his national political ambitions. I had met him only once, but even that brief meeting was enough to convey his vast energy and unhesitating convictions. He may have had some trouble distinguishing between money the state had raised through taxes and fees and money it had merely borrowed, but he certainly believed in good things. He believed in making higher education widely available. He wanted to bring health care to the needy. Years later, Carey told me that in 1965, when President Johnson was designing the legislation that established Medicare for senior citizens, Rockefeller was extremely important in persuading him to add Medicaid to the legislation to provide health-care coverage for the poor.

Rockefeller also believed in making housing available to poor families, as well as working-class and middle-class families. In this he was heir to federal and state housing policies that had their origins in the Depression, when President Franklin Roosevelt's administration first proposed that the federal government build and finance public housing for the poor. Southern senators objected to giving the federal government authority to decide where the poor in their states would live. Therefore, the New Deal's public housing legislation, as finally enacted, provided that local housing authorities would build the housing. The federal government, under contracts with the local authorities, would pay the debt service on the bonds that were sold to finance the construction. HRH built a significant amount of this type of public housing.

After World War II, as the sense grew that not just the poor but middle-class Americans could hardly afford new market-rate housing, a succession of New York governors tried to use the state's borrowing power to issue tax-exempt bonds in the hope of stimulating the construction of affordable middle-class housing. But this hope was increasingly disappointed. Under the New York State Constitution, like many other state constitutions, the state can unconditionally obligate itself to repay bonds by pledging its "full faith and credit" to the repayment only if the voters approve the issuance of the bonds. After the war, New York voters approved several of these general obligation bond issues to build housing for the poor. Over time, however, voters became more resistant. By the time Rockefeller took office in 1959, any ballot proposal to issue general obligation bonds for housing was almost certain to fail.

These constitutional limits on the states' borrowing authority were the legacies of state financing crises in the nineteenth century. By the twentieth century, the limits prevented states from raising capital for purposes that many had come to consider vital.

Which brings us to John Mitchell. When Carey called me in 1975, Mitchell, formerly President Nixon's attorney general, was on trial in federal court for crimes related to Watergate. But before Mitchell was associated with Nixon, he was prominent among the bond lawyers who enabled states and localities to borrow money in the nation's credit markets. The State of New York, under Rockefeller, was one of Mitchell's many clients.

As New York's bond counsel, John Mitchell is widely credited with having developed the moral obligation bond, an alternative device through which the state, and eventually other states, could borrow large amounts of money for public purposes such as housing. The state did not have a legal obligation to repay this type of bond, but it declared that it was morally obligated to stand behind it. In the housing area, for example, the only actual legal security for a moral obligation bond might be the rental revenues from the housing that the bond financed. But if these revenues came up short, the state was morally obligated to step in and ensure that the bondholders were paid.

The actual mechanism was this: the original bond amount would include a reserve fund, which contained enough money to pay one year's debt service. If the housing development did not generate enough revenues to cover the required debt service, the trustee for the bondholders could have the debt service paid out of the reserve fund. And if the reserve fund was impaired in this way, it was the moral obligation of the state to appropriate the money to replenish it.

Because the state assumed this contingent obligation to the bondholders, the markets had confidence in the bond. But because the state's obligation was only moral, not legal, there was no need for the state to undertake the increasingly difficult task of getting voter approval at the ballot box. The moral obligation bond, in short, was intended to provide for present public needs in the face of historically imposed legal constraints—and, for better or worse, to circumvent the voters.

In 1960 Rockefeller persuaded the state legislature to establish the New York State Housing Finance Agency to issue moral obligation bonds for middle-income housing construction—under strict constraints. The developer-owner of an HFA-financed project was required to make a minimum equity investment and, as with similar programs, to limit profits. Moreover, for bonds to be issued, HFA had to certify that the project's revenues would equal the sum of its operating expenses, its debt service payments, and the limited return on the developer's equity investment.

Acting within these constraints, HFA financed a number of middle-income housing projects in New York, including Co-op City, still the largest single housing development in the United States. HRH built many apartment buildings financed in this way.

But the scale of HFA's efforts did not satisfy Rockefeller. He wanted an enterprise that would not just finance housing projects for private developers but serve as a developer itself. More than that, he wanted the state involved not in just housing construction but also in the more comprehensive development process he thought was needed to reverse the deteriorated physical, economic, and social conditions in New York's major cities.

Accordingly, in 1967 Rockefeller proposed a new public corporation, the Urban Development Corporation, with powers far exceeding those of HFA. UDC would have not just borrowing authority but also the ability to acquire real estate by exercising the state's powers of eminent domain. UDC, unlike HFA, would be able to do its own building.

∂ρ

THE MAN ROCKEFELLER chose as UDC's chief executive was Edward J. Logue, a bright and attractive urban planner who, deservedly, had received much of the credit for renewal projects in New Haven, Connecticut, and Boston, Massachusetts. Rockefeller saw Logue as able, honest, and appreciative of fine architecture. Logue, like Rockefeller himself, thought big. Both men believed their mission noble in purpose and doable in practice. They were disdainful of people who stood in their way—or merely had more skeptical temperaments. Their argument for a powerful UDC gained force from the violent social unrest of 1968. That year, on the night when Rockefeller flew back to Albany after attending the funeral of Martin Luther King Jr., the New York Legislature approved his UDC legislation.

In between the original draft legislation and the final enactment, there had been changes. Despite opposition from local officials, UDC had been given increased authority to override local building codes and zoning ordinances. UDC had also acquired more independence in its financing. In the original draft legislation, UDC debt was to be issued under HFA's standards and oversight. But Logue persuaded Rockefeller otherwise. In the final legislation, UDC, unlike HFA and other state housing agencies, would not be required to have all the financing for a project in place before making final commitments and beginning work. And, unlike other agencies, UDC would not have to limit itself to issuing bonds secured by revenues from specific projects but would be able to issue its own general obligation bonds, which meant that no particular UDC assets or revenue streams would have to be set aside as security.

Friction arose almost immediately between HFA and the new UDC. HFA wanted UDC to show that there would be enough revenue from its projects to pay interest and principal on its bonds. UDC's revenue projections were optimistic; HFA's were more conservative. There were also squabbles between UDC and the state's Division of Housing and Urban Renewal over issues from estimates of expenses to the kinds of amenities to be included in UDC-sponsored apartments. Rockefeller and Logue procured new legislation that removed the commissioner of Housing and Urban Renewal from the review of UDC projects. Both UDC and the commissioner were pleased.

In 1968 Congress enacted Section 236 of the Housing Act, which authorized HUD to give interest-rate subsidies to qualified mortgage lenders—that is, lenders to projects that limited developers' profits—in order to ensure that the tenants, not the landlords, would benefit from the subsidies. These subsidies enabled these developers to pay interest at an effective rate of just 1 percent. The prospect of these subsidies enabled UDC to increase its projections of the number of moderate-income housing units it could develop. UDC's authority to override local regulations enabled UDC to project still faster completion.

Propelled by its extraordinary authority, the Urban Development Corporation got off to a fast start. By June 1969, it was negotiating fifty projects in twenty-three cities. A year-and-a-half later, it was negotiating for 45,000 housing units with a total cost of $2 billion, a price tag that was still bigger when one added the various commercial and industrial developments included in UDC's plans. UDC's chairman, George Woods, was also chairman of the First Boston Corporation, which became one of UDC's chief underwriters. After initial difficulties in establishing its credit in the marketplace, UDC issued its first bonds in January 1970.

UDC publicly emphasized the breadth of its powers, drawing invidious comparisons between itself and HFA, which UDC people characterized as a mere mortgage lender, in contrast with UDC, a developer and builder. But ambition had costs. The corporation's broad powers, including its ability to bypass local standards and ignore local demands, generated widespread suspicion and resentment. Later, when UDC's financing structure proved fragile and the corporation ran into trouble, the suspicion and resentment deprived it of political support it sorely needed.

⸉⸊

UDC's MOST AMBITIOUS project was the development of Welfare Island, a small island in the East River between Manhattan and Queens. Between the mid-nineteenth and mid-twentieth centuries, it was home to a penitentiary, the New York City Lunatic Asylum, a workhouse, a smallpox hospital, and several chronic-care facilities. In 1971 it was, understandably, in the process of being renamed Roosevelt Island. Ed Logue invited me to lunch to discuss the project.

We had known each other casually for some years because of our common interest in urban renewal and government-assisted housing. As we sat down to eat, Logue said he admired the plans for Waterside, then under construction, and its architect, Lew Davis. Flattery accomplished, he came to the point: would HRH consider becoming the agent and overseer of Roosevelt Island's development? HRH would supervise construction of the island's public infrastructure, such as roads and utilities. We would recommend developers for the island's individual housing projects and oversee their work.

Consider it? HRH had stretched its resources mightily to get Waterside built and repay a working capital loan from Chase Bank. Logue was offering a multiyear contract worth more than $3 million. It meant a respite from financial worries and a chance to expand our business. I left the lunch as excited as I'd been since my pre-Waterside brown-bagger with Lew Davis on the banks of the East River. I reported HRH's good fortune to Ray O'Keefe of Chase, who had arranged Waterside's working capital loan and mortgage, assuring him that Chase needn't worry about getting repaid. With Donald Schapiro, once my professor of legal accounting at Yale Law School and now my friend and counsel, I began negotiating the contract with Logue. I couldn't wait to sign.

But I also started studying the Roosevelt Island project, and reality set in almost immediately. For one thing, UDC's cost estimates were based on 1971 construction costs. But the projects would take years to finish. Over that time, construction costs would increase because of inflation, but the increase was nowhere to be found in UDC's calculations. More important, UDC's projection of its revenues from completed projects appeared to be substantially overstated. If it turned out that the revenues couldn't cover the estimated interest and principal on the bonds financing the project, UDC and the state were going to be in deep trouble.

When I told Logue about my worries, he asked me to meet with his numbers experts. They would reassure me, he said. They did not. The more I learned about the economics of the project, the more I worried. "If someone offers you a million bucks to try to get to the moon," I told myself, "and if you know that try as you might, you can't do it, don't take the money." But this wasn't one million; it was three.

Don Schapiro put it in more practical terms. He warned that if I simply took the job, I would be saying, in effect, that I could produce economically self-sustaining housing on Roosevelt Island. If I wasn't certain I could do so, my contract with UDC needed a clause stating explicitly that HRH was making no representations about the economic success of the project.

I was in agony, money warring with reputation in my Faustian soul. Finally, however, I told Logue I wanted the protective clause in HRH's contract. And that, as I'd feared, was the end of the deal: Logue had no wish to pay a consultant $3 million to do a job that the consultant didn't think could be done. Roosevelt Island would be built without HRH Construction, and HRH would somehow have to compensate for the loss of the UDC contract.

Only a few people at UDC and HRH knew about Logue's making and rescinding his offer, but I did have to call Ray O'Keefe at Chase and take back my assurances. Ray understood. He was interested in my views of the Roosevelt Island enterprise. Indeed, because Chase was deeply involved in UDC's financing, he asked me to share my thoughts with his boss, Chase chairman David Rockefeller. Word spread, as it always does in the tightly knit housing industry, that I had predicted UDC would have trouble meeting the debt service obligations on its bonds. But nothing appeared in the press. The Urban Development Corporation kept pursuing its projects throughout the state.

*

THUS, WHEN GOVERNOR Carey phoned me in January 1975, I was not exactly surprised about UDC's troubles. The next day, with Judah Gribetz, an extraordinary lawyer who was the governor's counsel, I drove up to Albany to meet Carey.

Judah was also my friend. I had met him in the early 1960s when he was deputy commissioner of the New York City Building Department under Mayor Wagner. HRH was finishing a building and needed a certificate of occupancy. A city building inspector was trying to extract a bribe for it. I called the Building Department to complain and ended up with Judah on the other end of the line. The problem went away. In the fifty years since then, there aren't many weeks when we haven't seen each other or talked on the phone.

Judah moved on to serve as regional administrator of HUD under Secretary Robert Weaver. Judah was one of the people who had recommended me to Carey; Bob Weaver was the other.

During the drive, Judah told me he hadn't known Carey before becoming his counsel. The same was true for David Burke, who was secretary to the governor, the top staff job in state government, and for Peter Goldmark, the governor's new budget director. In other words, Carey didn't think that being a political supporter or campaign contributor was a necessary qualification for an adviser in whom he could put his trust. Judah filled me in on Carey's team and Carey himself—a straight talker, Judah said, honest, smart, and tough.

At the State Capitol, we were shown directly to Carey's office. As soon as the handshakes were done, Carey reviewed the situation for us. In December 1974, the New York banks lent the Urban Development Corporation $30 million to cover the corporation's day-to-day expenses. The loan was due on February 20, 1975. After the election, Carey had said publicly that the State of New York would honor its moral obligations. But the banks would make no more loans to UDC or underwrite its bonds. In addition to the bank loan, payments of $104 million of bond anticipation notes—short-term financing issued in the expectation that it would be repaid by future UDC bond proceeds—were due on February 25. UDC had no apparent means of making these payments.

Carey said the issue had been at the forefront of his attention since his election. There were discussions about it between the outgoing administration and Carey's transition team. Early on, people hoped HFA would step in and provide much of the financing UDC needed. But HFA rejected that idea, noting that UDC was unlikely to have enough revenues to pay off the debt. There had been a number of task forces and all kinds of recommendations, most involving substantial state appropriations. Carey had asked the legislature to appropriate $178 million to cover UDC's short-term debts, but the legislature was cool to the idea.

Carey said he had decided that he would no longer continue to act on the basis of his predecessors' recommendations. He was going to have his own people review the situation. He wanted to know whether I would be one of them. He asked me to become chairman of UDC. As with every public post I was to hold in the years to come, I would not be paid.

I told him I first had to get a better understanding of UDC's situation, determine whether I had any conflicts of interest, and figure out whether I could afford the time and the potential personal liability entailed in representing and negotiating for a corporation whose ability to pay its debts had been seriously compromised.

When I left the meeting, I did not know the things about Hugh Carey that I was to learn over the months and years of our working relationship. He was a man who was easy to underestimate, an outwardly genial Irish pol who did not wear his emotions or his intelligence on his sleeve. He grew up in Brooklyn, one of six boys. He went into the Army before he finished college and became a highly decorated officer, fighting in the famous battle for the Remagen Bridge. He told the story of having been in the first contingent that freed the Nordhausen concentration camp and his reaction to being surrounded by so much death. Throughout his political life, he maintained a passionate objection to the death penalty.

In 1960 Carey ran for Congress in a district that had been heavily Republican. He won by just a few thousand votes. In the House, he became friendly with the leadership, and within a few years he was on the Ways and Means Committee. As an advocate of federal aid to parochial schools, he fought the Johnson White House over the issue. But his political ambition led him back to New York City, where he ran unsuccessfully for the presidency of the City Council in 1969. Not a man who wasted time in brooding over political loss, he ran for governor as a maverick in 1974 and won.

He was extraordinarily smart, capable of understanding the nuances of complicated commercial and financial transactions and explaining them to politicians in their own language, even though many of them had trouble grasping basic financial principles. He also had other dimensions. He was genuinely devout. He could make decisions on the merits in the face of fierce political pressures. He was honest; indeed, because he was incapable of dissembling, he made enemies when he didn't have to, a distinct liability for a man in politics. The same trait, though, made him the best of allies. Our personal friendship came later. But, at his insistence, until he left office in 1982, I would stay at the Governor's Mansion when I was in Albany. I would play basketball with his children, who adored him. He and I would stay up late talking about politics. In those days, the conversation never spilled over into anything personal.

What I got at our first meeting was an impression of Carey's straightforward seriousness—and a sense that he did not yet understand just how deep his inherited financial problems were. UDC's crisis was imminent, its bankruptcy would have enormous fiscal repercussions throughout the state, and its problems were enmeshed in serious public issues and highly partisan politics. Helping to deal with this crisis would be meat and drink for a man like me, whose temperament and entire course of public and private experiences seemed to have led straight to this point.

க

HOWEVER, MY LAWYERS were not so sure. When I got back to the city, the first person I phoned for advice was Don Schapiro, who offered his services, in this instance as he always did when his city and state were involved, at a significantly discounted rate. Within forty-eight hours, he and his firm had prepared a memorandum about the potential personal liabilities involved in holding the post of UDC chairman and the protections I would need. HRH had never done business with UDC, so I had no conflicts of interest. Still, I would need to learn more about the federal securities and bankruptcy laws, neither of which were among my strong points, and to start measuring my words in public.

But personal liability wasn't the only issue that had to be addressed at the outset. The partisan politics permeating the UDC issue would also have to be defused. UDC was the creature of a Republican governor, Rockefeller. When Carey first took office, some of his aides recommended that he simply blame the UDC mess on the opposing party and wash his hands of it. Carey was too much a statesman to agree. Besides, Rockefeller was now vice president, and Republicans controlled the White House. Who knew when we would need federal help? Closer to home, Republicans controlled the New York State Senate. We would have to find a way to unearth the causes of the financial chaos at UDC without more politics than necessary. Rockefeller, after all, was not the only one who had made the mistake of overestimating government's capacity to do good.

A week after my first meeting with Carey, I told him I would start seeking solutions to UDC's crisis but would not take office as its chairman unless and until it became clear that its bankruptcy was not inevitable. I asked him to propose a bill that would provide public officers' indemnity for me and the other new members of the UDC board and give me authority to choose UDC's chief executive officer and outside counsel. I also asked him to assign the investigation of the UDC crisis to a Moreland Act commission. The Progressive-era Moreland Act of 1907 authorized the creation of commissions with extraordinary powers to investigate the affairs of any state agency and recommend legislative changes. Carey agreed to all of my requests. He welcomed the idea of a Moreland Act commission. He, too, wanted to avoid having to allocate blame or engage in recriminations.

On February 5, at a press conference in Albany, the governor announced my appointment and named Orville Schell to head a Moreland Act commission to investigate the UDC crisis. Schell, the managing partner of a large New York law firm and a past president of the New York City Bar Association, filled the bill for nonpartisanship.

The *New York Times* approved. "No objective is noble enough to overcome fiscal imprudence," the *Times* opined, but "it would be ignoble to retreat" to a policy that "takes no calculated risks on the future." Therefore, the *Times* concluded, UDC's "long-term financing must be put on a sound basis." Vision and prudence both, the *Times* called for. Easier said than done.

∂ρ

MY FIRST JOB was to determine how much cash the Urban Development Corporation would need over the next two years, which was the length of time it would take to fulfill all of the corporation's existing contracts to finance the construction of new apartments. Although I was not yet officially connected with UDC, its staff and outside accountants cooperated fully. Everyone understood the stakes.

Some of the cash needs during this build-out period were easy to estimate. UDC would need $30 million to pay off the short-term loan the banks had made, $104 million to pay interest and principal on the short-term debt due February 25, approximately $80 million a year to pay debt service on UDC's outstanding long-term debt of around $1.1 billion, and about $1 million per month to cover operating overhead. Other needs were harder to estimate, especially the future costs of completing UDC's projects and the revenues likely to be generated by UDC operations during the build-out period. But we estimated that the net cost of bricks and mortar—that is, the overall cost reduced by the revenues the UDC could count on—would be around $370 million. In sum, the total cash UDC needed would be $690 million.

UDC could not reduce this number without either breaching its obligations to its lenders or the developers with whom it had contracts or abandoning projects that were already under development or construction. This last option was economic insanity. If the projects were finished, they could produce enough revenues to cover the cost of servicing the debt that would need to be incurred to complete them. But if they were abandoned before they were

So Much to Do   59

finished, they would produce no income at all. Their value would be totally lost.

Abandoning the projects would also make UDC potentially liable for claims by owners, developers, and contractors. Construction workers would have to be laid off. Suppliers who had dealt with UDC in good faith might be bankrupted. And the more than twenty thousand housing units not completed would deprive some eighty thousand people of safe, decent shelter at reasonable rents. So the next task was to find the money to finish the projects.

✥

We first made what we thought was an attractive offer to the banks to provide the money UDC needed, but their reaction made clear that we would need more than the banks to solve the problem.

UDC could not issue any more of its own general obligation bonds. Even if every UDC project was completed, there would never be enough rent revenue to service all the debt the corporation had incurred, and no one would buy debt based on the corporation's general promises. Therefore, to raise more money by issuing debt, it would have to be fully secured debt. We started trying to find out what UDC revenues were available to offer to the banks as collateral to induce them to provide the additional funds UDC needed to complete the projects already under way.

UDC held housing mortgages, most of its assets, which qualified for interest-rate reduction and rent subsidies from the federal government under Section 236 of the Housing Act. When the housing was completed, the federal government would pay the subsidies to UDC. The subsidies alone would provide enough revenues to support $500 million in new secured borrowing. I concluded—it was the most important idea I contributed to preventing UDC's bankruptcy—that the existing holders of UDC's general obligation bonds did not have a security interest in the federal subsidy revenue UDC would receive. Therefore, the subsidy revenue could be used to collaterize new borrowing.

True, if the UDC's new lenders were secured lenders, while the holders of UDC's general obligation bonds remained unsecured lenders, the new lenders would have a right to be paid before the old lenders. The old bondholders would be subordinated to the new ones. But we did not think this was a fatal problem in UDC's case because subordinating the old lenders would not decrease UDC's future revenues or its ability to pay its debts. Indeed, without the new cash that would enable UDC to complete its projects, it was highly improbable that the old bondholders would be repaid at all.

Moreover, even if UDC did not have enough revenues to pay debt service on its old general obligation bonds, the old bondholders were not without protection: these were moral obligation bonds. New York State, under its moral obligation, could be expected to cover the shortfall. In sum, the subordination of the old bondholders was of no practical consequence.

That was the case we made when we went to the banks with a proposal for a secured lending agreement, with the loan to be repaid when UDC's projects were finished. Neither Carey nor I thought there was any good financial reason why the banks should not lend the money we were asking against the collateral they were being offered.

But the banks balked. They saw our proposal as an attempt to strip UDC assets that rightfully belonged to the existing bondholders. They also asked skeptical questions. How certain was the value of the collateral? How reliable were the estimates of build-out costs? Moreover, in the banks' view, we were simply asking them for too much money. UDC was a creature of the State of New York, established for the benefit of the public. Why shouldn't the public contribute the needed cash?

This last question was a valid one, but there was no chance that the public would contribute all of the needed cash. Carey and state legislative leaders had already rejected the idea of appropriating the full amount that UDC needed. For understandable reasons, they did not think the taxpayers of New York would stand for the idea of laying out almost $700 million for UDC over the next two years. But the public would have to contribute something. UDC would get its money only if the legislature and the banks compromised. And it looked like that compromise would have to be made within two weeks, by February 25, when payment on the $104 million in short-term notes was due.

When I accepted Carey's UDC offer, I knew no one in the state legislature and had never met the heads of the commercial banks that had lent UDC money or the investment banks that had underwritten its bonds. But I was about to spend more time in their company than in my own family's—without the love. I shuttled back and forth between New York and Albany, sometimes more than once a day, in the state's plane.

I was in the eye of a storm. There were calls from legislators, contractors, architects, union representatives, mayors, and other local officials, all of them worried—for themselves, their clients, their members, or their communities—about the consequences of a UDC collapse. With the market value of UDC bonds declining, the anxious bondholders looked to me as their savior. If the negotiations with the banks and the legislature failed, I would become everyone's failed messiah quickly enough.

Under some circumstances I might have enjoyed this experience, but the pressure overrode the pleasure. The crisis threatened not only UDC's moral obligation bonds but also the moral obligation bonds issued by the sixteen other, separate New York state authorities and, in fact, moral obligation bonds issued by other states. In New York, the money raised by these bonds was being used to build public housing, schools, and hospitals. Tens of thousands of people were employed on these projects. A default of payment on the bonds would affect not only the state's credit but also the critical public purposes for which the debt was incurred.

The task seemed impossible, but I had accepted the challenge. It served me right.

I BEGAN THE work of building support in the state legislature, where, even though it was clear that the banks would not lend UDC money unless the state paid at least some of its debts, hostile questions were being asked. A first-term Democratic assemblyman named Charles Schumer intelligently noted that the state paid higher interest rates on its moral obligation bonds than on its full-faith-and-credit debt. Why was the state paying the higher interest rates on the moral obligation bonds, he asked, if in the end it had to back them up anyway?

From the beginning, Assembly Speaker Stanley Steingut, a Brooklyn Democrat, supported the effort to save UDC. More difficult to convince was Warren Anderson, the Republican Senate Majority Leader. He was a lawyer from Binghamton, in the state's southern tier, and a Rockefeller man who didn't want his ex-leader to take full blame for the UDC mess. I began to spend many hours trying to convince him that I had no partisan goals but wanted to strike a fair balance among the interests affected by the crisis.

Anderson eventually became one of my most significant allies, but he wasn't the only person that had to be convinced. Legislators called; their staffs called. How could they vote a big appropriation for UDC, many asked, without assurance that its projects would be finished? It wasn't possible to answer all their calls—the day has just so many hours—but I tried, knowing I would need the maximum possible legislative backing for a solution. Still, Carey and the legislators were firm: they would not appropriate the money to pay off the $104 million short-term debt until the banks showed they were prepared to lend UDC the funds it needed to finish the projects it had under way.

⊘⌀

WHEN I WASN'T seeing legislators in Albany, I was involved in negotiations with the eleven banks involved in the crisis; their deadlines were the most immediate ones. We met in the Federal Reserve's magnificent conference rooms on Liberty Street, near the World Trade Center. We had tried to obtain help from the Federal Reserve, which had statutory authority to make emergency loans to municipal corporations like UDC. Carey had phoned Alfred Hayes, president of the Federal Reserve Bank of New York, and asked whether the bank would purchase and hold UDC's short-term debt long enough to provide us with some additional time for negotiations with the banks. The answer was no. We got the conference rooms instead.

Chase was the lead negotiator for the commercial banks, First Boston for the investment banks. The Morgan Bank acted as trustee for existing bondholders and was potentially liable for a breach of fiduciary duty if it failed to represent their interests properly. The banks offered a dozen plans, but each of them depended on the state's first making an appropriation to pay off UDC's short-term debt, which the state had said it would not do. We were getting nowhere.

We were counting on the availability of federal interest-rate subsidies—enough of them so that the interest paid by UDC projects would effectively be reduced to 1 percent—to provide security for new UDC borrowing. But we learned that UDC was so compromised as a borrower that we were going to have to establish a new state entity to issue the debt. Moreover, if the subsidies were going to serve as security for the new borrowing, they would have to be made available to the new state entity before UDC's projects were actually completed. The federal Department of Housing and Urban Development (HUD) was going to have to bend its rules.

I called Carla Anderson, a law school classmate of mine. In one of those fortunate coincidences that have marked my life, Carla was secretary of HUD at the time. We met in Washington the next day and agreed that the arrangement I described to her—assigning the federal subsidies to a new financing agency before the UDC projects were finished—would serve the purpose of the subsidies, which was to aid the families to whom the apartments would be rented. It would take another week for our lawyers to work out the wording of the agreement, but I returned to New York feeling flush with success and newly confident.

At UDC's New York offices, less than a week before the February

25 deadline for the payment on the $104 million of bond anticipation notes, I presented the banks with a revamped proposal. The state would appropriate money to pay UDC's short-term debt and ensure the maintenance of a reserve fund for the repayment of the long-term debt. In return, the banks would lend UDC $300 million to complete its projects. We discussed the plan late into the night, but the next day there was bad news: of the eleven banks, only Chase and Irving Trust were willing to agree. The rest insisted that the federal subsidies funds were UDC revenues and that if the banks allowed them to be used as security for the new bondholders, they would be liable to the old ones.

I reported the news to Governor Carey. He phoned Treasury Secretary William Simon, who had been a leading municipal bond underwriter at Salomon Brothers and had underwritten hundreds of millions of dollars of bonds for New York City. Carey asked Simon whether a default by UDC would have a significant negative impact on the municipal bond markets. Without hesitation, Simon said it would. He suggested that I try to meet privately with Walter Wriston, chairman of First National City Bank. On the morning of February 25, I went to Wriston's office. Pat Patterson, CEO of the Morgan Bank, joined us. If I could persuade these men, arguably the two most powerful bankers in New York, to give us their support, I could persuade the others.

But I couldn't. It was a long meeting. Wriston left the room several times to talk, he said, with Arthur Burns, chairman of the Federal Reserve Board in Washington. In our discussion, Wriston said the state should pay its debts before it asked for additional loans. I answered that the banks had made the original loans with a full understanding that they were not backed by the full faith and credit of the state; that understanding was reflected in the higher interest rates the banks had charged. Wriston countered that UDC was a child of the state, and honorable people pay the debts of their children. I answered that it is not honorable for a democratically elected government to pay its money creditors while leaving its trade creditors with only a hope that they might be paid in the future. We ended at an impasse.

When I phoned Carey to let him know, he said I should come to Albany immediately on the state plane waiting at La Guardia Airport. When I arrived at the State Capitol, he was totally supportive. He said members of the legislature had gathered on the Assembly floor. He wanted me to bring them up-to-date on the events of the past twenty-four hours. With anger overcoming fatigue, I told the legislators, "The banks of New York have closed their doors to the people of New York."

∂℘

THE CENTER OF the drama moved, briefly but decisively, back to Albany. That night, Governor Carey sent the legislature a bill to create a new Project Finance Agency, to which HUD could assign the federal subsidies whose release I had negotiated. The new PFA would buy UDC's mortgages, issue debt secured by the federal subsidies, and transfer the funds to UDC. The funds would enable UDC to finish its projects. Carey hoped the creation of the new agency would put more pressure on the banks to enter into the partnership we were desperately seeking.

On the Senate floor, Anderson urged that the bill be passed. It was not the remedy for the UDC crisis, he said, but an essential first step in getting people outside government to make appropriate decisions. His meaning was clear: UDC had to be and was going to be saved. There was virtually no partisanship in Albany that night. The bill passed overwhelmingly.

It was a brave step. But UDC was closer than ever to bankruptcy, and we couldn't keep this possibility from the press. "UDC Collapsing," a *New York Post* headline screamed. Other papers, including the *Times*, reported that bankruptcy was inevitable. In Albany, bickering began over just how much money the state would provide to the Project Finance Agency, with Republicans seeking to hold down spending and Democrats wanting to give Carey everything he had asked for. But none of the participants was fundamentally challenging UDC's goals. The absence of vitriol then is almost unrecognizable to observers of politics now.

ॐ

ON FEBRUARY 26, the UDC's notes went into default. On Friday, February 28, the commercial banks finally demanded repayment of the $30 million loan they had made in December to keep UDC solvent. The corporation informed the banks that it simply did not have the money. The banks responded by "setting off" against UDC's bank accounts, taking money that UDC was holding for general purposes. UDC could no longer pay its employees or advance the loans needed to continue construction on its projects. When the situation became public, word spread that UDC was going to have to fire five hundred employees and that contractors were abandoning UDC projects throughout the state.

We were at the end of our options. The banks claimed that their position was grounded in their concern about their liability to UDC's existing bondholders. I knew the only place in which that liability could finally be determined was a bankruptcy court, where the bankers themselves would be uncertain of the outcome. With Governor Carey's approval, I called the bankers to a meeting at his New York office on Sunday afternoon. I had hired bankruptcy lawyers and asked them to have a bankruptcy petition ready to present to a judge on Monday morning.

The day before the meeting, the gravity of the coming confrontation—and what at that moment seemed like my presumptuousness—became palpable. If the banks did not free up cash for UDC, we had to make good on our threat and file for bankruptcy.

However, I had to give Carey one more opportunity to consider the risks. That evening we met for dinner at Roses Restaurant, a none-too-fancy Manhattan bistro on 52nd Street, next door to the elegant "21," which would have been a more fitting location for a governor. But the restaurant was quiet, and we could talk undisturbed. I admitted my shakiness and self-doubt and asked Carey whether someone with more gray hair and experience should join the team. I have a vivid memory of his response. No sentimentality, just straight talk about why he'd chosen me for the task, how much confidence he had in me, and how fully he agreed with the course I had taken. He would be known, he said wryly, as either the guy who made the state go broke or the guy who cleaned up Rockefeller's mess. I can't remember ever feeling so buoyed, supported, necessary. We would wage the battle together.

On Sunday, the bankers filed into a conference room in the governor's office. On the table in front of each man's seat was a copy of UDC's bankruptcy petition, ready for filing. The banks blinked. They agreed to withdraw their set-offs against UDC's accounts.

ঞ৷৵

I WAS REDEEMED, though hardly triumphant, because the banks still refused to lend UDC any new money. They must have known they would have to invest in debt of the new Project Finance Agency sooner or later, but they left the meeting still insisting that they would make no further loans until the state paid the existing short-term UDC debt. There would be one more round—or set of rounds.

So Monday morning, I was back in Albany. The governor asked the legislature for a $110 million appropriation to make mortgage advances to developers so that construction could continue at eighty UDC construction sites. The legislators approved the bill, but their antibank feeling was so intense that they insisted on a provision in the legislation stating specifically that not one penny of the appropriation could be used to pay existing UDC debt.

The back-and-forth with the banks went on for two more months. Finally, after a group of New York savings banks agreed to buy PFA bonds that would "take out"—pay off—the commercial banks at a later date, the commercial banks agreed to do the very thing they had refused to do before UDC's notes went into default. On April 30, the state appropriated money to pay off UDC's short-term debt, and the banks loaned PFA enough new money to keep UDC functioning. The ratings agencies gave the PFA's debt an AA rating, and PFA started arranging the take-out financing to which the savings banks had agreed. Then, at last, I was sworn in as chairman of UDC. I hired a new president and CEO to replace Ed Logue and remained in the chairman's post until 1977.

ഇ

IN THE END, there was a sense of accomplishment but not of victory. The bruising fight caused short-term problems, long-term problems, and serious reconsiderations. In the short run, the drama of the UDC crisis and the possible consequences of the state's not paying UDC's debts diverted so much of Carey's attention that he barely had time to prepare the state budget that was due on March 31. Nor, despite scrambling, could he fill all the key posts in his administration.

In the longer run, many people since that time have asked whether UDC's default on its debt impaired investor confidence in the municipal bond markets and thereby contributed to the New York City fiscal crisis a month later. That is too unqualified a judgment, but the UDC crisis certainly prompted banks and the investing public to look more critically at the financial strength underlying state and local obligations. The default also demonstrated that the financial resources of a state, even the State of New York, had their limits and that a state faced with a choice between paying certain debts and maintaining essential government programs just might postpone the repayment of debt, no matter what the nature of the obligation was.

The crisis should have taught us that investor confidence in municipal securities cannot, in the end, be sustained without a sense that the expected revenues underlying these securities are adequate to meet the obligations. If they are not, the government raising the money must have both the resources and the political will to make up the shortfall. Whether people learned these lessons adequately remains an open question.

For people like me, who had a major interest in housing policy and cared about social issues, the UDC crisis and its outcome had deeper repercussions. For the first time, we began to wonder whether the costs of the approach we had originally taken were too great and whether other forms of housing subsidy to the poor and middle class would be more effective. Since the UDC's temporary default in 1975, neither the State of New York nor any other state has been able to issue bonds for public housing without the added security of some kind of outside credit enhancement like Federal Housing Administration mortgage insurance or privately financed bond insurance.

For people who were not sympathetic to these public objectives in the first place, the UDC story seemed to support the view that no matter how socially desirable a government program was, it had to be economically self-sustaining and should not be financed through state borrowing unsupported by project revenues.

Politically, the upshot of the UDC crisis was more encouraging. Both sides took a hit. If UDC hadn't drastically reduced its staff and cut back on future projects, the state legislature wouldn't have agreed to the new appropriations that formed part of the solution. And if the banks hadn't softened their position, no level of state effort would have helped.

We learned, as we will probably have to relearn repeatedly, that a functioning political system can keep a seemingly insurmountable problem from becoming an active disaster—and that the political system does not have to compromise democratic principles in order to do so. But a functioning political system is not a condition to be taken for granted. In the 1975 UDC crisis, partisanship and grandstanding ultimately bowed to common necessity. Individual legislators may have voted out of political bias or to please a benefactor or, occasionally, out of pure ignorance, but they were in the minority. During the crisis, no one ever asked us for anything inappropriate or based a vote on any false promise we had made.

Yet, if the UDC crisis showed that such behavior is possible in politics, it also showed that the possibility depends on strong leadership. At the time, we had such leadership in the legislative leaders and, above all, the governor. We have not always been so fortunate.

The experience was exhausting and exhilarating. Almost thirty thousand apartments got built. All the notes and bonds eventually got paid, with interest. I was able to use what I knew about finance to help steer the ship of state past some dangerous shoals.

But even that crisis was incomplete preparation for what was about to happen to the City of New York.

4

City on the Brink

O N THE MORNING OF MAY 2, 1975, I was at my desk at the HRH offices in Midtown, digging out from under the business issues that had piled up during the Urban Development Corporation crisis, when Governor Hugh Carey's private secretary, Kate O'Connor, called. The heads of New York's three largest banks—Citi, Chase, and Morgan—had asked to meet with the governor that afternoon at the state's offices on East 55th Street. She didn't know what the meeting was about, but it had to do with banks. With the UDC crisis fresh in her mind, she, on her own initiative, thought the governor would want me to be there.

With UDC's problems in abeyance, everyone expected the next trouble to involve New York City. Its credit was shaky, and the banks had been delivering public warnings about it ever since Abe Beame had replaced John Lindsay as mayor in January 1974. In February 1975, Charles Sanford, president of Bankers Trust Company, pulled the plug on a proposed sale of city notes because he could not get a clean opinion from bond counsel confirming that the city would have the revenues to pay the notes that his bank was being asked to underwrite.

The meeting between Carey and the bankers was scheduled for 2:30 P.M. When I arrived at the state's drab, utilitarian offices—a stark contrast to the splendors of the executive suite on the second floor of

the State Capitol in Albany—the bankers were already there: Walter
Wriston of Citibank, Willard Butcher of Chase, and Pat Patterson of
Morgan, making strained conversation with one another. They gave
me a perfunctory hello, and we sat in silence to wait for the governor.
I was deeply anxious. The financing for UDC had been negotiated
but had not yet actually closed, and I thought something must have
gone gravely wrong.

Something had indeed gone gravely wrong, but it was much bigger than UDC. When Carey arrived, the bankers, wasting no time,
announced that they would no longer underwrite the notes and
bonds of the City of New York. This statement turned the city's
heretofore looming crisis into an immediate one.

There wasn't much time for reflection. When the bankers left,
I phoned the city comptroller, Jay Goldin, and asked him to come
to the governor's office to brief us on the city's cash position and
the schedule of its maturing debt obligations. The governor asked
his budget director, Peter Goldmark, who for months had kept a
worried eye on the city's fiscal situation, to fly down from Albany.
That morning, the newspapers had reported that a man named Paul
Volcker was going to be the new president of the Federal Reserve
Bank of New York. I noticed the item and remembered from the
UDC crisis that the Federal Reserve System had authority to make
certain kinds of emergency loans to municipalities. I contacted Volcker through Ed Cohen, the father of the Ed Cohen I had brought
to UDC as president; the elder Cohen was a tax partner at Barrett
Smith and had worked with Volcker at the Department of the Treasury. That night, Volcker, Goldmark, and I had dinner at a New York
steakhouse, Christ Cella. It was a cordial enough meal, but none of
us knew enough about the facts to understand what might happen if
the city lost its access to credit, let alone the information we would
have needed to fashion solutions. Volcker was appropriately cautious.

⁂

A PERIOD OF COMBINED personal and public upheaval began. Only weeks after my meeting with the governor, I got the news that Saul Horowitz Jr.—my partner, cousin, and best friend—had been killed in a plane crash as his Eastern Airlines flight from New Orleans was landing at Kennedy Airport. I drove straight to his family's home in Scarsdale. There was never a question in my mind but that my responsibilities to them and our business were now at the top of my list of priorities. I've always had profound doubts about the kind of person who cares more about humanity than he does about the human beings who are closest to him.

But it was equally clear that the demands of public life were going to become more rather than less pressing. Luckily, Ed Cohen was taking hold quickly and effectively at UDC, and I had support at home and at work. But I still had to finish securing UDC's refinancing and assemble a staff to complete its projects. And, as the New York City crisis escalated, Governor Carey had me take on jobs large and small. He was very considerate; but he didn't hesitate to ask, and he kept asking.

Thus, though I held no state or city office, I became a sometime player in the New York City crisis that began in 1975. I was the quintessential participant-observer. I saw the state and city political systems survive one fiscal cliffhanger after another and, in the end, resolve seemingly insurmountable fiscal problems without surrendering their democratic character.

જ0

NEW YORK CITY was driven to the edge of bankruptcy, then pulled back from the brink partly by significant events in the country as a whole and partly by the individuals who had to grapple with them. Throughout the crisis, one of those individuals was Governor Carey, who behaved in this matter, as in every public matter in which I saw him involved, with honor and acumen. But there were many others, some who got the city into trouble and some who helped extricate it.

During the years from 1954 to 1965, when Robert F. Wagner Jr. was the city's mayor, the vast migration to the city from Puerto Rico and the American South caused huge changes in the city's demography, economy, and politics. At the beginning of this period, New York's Democratic machine was powerful enough so that it effectively chose the city's officeholders, including Wagner. But the tools that the machine had traditionally used to control voters were losing their strength. Television's reach was growing. Government programs were replacing the political clubs as sources of jobs and support for the poor. The clubs' influence declined correspondingly.

The early 1960s also saw the rise of the reform Democrats, better-educated New Yorkers dissatisfied with the party's existing power structure. In 1961 Wagner, once the choice of the machine, ran for reelection as a reformer and defeated the machine candidate. Once reelected, he increased city services in areas such as health and higher education and executed the first collectively bargained contract between the city and its public employee unions. He began New York's transition from a system dominated by political organizations to one that was shaped in equal parts by money, media, and organized labor.

The Republican John V. Lindsay, elected in 1965 to succeed Wagner after representing an Upper East Side district in Congress, accelerated the transition. Lindsay was an honest, telegenic man aligned with liberal causes such as the civil rights movement and concern for the poor. When he took office, optimism about government's capacities had not yet faded. Many saw him as another Fiorello La Guardia, New York's mayor from 1934 to 1945, who commanded political support across party lines. Lindsay's Kennedyesque presence and optimism, they hoped, would transcend machine politics, bring a new force of talented young people into city government, and transform New York's public services.

The early years of the Lindsay administration were also the years of Lyndon Johnson's War on Poverty, and increasing federal funds allowed Lindsay to keep up with the city's rising costs. In 1969 he lost the Republican primary but was reelected as an independent, vigorously supported by a municipal labor movement that had grown exponentially since the Wagner years. In the same year, however, a recession began. In the hard economic times that followed, Lindsay's upper-class style steadily lost its charm; New York grew disenchanted with him.

In 1973 New York chose a very different mayor, Abe Beame, the city's comptroller, who had lost the mayoralty to Lindsay in 1965. Beame, a product of the Brooklyn Democratic organization, was an accountant who was viewed as a budget expert and fiscal watchdog, no small irony for the man who would preside over the city's financial collapse.

⁂

HOWEVER, ELECTED officials were not the only, or perhaps even the most important, players in the New York City fiscal arena. At least as critical were the representatives of business and labor. The denizens of the financial services industry—the bankers, along with their lawyers, and the credit rating agencies—had a very real concern for the well-being of New York and a very particular view of what that well-being required. The most prominent of the bankers were David Rockefeller, chairman of Chase, and Walter Wriston, chairman of First National City Bank, soon to be renamed Citibank. Rockefeller was in many ways the leader of the banking community, but he was a modest man. He was also very conscious of the fact that his brother was President Ford's vice president and had been governor of New York when many of the problems facing the city had begun. More outspoken was Wriston, who had developed the largest bank in the country. He was a man of very conservative politics and very straight talk.

Only a few blocks separate them, but Wall Street is a long way—in income, culture, and organizational style—from City Hall. But the multimillion-dollar underwriting business is a vital link between them. Cities need access to the credit markets for two reasons that are respectable and one that is not. The first respectable reason is that even a city with a balanced budget will have mismatches during any fiscal year between the times when revenue comes in and the times when payments must go out. Cities must engage in short-term borrowing to cope with these timing differences. The second respectable reason is that cities must borrow long-term to fund capital projects, investments in infrastructure that will serve and should be paid for by more than one generation. The third, more dubious reason for going to the municipal credit markets is that cities often borrow to cover operating deficits they incur. Banks earn substantial underwriting fees from all these borrowings, the dubious as well as the respectable ones.

Then there were the unions, specifically the leaders of the five major municipal unions, representing police, firefighters, sanitation workers, teachers, and the rest of the city's employees. The leaders who played the biggest roles in the city crisis were Al Shanker and Victor Gotbaum. Shanker was president of the United Federation of Teachers; I had met him during the March on Washington. Gotbaum was president of District Council 37 of the American Federation of State, County, and Municipal Employees; I had met him during the Lindsay campaign. AFSCME's members were less affluent and more racially diverse than those of the UFT. Jack Bigel, whose day job was running a New York health insurance company, served as intellectual guru to the Uniformed Sanitationmen's Association and all-around expert on municipal labor issues.

Gotbaum and Shanker barely talked to each other. In 1969, a year after a long teachers' strike in Ocean Hill–Brownsville became a racial conflict because the teachers were largely white and the parents largely black, Shanker and Gotbaum waged a nasty contest to represent the paraprofessionals who worked for the city's Board of Education. Most of the paraprofessionals were nonwhite, and Gotbaum's campaign to represent them placed a lot of emphasis on race. But the teachers' union won the vote hands down: race was less important to the paraprofessionals than the benefits of belonging to a professional union like the UFT. Before the city crisis was over, I would bring Shanker and Gotbaum together at dinner in an effort to be a peacemaker. But that was later.

⌀

THE STATUE OF LIBERTY, Wall Street, Broadway, seven hundred miles of subway tracks, the headquarters of the major national news media, and a culture and politics attracting people from all over the world: for better and worse, these features made New York City a very special place in reality and in the eyes of the rest of the country. New York had the largest population of any city in the United States because of all its attractions, the greatest of all being the sense that wherever you came from and whatever language you spoke, you could get a job, build a career, and, if you had the talent, make it big.

The early- to mid-1960s was an optimistic time in the city and the country as a whole. To many, it seemed there were no limits on what government could do to generate benefits and opportunities for its citizens. For liberals, the paramount domestic issues revolved around segregation—uprooting discriminatory practices that had no place in a country that prided itself on being the world's greatest democracy and addressing the consequences of those discriminatory practices. Even when these New Yorkers decried the urban crisis, they thought of it as a problem that government could solve.

In those years, the city added jobs, but over a third of them were for public employees. In the Lindsay administration's first term, the municipal labor force grew by more than 100,000, from 250,000 to 350,000. The cost to the city of each employee grew by almost 8 percent annually. New federal programs, whether in health care or, as part of the War on Poverty, brought new federal funds to the city. But those programs generally required the city to contribute matching funds, and the programs were inevitably accompanied by federal mandates that required the city to spend still more of its own money. Nelson Rockefeller, who was then governor, shared Lindsay's liberal outlook and was similarly eager to expand the services and facilities available to the poor. As a result, during Lindsay's first four years in office, city spending went up by almost 50 percent, much of the increase driven by mandates under the state's expansion of programs like Medicaid.

Both the state and the city had enacted income tax laws that were generating increased amounts of revenue, so at first there was little serious opposition to the rapidly expanding size and scope of local government. But while this growth was occurring, less benign changes were also taking place. Blue-collar jobs were declining. White-collar jobs were increasing, but many of the new immigrants did not have the skills these jobs required. As the 1969 recession created revenue problems for governments in Washington and Albany, both capitals began to show a diminished interest in any further expansion of government.

Then, in the first part of the 1970s, New York City hemorrhaged private sector jobs. By 1975 it had lost more than 500,000 of them. It had over a million people on welfare. There was a consequent rise in government spending, accelerated by the increased costs of unionized public employees.

There was no commensurate growth in city revenues. Because the economy was weakening, politicians became less willing to enact new taxes. Private jobs had been replaced by public jobs, which did not generate as much in tax revenues. And although the value of the city's real estate may have increased, there was no corresponding increase in its assessed, or taxable, value.

With commercial property, the real estate industry convinced the city that it couldn't raise real estate taxes if it wanted to keep businesses in New York. With residential property, the single-family homes in the outer boroughs were considered politically sacrosanct, largely immune from increases in assessed values. Residential property that was made up of rental housing was not politically immune, but here the city faced another barrier to increased assessments: rent-control policies had depressed the value of apartments throughout the city.

In fact, as the value of rental apartments declined, landlords began to convert them to co-operative apartments that would be owned by their occupants. The landlords making these conversions got the tax laws changed so that the apartments continued to be assessed on the basis of their depressed value as rent-controlled rental apartments before their conversions. Because the apartments were lightly taxed, the landlords who were selling them got higher sales prices, while the buyers who became the owners of the apartments got the tax benefits. The city treasury suffered.

cﬡﬡ

AMID THE CONSENSUS that the city should be an agent for social change, almost no attention was paid to the cost of this change, which was reflected in the city's rapidly growing annual deficits. And as the gap between expenditures and revenues grew, the city began to deal with it in ways that made some form of insolvency inevitable and should have made it obvious.

The elected officials who approved the city's budgets were far more concerned about allocating city spending among various constituencies and interest groups than they were with the question of whether the expenditures were matched by recurring revenues. Union leaders, then as now, earned their salaries by using their political clout to get more benefits for their members. The banks profited from underwriting city debt. The major players shaping city politics pursued their separate purposes with probably not much understanding of the consequences of their actions while remaining convinced, or at least asserting, that they were acting in the city's best interests.

Meanwhile, there were no clear rules governing the city's budget process. City budgets were opaque, and learning about them was not uppermost in the public's mind. When budget stories appeared in the press, they generally reflected the self-serving agendas of the people in city politics who wanted the stories published. It was relatively easy, therefore, for city government to adopt budget devices that hid the deficits and allowed officials to say the budget was balanced—which state law required it to be—when in fact it was not.

Many budget and accounting gimmicks were employed to kick the deficit can down the road. All of them were engineered by people who were trying, for reasons they thought legitimate or even admirable, to avoid imposing higher taxes or making painful cuts in what they viewed as essential public services. Occasionally, public officials questioned some of these practices, but they were not prepared to fall on their political swords to defend their positions.

One way of masking the deficits was to overestimate revenues. Throughout the period after Lindsay's first term that preceded the crisis, there were persistently optimistic revenue forecasts. In the short run, they led to overspending. In the long run, they led to underfunding the city's growing employee pension obligations.

Another pervasive technique for masking deficits was using the city's capital budget to pay for recurring operating expenses—something like paying for your nightly dinners with the money you got by mortgaging your home.

Yet another technique was used by the city to finance its middle-income housing program. Instead of shifting to long-term financing after the construction of these projects was completed and their operating costs were known, the city continued to borrow in the form of short-term notes. By doing so, the city kept its interest rates unrealistically low. In turn, the artificially low interest rates allowed the city to avoid increasing rents for its limited-income tenants. This was the same practice that had contributed to the near-bankruptcy of the state's Urban Development Corporation.

The city's most egregiously misleading gimmick, however, was to treat the proceeds of borrowing as revenues and to use these revenues to claim that the budget was in balance. Compounding the recklessness, the city was ingenious in circumventing the rules that purported to limit this borrowing. Under the state constitution, the city could borrow long-term for capital purposes, but the amount of the borrowing was limited to a percentage of the assessed value of the city's real property. In contrast, the city could borrow short-term without any general limit on the amount, as long as it repaid these short-term loans within twelve months, out of taxes it collected or state and federal aid it received. There was only one limitation on this short-term borrowing, but it was critical: the city could not borrow more than the amount it had actually received in revenues in the previous year.

In 1965, at Mayor Wagner's request, Governor Rockefeller got the state law on short-term borrowing changed: instead of the city's being able to borrow up to the amount of revenue it had actually collected in the preceding year, it would now be able to borrow up to the amount of revenue that the mayor estimated the city would collect in the following year. The mayor's chief of staff candidly summed up the philosophy of municipal finance underlying this change, "A bad loan is better than a good tax."

From the time the law changed, the city issued short-term notes on the basis of the mayor's estimate of the revenues or taxes that would be collected in the year to come. If there was a single phenomenon that marked the beginning of the New York City fiscal crisis of 1975, it was this change in the municipal finance law ten years earlier. The change passed unnoticed by the press, and no one on Wall Street challenged it.

The decade that followed saw repeated allegations of fiscal impropriety in city government. When Lindsay became mayor, he leveled these accusations at Wagner and Wagner's comptroller, Abe Beame; when Beame ran to succeed Lindsay in 1973, he said the same things about Lindsay. But beyond the personalized rhetoric, the city was facing several kinds of acute financial problems. The first problem was the underlying fact that the city's recurring expenses exceeded its actual recurring revenues. The second problem was a developing crisis in financing: the banks were becoming reluctant to lend money against city revenues that were merely aspirational. The third problem was a crisis of political culture: none of the people with power to manage the city's affairs was willing to face the first two crises and change the behavior that produced them.

The 1974 recession further weakened the city's financial condition.

In the months leading up to the bankers' May 1975 announcement to the governor, alarm had grown in many quarters. The governor's budget director, Peter Goldmark, told Carey in March that the city had no present capacity to repay its short-term debt. He said the debt would have to be restructured, the state would have to involve itself in the city's governance in ways no one had anticipated, and it might take the Federal Reserve System to provide the credit needed to avoid a city bankruptcy. Like all of us, Carey had complete and well-founded confidence in Goldmark's conscientiousness and judgment. Of all Carey's advisers during the city crisis, Peter was probably the most important.

Academic and civic organizations were also calling attention to the unsustainability of the city's fiscal practices. The press was now paying more attention to budget news, especially as it included Mayor Beame's threat to fire seventy thousand city workers. Some politicians asked why the city couldn't avoid this evisceration of city services through default or bankruptcy. Others answered that a default would be an admission of the city's incapacity to deal with the most fundamental issues of democratic self-governance.

Because the city budget was so opaque—incomprehensible, in fact—the May crisis produced chaos. For anyone who had not worked with the budget on a daily basis, there was blanket confusion about what the city's deficit actually was. We knew the city needed $500 to $600 million every month to pay off the maturing notes it had sold a year earlier. We were told that the deficit for the fiscal year that would end on June 30, 1975, was more than $400 million. We knew, though the mayor changed his mind from time to time, that the deficit projected for the next fiscal year was more than a billion dollars.

Beame proposed layoffs of city employees, state authorization for new city taxes, and substantial increases in federal and state aid to the city. Republicans in the state Senate would not support more state aid without getting, in return, increases in state education aid to localities outside New York City. The banks insisted on a combination of personnel reductions and new revenues before they would lend the city any further funds. Union leaders cursed the banks; one of them declared Citibank "public enemy number one." The mayor was regularly advising the public that the banks' recalcitrance was a gross interference in the democratic process. He said the city's problem was merely one of cash flow. If the city went broke, it would be the banks' fault.

It was clear to Carey, Goldmark, and me that the state's decision earlier in the year not to pay the debt of the Urban Development Corporation when it came due had had the unintended consequence of shaking the financial community's confidence in the state's ultimate willingness to pay the debts of other "creatures" of the state, including public authorities and local governments like New York City. The bankers' announcement that they would no longer underwrite city debt reflected not only a general judgment that the city wasn't entitled to credit but also their concrete fear that city debt actually might not get repaid. And if it was not paid, they were afraid that the financial institutions that sold this bad debt to customers might be liable under the fraud provisions of the federal securities laws.

The obvious first step was to join in the efforts to persuade the federal government to help the city. The banks were importuning the Treasury Department for help, offering to provide additional loans to the city if the federal government would step in with aid. But on May 10, Treasury Secretary William Simon, the former underwriter of New York municipal securities, announced that the federal government would not step in. "The fundamental solution to the city's financial problems," he said, "does not lie at the federal level." The administration did not believe that a city default would significantly affect the financial markets. Moreover, federal help to the city would require congressional approval, which was not likely. Finally, the precedent of federal aid to New York could give rise to similar demands from other cities. President Ford met with Carey and Beame and repeated the administration's position. Afterward, he wrote a letter confirming that no federal aid would be forthcoming. "The proper place for any request for backing and guarantee," he said, "is with the State of New York."

On the one hand, the economic downturn and its effect on revenues had created serious budget issues for the state's localities and public authorities, UDC among them; Carey's first responsibility was to protect the credit of the state from being harmed by these issues. On the other hand, the credit of the state would also be in jeopardy if the city defaulted on its debts, including its debt to the state. The state's fiscal year began on April 1, the city's fiscal year on July 1. In April, after the state's new fiscal year had begun, the state would customarily lend the city money to tide it over for the remainder of the city's old fiscal year. When the city's new fiscal year began on July 1, the city would repay the state. But if the city could not pay off its debt to the state in July, the state would have trouble borrowing to pay off its own short-term obligations. Even more immediately, some $750 million in New York City notes would mature on June 11. If they were not paid off or extended with the lenders' consent, neither the city nor the state would have access to cash for its operations.

After conversations with Goldmark, me, and David Burke, Carey concluded that he had to find a way for the state to restructure the city's debt without impairing the state's credit in the process.

*

THUS BEGAN THE process of extricating the city from its crisis. It did not happen in a single episode of conflict, crescendo, and resolution; instead, it happened in stages. After each purported solution was reached, its inadequacy would become clear, and we would have to try again. That is the way public problems are resolved, more or less.

The solution to the city's crisis would have to include more borrowing from the banks; otherwise, the city would not be able to finance its essential operations, let alone pay its pre-existing debts. The same banks already owned more than $1 billion of city debt,

representing over a quarter of their equity capital. The city's first deputy mayor, James Cavanagh, thought the situation placed the banks
and the city in a "community of interest: if we go down, they go
down."

Governor Carey was not so sure. He urgently needed the advice
and support of the banks and the business community, but he also
needed the support of the political players who denounced the business community as anathema. While David Rockefeller was urging
a wage freeze for municipal employees, the unions were defiantly
withdrawing their funds from the clearinghouse banks. With anger-
fueled rectitude flying in all directions, Carey was going to have to
persuade a whole range of interest groups to agree to actions they
considered unthinkable.

On May 21, Carey announced the appointment of an advisory
group from New York's commercial world. It included former federal judge Simon Rifkind, Metropolitan Life Insurance Company
chairman Richard Shinn, AT&T CEO William Ellinghaus, and investment banker and Lazard Frères partner Felix Rohatyn. None
of them had any previous exposure to the city's budget and fiscal
issues. But they were fast learners, and their credibility was crucial to
gaining widespread acceptance of the recommendations that Carey
hoped would emerge from their discussions.

Rohatyn became the group's most active and forceful participant.
His skills as a financial engineer were well known. Less well known
but at least as important was the fact that he was a refugee. His family
had fled Austria for France in 1935, then left France in 1940, traveling
to Casablanca, Lisbon, and Rio de Janeiro before finally arriving in
the United States in 1942. His commitment to the success of the
country's democratic processes ran deep. The city's eventual rescue
was due in no small part to his rhetorical skill and his credibility in
deploying it.

Out of Carey's consultations with the advisory group and others
came the idea for the state legislation that created the Municipal

Assistance Corporation—it quickly became known as Big MAC—to borrow the funds needed to restructure the city's debt.

As with the UDC crisis, the first challenge was to identify a stream of public revenues that could be pledged as security for the new lending the city needed. Raising the revenue through new state taxes would have been another blow to a struggling economy and, in any event, was politically impossible. So it was decided to take certain taxes that were currently being paid to the city and make them payable to MAC instead—just as we had taken certain revenues payable to UDC and transferred them to the new Project Finance Agency.

If the idea bore a great similarity to the UDC plan, so did the resistance to the idea. In the beginning, the banks vigorously objected to MAC, claiming it would strip revenues rightfully belonging to the holders of the city general obligation notes and bonds that the banks had already underwritten. Underlying their argument was their worry that they might be liable to these bondholders for not having disclosed the lack of a security interest in the city revenues that were going to be assigned to MAC. I reminded the governor that this issue had been raised and resolved in the case of UDC. In the end, the financing provisions of the MAC legislation followed the model we had used for the UDC rescue.

There was, however, a crucial difference. MAC's designers concluded that the new body could not be just a financing mechanism; it also had to have the power to ensure that the city would actually balance its budget. The city would have to adopt proper accounting practices and provide accurate financial information. The budget gimmickry that had kept it going in the years before the crisis would have to end. Rohatyn made it abundantly clear that unless MAC had the power to impose fiscal discipline, the city would not be able to borrow the money it needed.

Some players, for reasons of principle or self-interest, said that giving MAC this kind of authority was undemocratic. Mayor Beame called MAC's proposed control powers humiliating to the city and an infringement of the principle of home rule. Some elected officials said it would be better to default and face the consequences. Republicans who controlled the state Senate wanted seats on the MAC board. The unions were trying to extract a commitment from the governor that there would be no layoffs.

Finally, Rohatyn announced dramatically that if MAC was not in business by June 9, 1975, "You're all finished." The ultimatum worked. The governor relented on his insistence that MAC have the power to approve the city's budget directly. The state accelerated transfers of funds to the city. The city agreed to turn its sales and stock transfer tax revenues over to MAC, to stop using its capital funds for operating expenses, and to reform its budget accounting. The banks agreed to exchange a substantial amount of their city bonds for MAC bonds. The MAC legislation passed, and the city avoided a disastrous default because, in the end, all the participants in the process did what only days before they had sworn they would never do.

⊙∫ρ

THE INITIAL EUPHORIA after the enactment of the MAC legislation didn't last long. Beame had insisted that unless the state authorized the city to impose new taxes, he would have to lay off tens of thousands of city employees. Carey and the state legislature, fearing the damage a tax increase would do to the economy, turned him down. The mayor announced a wage freeze and forty thousand layoffs. The unions were enraged. They accused the banks of benefiting from the fiscal crisis by charging the city excessively high interest rates and argued that, if the rates came down, no layoffs or wage freezes would be necessary. Off-duty police blocked traffic. Firemen called in sick. The sanitation men went on strike, and tons of garbage piled up in the city's streets. The display of public discord chilled the market's interest in buying MAC bonds. Another crisis loomed.

Carey convened the legislative leaders in Albany and engineered another compromise, producing another short-term fix. The city got additional taxing power. The state increased its aid to education. The unions, bowing to the banks, agreed to a voluntary wage freeze, except for police and firefighters. The banks, their condition largely met, extended a bridge loan to the city so that it could meet its July payroll.

By now, though, it was apparent that New York City was merely lurching from crisis to crisis. The early public discussion of the city's fiscal situation was dominated by confusion and ignorance. But press coverage improved when the *New York Times* assigned the story to a couple of talented reporters who made it their business to understand and report on what was going on; and Mike O'Neil, the estimable editor of the *Daily News*, made sure his paper covered the story in depth. Now the *Times* called the city a "national model of municipal mismanagement." Not many people disagreed.

MAC was offering to pay high interest rates on its bonds, but there was no real market for them. The city had $9.5 billion in long-term debt and $2.6 billion in tax and revenue anticipation notes outstanding. It needed to borrow around $1.5 billion for the legitimate purpose of smoothing out cash flow, and another $756 million in notes would have to be sold for the more dubious purpose of covering the projected deficit for the fiscal year beginning July 1. There were $1.6 billion in bond anticipation notes outstanding, and the city was proposing another $2 billion to prevent all municipal construction from coming to a halt. If the city stopped using funds from its capital budget to finance its operating expenses, the deficit in the operating budget would increase by another $700 million. And an $800-million city note was coming due in September.

It was remarkable that the prospect of losing access to the bond markets had not sent alarms throughout the business and labor communities long before the summer of 1975. Something more radical had to be done.

જ્ર

CAREY, CONSULTING mainly with Rohatyn and Rifkind, devised a new plan to create a state-controlled board that would exercise financial and management powers over city operations. They arranged to have the plan proposed by MAC rather than by the governor in order to leave the governor room to negotiate the final bill. The legislature, the mayor, the unions, the banks, and the public began to weigh in on a proposal for a fundamental change in the governance of New York City.

The new Emergency Financial Control Board would be made up of the governor, the mayor, the state and city comptrollers, and three private citizens chosen by the governor. The board would not have direct authority to tell the city how to spend its money, but the city would be allowed to spend its money only in accordance with a financial plan submitted by the city and approved by the board. The city's financial plan would have to cover three years and, by June 30, 1978, present a budget that was balanced according to generally accepted accounting principles. The city could not change its revenue estimates, issue debt, or execute labor contracts without board approval. There would be a wage freeze, and a special deputy state comptroller would be appointed to audit all city operations.

The plan also included new financing. The state would borrow $750 million to advance to the city, and banks and city pension funds would buy MAC bonds in the amounts needed for the city's board-approved debt repayment and capital spending. But the financing was embedded in a framework based on what had become an accepted principle: the city could not govern itself in a fiscally responsible fashion, and external discipline was necessary to ensure rational governance.

In light of the breadth of the change proposed by the legislation, opposition was surprisingly muted this time around. True, voices on the right and left called for bankruptcy instead of a control board. The right favored bankruptcy in order to break the unions, the left in order to break free of control by the banks. But the unions had finally come to understand that under bankruptcy they might lose their collective bargaining rights altogether, while the banks, despite misgivings about their legal and financial liabilities, did not have much choice but to support the legislation. Wall Street was increasingly concerned about the impact a city default would have nationally on the municipal bond markets. No one knew how a bankruptcy court might adjust the city's contract obligations and the competing claims of its creditors. There was a growing awareness of the systemic failure that a bankruptcy would represent.

The state legislation passed on September 9, 1975. We were optimistic that MAC bonds would now sell and that the federal government would step in with aid to reduce the city's interest costs. The governor asked me to be the executive director of the Emergency Financial Control Board. Because of Saul's death and the family and business burdens that had come in its aftermath, I could not take the job. But, as before, Carey kept me informally involved as his consultant in the approach to the federal government and the sale of MAC bonds.

Neither one went smoothly.

ல்ல

THE STATE AND city began a campaign to secure federal credit aid for New York. The governor and the mayor lobbied the White House. New York businessmen asked their contacts in other parts of the country to get in touch with their congressmen. Foreign banks expressed concern about a possible New York City bankruptcy, and Rohatyn used his connections with international financial leaders to build support. He also spoke with Helmut Schmidt of Germany and Valéry Giscard d'Estaing of France, who, in turn, spoke to President Ford at a meeting of the G-8.

Carey was aware that I knew Henry Reuss, chairman of the House Banking Committee, and Howard Shuman, staff director of the Senate Banking Committee, who had been chief of staff of the National Commission on Urban Problems. Carey asked me to go to Washington and brief both committees. Accompanied by Goldmark and Burke, I did so on October 16.

When we arrived back at La Guardia and Burke called the governor to check in, we got a disturbing message. After the enactment of the control board legislation, with the market for MAC bonds shaky, the banks and union pension funds had agreed to a schedule on which they would make purchases of the bonds. Carey told Burke that Al Shanker had just phoned and told him that the Teachers' Pension Fund would not be making its scheduled $200-million purchase of MAC bonds the next day. Without the purchase, the city would not have the cash to repay a revenue anticipation note that would mature on the same day. We were thunderstruck. The city was on the verge of default tomorrow. It looked like we had finally run out of last-minute solutions.

The news was not yet public. That evening, as scheduled, I went to a dinner given by Gus Levy, chairman of Goldman Sachs, for the trustees of the Federation of Jewish Philanthropies. It was an opulent party, but I was exhausted, depressed, and incapable of enjoying it. I left early, went home, and was in bed by 9:00 P.M. But at 10:00 I was awakened by a phone call from Carey. He, too, had just finished an evening engagement, the annual white-tie Alfred E. Smith dinner in the city. He had returned to his office and wanted me to join him there as soon as I could. When I arrived, he told me to find Al Shanker and get him to change his mind.

I had remained friends with Shanker after we met in the 1960s. I knew about his wide reading, his serious cooking—he favored Moroccan—and his polymorphous love of music. Years later, he gave me my first CD player, before I knew what the thing was used for.

I wondered how Carey knew I was friends with Al; I didn't recall ever having mentioned it. Years later, Carey reminded me that a few months before the crisis, Shanker had tried to have my wife, Diane, appointed to the New York State Board of Regents. She had written a respected history of public education in New York City, *The Great School Wars*. Its description of the 1969 teachers' strike was sympathetic to the union. Carey allowed that when he'd asked me that night to approach Shanker because I knew him, he might have been thinking of the wrong Ravitch.

When I arrived at Al's apartment that October 17, I saw that he was genuinely distressed by his decision not to buy MAC bonds. He knew the risks to the city, but he believed his primary obligation was his fiduciary responsibility to his teachers. As city employees, they had already been put at risk by the city's fiscal crisis. It was no small thing to make their pension money subject to the same risk.

We talked until five o'clock that morning about whether an individual's decision can really make a difference in history and why so much had come to ride on our conversation. Al wanted assurance that there were no circumstances under which MAC would fail to make its payments on its bonds. I couldn't give him that assurance. At 5:00 A.M. he said I should go home; he had a few people to consult and would phone me in the morning. The State Police drove me back to my apartment, where I waited. Al's call never came. At 9:00 that morning I turned on the television and heard the news that the city would be going broke that day.

I took a taxi to the governor's office on East 55th Street, which was filled with reporters and television crews. Soon afterward, we got Shanker's call. He was with Mayor Beame and former Mayor Wagner at Gracie Mansion on 88th Street and East End Avenue, the mayor's official residence. Shanker wanted to meet with Carey and me in a place where we wouldn't run into the press. I suggested my apartment at Park Avenue and 85th Street.

Carey, the governor's counsel, Judah Gribetz, and I walked down the back stairs of the office building, got into an unmarked police car, and arrived at my place just as Shanker and Wagner were getting there. They were accompanied by Sandy Feldman, who would later succeed Shanker as president of the teachers' union, and Harry Van Arsdale, head of the city's AFL–CIO Central Labor Council. Judah warned that we shouldn't let Carey and Shanker talk privately, because Al might want to raise the question of whether the financial control board was going to approve the contract that the city had just negotiated with the teachers. Judah wanted to protect Carey from the pressure. He needn't have worried. Al never raised the subject.

My family wasn't home, and we all sat around nibbling on whatever we could find in the refrigerator. Carey called Rifkind, who came over to join the meeting. If the city filed for bankruptcy, Shanker asked, would the MAC bonds be paid ahead of the general obligation bonds that the city had previously issued? Rifkind said they would. It never came to that, which was fortunate, since the question of how a court would rule in such a case has never really been settled.

Around one o'clock in the afternoon, after several hours of a conversation in which no issues were sharply joined and it seemed that nothing dramatic was said, Al's mind seemed, finally, to come to rest. He announced to all of us that the trustees of the pension fund would vote that afternoon to make their scheduled investment in MAC bonds, which would enable us to pay the city note maturing that day.

We were thrilled with the news. Everyone rushed out of the apartment, leaving me alone. I suddenly realized the banks might not stay open long enough to assure that payment could be made to the holders of the maturing city notes. I phoned the State Banking Superintendent to ask whether he could keep the banks open beyond their normal closing time of 3:00 P.M. He said his direct jurisdiction was limited to a single state-chartered bank. The only person who could keep the other banks open was the Comptroller of the Currency in Washington, DC. And in the superintendent's opinion, the only person to whom the comptroller would listen on this matter was the head of the clearinghouse in New York.

That was Pat Patterson, chairman of Morgan. When I phoned his office, his secretary said there was no way he could take my call, because the City of New York was going broke that day. I told her that the governor and Al Shanker had just left my apartment and that her boss would want to talk to me.

The banks stayed open until midnight. Everyone got paid. A few hours later, Al phoned to invite me to the union's headquarters to help him enjoy all the food and wine that members of the public had sent to thank him for helping to save the city.

Afterward, Al and I talked many times about the events of October

17. In the years since the crisis, there has been a lot of public speculation about how his decision was made. To this day, some people who consider themselves sophisticated about the workings of politics refuse to believe that Shanker's decision wasn't the result of some nefarious secret deal for the benefit of the teachers' union. Others have tried to minimize the importance of what Shanker did, claiming there was an understanding that if he did not step in to buy the bonds, some other union would pick up the slack.

But, even with the benefit of hindsight, it is the sophisticates who have an incomplete understanding of what moves human beings in politics. The truth is that Shanker was troubled by exactly the question that should have troubled him: if the city ultimately went bankrupt, would he have breached his responsibility to his teachers by putting their pension funds into shaky securities? The truth is also that there were no orchestrated understandings. Shanker's decision was courageous; and, like almost all the decisions that were made during that year of crisis, it was made in uncertainty at the last possible minute.

Indeed, the most important feature of that day was not its drama but the overwhelming evidence that all of us were still operating on a day-to-day basis. The problem of New York's insolvency had not been solved. There was no sense of stability within the city's government, there was no market for its paper, and there was growing anxiety that the disorder would drive businesses out of New York and shrink the city's tax base.

The bad news was that there would have to be more taxes, more borrowing, more discipline, and more state resources committed to the city. The good news was that banks, unions, and politicians had more or less stopped criticizing one another and begun focusing, together, on how to get federal aid.

⁊⁊⁊

AT FIRST, THE resistance from Washington seemed firm. In an October 29 speech President Ford denounced New York City's "bad financial management," citing a "steady stream of unbalanced budgets, massive growth in the city's debt, extraordinary increases in public employee contracts, and total disregard of independent experts who warned again and again that the city was courting disaster." The president said he was preparing legislation to enable New York to file for bankruptcy. He implied that federal resources might be available to ensure continuation of the city's essential services. But, he said, "I am prepared to veto any bill that has as its purpose to bail out New York City to prevent default."

The next day, Mike O'Neil put it in a memorable *Daily News* headline composed by the paper's managing editor, Bill Brinks: "Ford to City: Drop Dead." The public applauded the paper's spirit. (Carey later said he thought the headline was unfair.) Tension grew in the city. Federal aid was the last piece of the puzzle but a critical one.

Finally, federal resistance began to soften. Mayors and other local officials expressed their worry over the precedent of the federal government's abandoning a city in trouble. Around the country, banks that held New York securities urged their congressmen to put pressure on the administration. Congressmen wrote to the White House. Within the administration, differences of opinion began to surface. Vice President Rockefeller became a voice for federal help. Others in the White House, looking to the next year's presidential election, were concerned about Ford's chances if he continued to stonewall New York. Rohatyn continued to play his role in publicly clarifying the choices that needed to be made. At a critical point, Carey flew to Washington to play golf with Secretary of Defense Melvin Laird, a former House colleague of Carey's and a man as close as anyone to the president. Carey later said that the outing played a key role in moving President Ford closer to a willingness to help.

On November 14, the governor and state legislative leaders presented the Ford administration with the city's new budget plan. It included $2.3 billion in "seasonal" federal loans, needed to ensure the city would have enough cash to cover gaps between receipts and disbursements at various times during the year even when the city's budget was in balance. The plan also included MAC, the Emergency Financial Control Board, and a new deputy mayor for finance; new city and state taxes; layoffs, wage deferrals, employee contributions to their pension funds, and increased commitments by the pension funds to invest in city debt; an independent audit of the funds' actuarial soundness; and a reduction in subsidies like the city's support for its higher education system.

Perhaps the most important and certainly the most controversial part of the plan was that the state legislature, as a condition of the federal loan, enacted a three-year moratorium on the payment of all short-term city obligations that were outstanding on November 15. But there was an exception, the price paid for the banks' support: holders of short-term city debt could exchange their debt for MAC bonds, and the payments on the MAC bonds would continue to be made.

As Carey had reason to hope, these steps changed the president's mind. On November 26, Ford announced that he was endorsing legislation including federal loan guarantees. He cited all of the steps, including the moratorium, that the city and state had taken and were taking to put New York's fiscal house in order.

The terms of the federal loan were tough. The city was charged a 1 percent higher interest rate than the rate Treasury paid on its own comparable borrowings. The secretary of the Treasury could specify the city assets that would serve as collateral for the loan. If federal funds were appropriated to the city under other federal legislation, Treasury could withhold those funds to ensure loan repayment. Despite these protections for the federal government, the vote in Congress was close; there was just a ten-vote margin in favor in the House, and it required a cloture vote in the Senate to circumvent a filibuster. Finally, on December 9, the New York City Seasonal Financing Act of 1975 was passed.

THE LEGISLATION did not end the city fiscal crisis, far from it. We would get into trouble again in the following year. There were unresolved questions and Sisyphian tasks to perform, including the hard, exciting job of building a new budget system and budget culture.

But New York City emerged from its 1975 fiscal crisis because politicians, notwithstanding their intentions to run for office again, managed to solve a complex problem that appeared unsolvable to most people. True, the two politicians who were most important to the solution, Governor Carey and President Ford, relied on experts—the president on noted economists inside and outside the government and the governor on businessmen and the critically important legal services provided by New York law firms. But it was elected politicians who ultimately made the critical decisions.

Those decisions reflected the politicians' personal values, sense of right and wrong, judgments about what was in the best interests of their constituents, and assessments of what they could and could not get their legislatures to do. It is doubtful that President Ford could have persuaded Congress to approve federal aid to the city any sooner than it actually did. And if he had managed to do so when the crisis first erupted in the summer of 1975, New York City would never have taken the tough and necessary steps it took throughout the fall.

In fact, it is disconcerting to wonder how much of the city's recovery was due to the individual character and acumen of Hugh Carey and Gerald Ford and how much worse the outcome would have been if those particular men had not held office. One can only be grateful for their presence.

The city also had other kinds of luck. The institutions that monitored the city—MAC, the control board, even the Treasury Department—generally did not act in a manner that was hostile to the interests or opinions of most elected officials. Instead, these institutions provided an external discipline that the politicians privately welcomed, because they could point to the monitors as the reason why services or benefits had to be cut or taxes had to be raised.

Similarly, union leaders could tell their members that if they did not agree to cuts in employment, wages, or benefits, the control board would not approve their contracts and, thus, would effectively abrogate their collective bargaining rights.

Even more important than the reasonableness of the external monitors, however, was improvement in economic conditions. Some of it was due to inflation and some to federal aid, but the rest reflected the city's fundamental strength. Revenues began to exceed estimates, and the budget was balanced in three years instead of the promised four. By the mid-1980s, the city once again had full access to the credit markets.

New York City's next twenty-five years were mostly prosperous and upbeat. Population grew; so did investment in the city's infrastructure. New York became even more of a magnet for people from all over the world. Though questions remained about the effectiveness of the educational system, the city continued, at an accelerating pace, to absorb generations of immigrants. The Cold War ended; the hegemony of the United States seemed secure; the level of optimism reflected the conviction that trees would always grow to the sky.

But while New York had a right to be proud of how it got out of its seemingly overwhelming crisis, it also had an obligation to try to make sure this kind of debacle did not occur again. There was not much confusion about why the city made the mistakes it did: everyone understands that a politician generally doesn't get elected by running on a platform of taking things away from voters. But the city's institutions had failed, and not just the political ones. The federal Securities and Exchange Commission later issued a report on the city crisis that was critical of not just government mismanagement but also the financial institutions on which the city depended. During the six months just before Wall Street's decision to stop lending the city money, the ratings agencies had actually upgraded the city's credit. Most bond counsel had opined that holders of the city's general obligation debt had a first lien on all its revenues, which was probably not true. In those six months, Merrill Lynch and the city's six largest banks underwrote more than $4 billion in city debt despite New York's lack of a truly balanced budget in over a decade.

As the crisis ended, we saw these things—and told one another that we wouldn't repeat our mistakes.

5

New York and America
After the Storm

T HE YEAR 1975 CHANGED MY LIFE. I fulfilled a long-standing ambition to play a part in important public events, and I became something of a public person, which I wouldn't admit to enjoying. When the Urban Development Corporation and New York City crises quieted down, I made an abortive attempt to return to what I considered my private routine. But it was too late: I was hooked on politics and government, and my professional life would never again be without a healthy—or, sometimes, unhealthy—dose of public activity.

Part of the reason I thought it was time to get back to business was that HRH Construction required more of my attention. After my cousin Saul's tragic death, I had amicably bought out his interest in the firm; now I had to run the enterprise without his wisdom and collegiality. Also, business was slow.

One reason was the recession that began in 1973; another was the continuing uncertainty about New York City's future financial health. Still more important, almost all of the current housing programs that were the major source of our business were coming to an end. There was a generally reduced political appetite for spending public money on housing, and the UDC collapse and the factors that caused it made the bond markets unwilling to rely on the rent projections that state and local governments presented to support their issuance of tax-exempt housing debt. It was difficult, if not impossible, to market municipal bonds for housing that did not have some kind of credit enhancement from the Federal Housing Administration or a private financial institution.

Along with these pressures, there were the demands of the civic life of a private citizen. I was the chairman of the board of my sons' school at a time when it was engaged in replacing the headmaster, an exercise as intensely political as anything I had seen in Albany. I was a trustee of the Federation of Jewish Philanthropies. I helped organize and served as the first president of New York's Jewish Community Relations Council. I joined the board of the Bowery Savings Bank, the city's largest mutual savings association.

But 1976 was an election year, for both the US presidency and one of New York's seats in the US Senate. As always, I had a hard time staying away from the politics and the issues.

⚜

IN THE 1972 presidential election, the Democratic Party carried exactly one state and the District of Columbia. After that debacle, I helped set up the Coalition for a Democratic Majority, a group that aimed to keep the party from repeating the mistake of choosing a candidate who could not possibly win in a general election. Lane Kirkland, by then secretary-treasurer of the AFL-CIO, was part of the effort; so were Daniel P. Moynihan, Senator Henry "Scoop" Jackson, and Ben Wattenberg. I was introduced to yet another world.

One day in early 1976, I got a call from a young real estate developer named Landon Butler, who had heard about the integrated housing that HRH had built in Washington and wanted to do the same with the first integrated housing development in Atlanta. Butler made a trip to New York to ask whether HRH would be his partner in the venture. When I later saw him in Atlanta, he asked whether I wanted to meet the former governor of Georgia, who

Butler said was going to be the next president. But everyone knew Jimmy Carter didn't have a chance, so I took an early plane home instead. Butler later became President Carter's deputy chief of staff, and after he did so I got the opportunity to laugh with the president about my lack of political perspicacity.

I also wanted to be involved in electing people to national office who would help New York City. With Daniel Patrick Moynihan, I got that opportunity and more, as we struggled with both the city's travails and the nation's geopolitical insecurities throughout the 1970s.

Pat had many public roles and identities in his life, but he was, perhaps above all else, a product of New York City, a serious intellectual raised in Hell's Kitchen. In 1965, as assistant secretary of Labor in the Johnson administration, he produced a report, *The Negro Family: The Case for National Action*, which argued that poverty in urban black communities was partly due to the relative absence of two-parent families. The report was sympathetic to the families whose plight it described, and its diagnosis was fundamentally sound. But it suggested that culture, not just economic discrimination, played a significant role in the persistence of social inequality. It created a firestorm.

Moynihan's report, appearing at the time of the Watts riot, had a broad influence on the national discourse. It alerted policy makers and the attentive public to what was then called an "urban" problem, the combined result of the civil rights revolution and the jobs this revolution had left undone. It was no accident that the year 1965 saw the federal government's creation of a new cabinet department called not just a department of housing but a Department of Housing and Urban Development, even though most of the housing it financed lay outside central cities. The next year, Johnson's secretary of Health, Education, and Welfare, John Gardner, resigned to become chairman of the newly formed Urban Coalition. Schools of Urban Affairs were formed; degrees in Urban Affairs conferred.

But the controversy over the report changed Pat's political life. Estranged from some of his fellow liberals, he went to work for a

Republican president, Richard Nixon. While in the Nixon White House, Pat wrote a memo observing that the issue of race in American politics could benefit from a period of "benign neglect." Those who had been offended by *The Negro Family* found another reason to take offense. After Pat returned from being Nixon's appointee as US Ambassador to India, he triggered the same kind of uproar in American diplomacy, arguing in an article in *Commentary* that the world's democracies were becoming a minority in international bodies like the United Nations and had better get ready to defend their positions.

Largely because of this article, Pat was named US ambassador to the UN by President Gerald Ford in 1975. So Pat moved into the US ambassador's quarters in the Waldorf-Astoria Towers and became a citizen of New York again. He ardently defended the American democracy, as well as the Israeli democracy, because he became aware of how closely connected the two allies were. When the UN General Assembly passed a resolution declaring that Zionism was a form of racism, Pat's speeches expressed the widespread indignation with which most of America reacted.

◦∬◦

THE US SENATE seat from New York that was up for election in 1976 was occupied—anomalously, in a liberal state like New York—by James L. Buckley of the Conservative Party, who had won the seat through a series of highly unusual events. When Senator Robert F. Kennedy was assassinated in 1968, Governor Rockefeller appointed Republican Congressman Charles Goodell to fill out the balance of the term. In 1970 Goodell ran for election to the seat in his own right, but he and his Democratic opponent, Richard Ottinger, split the liberal electorate, allowing Buckley to win with 39 percent of the vote.

In 1976 the Democrats were poised to retake the seat, and the primary campaign for the Democratic nomination was going to be fierce. The most prominent candidate was Congresswoman Bella Abzug, a leading politician of the New Left.

I wanted to talk with Pat about his entering the Democratic primary race, and he invited me to dinner at the Waldorf Towers. We talked for a long time about the practical problems of running, the risk of his losing his tenured faculty position at Harvard, and his anxiety about whether he could gain any support from the African American community after the Moynihan report and "benign neglect." At the end of the conversation, he suggested that I get together with two people who he thought shared my view: his special assistant at the UN, Suzanne Weaver, and his friend Leonard Garment, who was US representative to the UN Human Rights Commission and counselor to the US delegation to the UN.

A few nights later, I had dinner with Garment and Weaver, and we agreed that it was important for Pat to run. We thought his candidacy would generate support in many different quarters. But first we had to find out whether he could raise the money to run a credible race.

The hunt for dollars started in my business office in Midtown Manhattan with my phone and Rolodex. The first people I called were Jewish New Yorkers who had seen what Pat's speeches in the UN and elsewhere had done for both American Jews and other Americans who felt that democratic principles were under attack. But I soon found that Pat's appeal was much broader than that. The eclectic nature of his life—he was part Irish pol, part Harvard intellectual—made him different from all the other candidates. More than that, New Yorkers saw in him a reflection of their own diverse, vibrant selves. Also, as Moynihan taught me, there is a more powerful connection than most people think between the world of ideas and the world of practical politics. Sometimes in an electoral race, a good idea is worth more than money.

Still, the race was hair-raisingly close. Pat's was not exactly the most efficient campaign in American political history. Pat himself was constitutionally disorganized. He had the good fortune to have a devoted wife, Liz Moynihan, who often made order out of his chaos; but most of the people involved in the campaign were new to Pat, and the crises were frequent.

One day during the primary campaign, in late August, I was fishing with my sons on a small boat off Martha's Vineyard when I got a message from my wife saying it was urgent to get in touch with Liz. I called her on the boat's ship-to-shore radio, which is audible to anyone on the high seas who happens to tune into the right frequency. Liz said the campaign needed cash to pay for the last week of television advertising. The Moynihans had applied for a loan from Citibank, as it had recently been renamed, that would be secured by a mortgage on their upstate farm, but would take two days to get an appraisal. The campaign couldn't afford to wait.

From the boat, I managed to get through to Citibank CEO Walter Wriston by phone. I warned him that we were having a conversation open to the world and asked him whether he could help. He told me that he was a Republican—no great secret—but greatly admired Moynihan. Several hours later, Liz phoned me to say that the bank had made the loan and the TV time was paid for.

Toward the end of the campaign, there was an intense battle for the *New York Times* endorsement, generally considered critical in this kind of closely contested Democratic primary. The editorial page editor, John Oakes, was enamored of Bella Abzug. The paper's publisher, Arthur "Punch" Sulzberger, was not. While Oakes was on vacation on the Vineyard, the *Times*, at its publisher's behest, endorsed Pat in an editorial written by Max Frankel, who was then editor of the Sunday *Times* and would later succeed Oakes on the editorial page. From the Vineyard, Oakes wrote a letter of protest to his own newspaper, which printed it.

Pat won the primary and went on to defeat Buckley, significantly outpolling Jimmy Carter in New York. During the campaign, Pat said that if he were elected, he would get himself appointed to the Senate Finance Committee and use his position to ensure that New York received its fair share of federal money. He did just that, becoming a supremely articulate advocate for the state. Many of the people who were active in Pat's campaign were interested in broader issues: race, education, the safety of Israel. (Some of my friends in the real estate business, from whom I had solicited campaign contributions for Pat, had second thoughts a decade later, when he allowed accelerated depreciation, a tax subsidy strongly favored by the industry, to expire as part of his and Senator Bob Packwood's comprehensive tax reform.) But those of us who were still struggling to keep the city out of bankruptcy realized our hopes that he would be New York's champion.

⸱⸱⸱

WE NEEDED ONE. Throughout 1976, there was continuing tension among the banks, the unions, and the state's politicians, with members of Congress chiming in from time to time. The unions and the banks had agreed on the need to do painful things, but it was not until they actually had to do them that the level of pain became apparent. Then, in late November 1976, the New York State Court of Appeals rendered a decision that put New York City's delicately structured recovery plan in serious doubt once more.

The opinion came in the case of *Flushing National Bank v. Municipal Assistance Corporation*. The bank had filed suit claiming that the moratorium on the payment of the city's short-term debt, imposed as part of the federal loan agreement, was unconstitutional. The bank acknowledged that the city literally did not have enough funds on hand to pay the notes. But the notes were backed by New York City's "full faith and credit." Therefore, the bank argued, the city was required under the state constitution to meet its obligation, even if it had to exercise its taxing power and impose new taxes on its citizens to raise the funds to pay the notes. The Court of Appeals, the state's highest court, sided with the bank.

There were several dissenting opinions, and most legal scholars believe that there has been no definitive answer to the central question raised by the case: in a community-wide fiscal emergency, should a government be allowed to defer the payment of its obligations, or should it be required to raise taxes to fulfill those obligations, no matter what the effect of the taxes might be on the community? In larger terms, which is the greater danger to a democracy, an unfulfilled debt obligation or confiscatory levels of taxation?

Apart from the long-term dilemma that the case exposed, the court's ruling had a very concrete short-term effect: the $2.4 billion of notes on which the moratorium had suspended payment now became immediately due and payable. President Ford pointed to the terms of Washington's loan agreement with New York City and indicated the federal government would withhold its seasonal loans to the city until the moratorium issue was resolved.

The banks, empowered by the court's decision, went further. When the moratorium was initially imposed, and the banks were allowed to escape the consequences if they exchanged their notes for MAC bonds, they did so in substantial amounts. After the court ruled in *Flushing* that the city had to repay the $2.4 billion in short-term notes, the banks contended the city should also be required to repay the MAC bonds that the banks had taken in exchange for these notes. The banks also demanded the creation of yet another fiscal monitoring body, this one without any elected officials on it—to "build a fence," they said, around the discretion of state and local politicians.

Mayor Beame denounced the demands as "blatant overreaching." The unions were furious and threatened to renege on their promise to have their pension funds buy $2.7 billion in MAC bonds. Once again, however, rational self-interest gradually overcame angry self-righteousness. The state agreed to assume the costs of the City University of New York and the New York City court system. The life of the existing Emergency Financial Control Board was extended until the year 2000. The federal government provided additional credit assistance. The union pension funds bought their $2.7 billion of MAC bonds.

Governor Carey visited President-elect Carter in Atlanta. Carter made a reassuring statement: "Bankruptcy is not a viable alternative for New York City, and we have eliminated that as a possibility for the future." Carter's statement calmed the markets, and people once again started doing what had to be done to enable the city to meet its obligations to creditors and citizens.

ॐ

THEN, ON THE heels of the Moynihan excitement and the city crisis aftershock, came the problem of Co-op City in the Bronx, the country's largest cooperative public housing project.

Co-op City includes 15,372 apartments that house more than sixty thousand people. It sits mostly on marshland that was used primarily for farming until developer Bill Zeckendorf built an amusement park there in 1960. The park was called Freedomland USA, and it went bankrupt within five years. Then the nonprofit United Housing Federation, created by the Amalgamated Clothing Workers union, proposed building a co-op project on the site to house thousands of recent immigrants to the city who wanted to move out of their shabby tenement apartments.

The construction of Co-op City began in May 1966. Residents began moving in at the end of 1968, and construction was finished in 1973. The mortgage on the development, more than $250 million, was held by the state's Housing Finance Agency, which, of course, had raised the money by selling tax-exempt bonds.

Unfortunately, the project was badly mismanaged. The construction was shoddy. Physical problems soon emerged in the buildings, interfering with the tenants' ability to live comfortably. They sued the developer over building flaws but were unsuccessful in the end.

At the same time, it turned out that the estimates of the monthly carrying charges the apartment owners would have to pay had been grossly inadequate. The owners had each paid somewhere between $3,000 and $5,000 for their apartments. The difference between the amounts they paid and the total cost of the project was made up by the $250-million mortgage held by the Housing Finance Agency

(HFA). The apartment owners' monthly carrying charges were meant to cover the buildings' operating expenses, real estate taxes—which were extremely low—and the debt service on the HFA mortgage. When the owners bought their apartments, they were told that their monthly carrying charges would average less than $200 per month. Soon after moving in, they were informed that the charges would have to double.

The situation had all the ingredients for a crisis, which proceeded to occur. In June 1975, a nasty rent strike began, led by a man euphemistically described by the *New York Times* as a son of "Eastern European immigrants with strong Communist sympathies." The HFA got an injunction against the strike, froze the bank accounts of the strike leaders, and began a proceeding to take title to the development back from the co-operative. State politicians were faced with the prospect of having to foreclose on sixty thousand people.

Secretary of State Mario Cuomo, on his own initiative but with the governor's blessing, stepped into the mess and negotiated a short-term accommodation. The striking tenants turned over the checks they had withheld from the state, and the co-op made a substantial payment to HFA in order to keep control of the property. But this arrangement would continue for just six months, by which time the state was supposed to come up with a permanent solution.

I was in the room when Governor Carey was briefed on Co-op City, including the fact that the state was now tasked with finding a permanent solution. He turned to us and asked hopefully, "How soon does my term end?" In a letter of July 21, 1976, he asked me to find the permanent solution that the state had promised.

I had once again entered a morass that all the elected officials were assiduously trying to avoid, while occasionally expressing sympathy to me sotto voce. Critical policy issues were at stake; so were the human pressures on many Co-op City tenants. Tens of thousands of people owed the State of New York large sums of money they could not pay, and the cost of continuing to live in the development had become greater than many tenants could afford. Meanwhile, a state agency, HFA, had sold hundreds of millions of dollars of moral obligation bonds to the public with little prospect of being able to collect repayment from the entity that had borrowed the money.

In the wake of the New York City crisis, an intense effort was under way to stabilize the state's credit. Now the prospect of a default on the Co-op City bonds threatened that effort. The state had clearly failed in supervising the development company that had borrowed the money to build the project. The developer was for all practical purposes insolvent. And Co-op City's sixty thousand tenants included tens of thousands of voters, a number that no New York City politician could ignore. Even worse, the problem at Co-op City existed in more or less attenuated form among most of the 430 Mitchell-Lama projects around the state, some 66,000 apartments housing close to half a million people.

In examining the Co-op City physical infrastructure, studying its books and accounts, and above all talking at length with the residents and their leaders, it became clear that it was simply impossible to achieve operating savings or produce revenues from sources other than rents in anything near the amounts that would have been needed for the project to meet its financial obligations.

Equally clear, if the carrying charges were increased immediately by amounts large enough to bring current revenues into line with current expenses, tenants would have to spend a far higher percentage of their incomes on housing than the Mitchell-Lama law had contemplated. And, law or no law, such increases would not have been fair by any standard that even a hard-nosed landlord could support.

In January 1977, I presented recommendations to the governor. They were conceptually simple. For each Mitchell-Lama project, there would be something called an "economic rent roll," an amount of rent for each apartment that would produce, in total, enough funds to cover the costs of operating the project, including debt service. The actual rent for each existing tenant would be raised by stages until it equaled the amount on the economic rent roll, except that no tenants would be required to spend more than 25 percent of their incomes on rent.

When apartments became vacant, they could be rented to people with incomes higher than the current income ceilings allowed. These higher incomes would produce higher rent revenues, which would offset the shortfalls created by the limits on the rent paid by poorer tenants. And people with income above certain levels would not be entitled to the 25-percent-of-income limitation at all.

The governor and state budget director supported the recommendations, and the press praised them. However, even after many trips to Albany and many discussions, the state legislature heatedly opposed the plan. It was never enacted. Co-op City's financial problems continued for years.

So did problems with other Mitchell-Lama housing. For instance, under its Mitchell-Lama program, New York City had made $2 billion in mortgage loans that were in default; but the city couldn't foreclose on the borrowers because, in its regulatory capacity, it had prevented the owners from raising rents enough to cover the properties' operating expenses and debt service. Thus, many of the mortgages were in default. With Carla Hills at HUD, I worked out an arrangement for refinancing the city's mortgages: the FHA would insure mortgages up to the amounts covered by the available cash flow for each project. For the balance, the city would take back second mortgages, subordinate to the FHA's mortgage claims. The second mortgages, like the primary FHA mortgages, were eventually paid off.

You could not watch the unfolding of these troubles without understanding that while a generous society can and should provide the necessities of life to its poorer citizens, we owe it to ourselves to be honest about the costs. As fiscal pressures grow, such honesty is all we have to keep us from relying on bailouts that the political system may be unwilling or unable to provide.

∂ρ

My mother, Sylvia, my father, Saul, and their adoring son, around 1939.

I know that I am without a doubt one of the luckiest people on the face of the earth. I have a beautiful, loving wife, two spectacular sons, three stepdaughters, four grandsons, and nine step-grandchildren, all of whom I adore.

Having finished law school in 1958, I became an assistant counsel to the Subcommittee on Military Operations, where I helped the general counsel prepare for congressional hearings on the separate ballistic missile programs then being pursued separately by the Army, Navy, and Air Force.

In 1963 I volunteered to help, in a very minor way, in the organization of the March on Washington. I had the thrill of standing in front of the Lincoln Memorial and hearing Martin Luther King Jr. declare, "I have a dream." I also became friendly with the civil rights giant Bayard Rustin.

The process of securing city support for the Waterside development was a microcosm of the complexity of New York politics. All it took was redefining the navigable status of the East River, fighting off Laurance Rockefeller, and negotiating the politics of race and ethnicity. Mayor John Lindsay and former Mayor Robert Wagner enjoyed the opening celebration with me, having played critical roles in Waterside's creation.

Pat Moynihan had many public roles and identities in his life, but he was, perhaps above all else, a product of New York City, a serious intellectual raised in Hell's Kitchen. Pat taught me that there is a powerful connection between the world of ideas and the world of practical politics. Sometimes in an electoral race a good idea is worth more than money.

I was at Governor Hugh Carey's side in 1975, when Walter Wriston of Citibank, Willard Butcher of Chase, and Pat Patterson of Morgan sat down with us to say they would no longer underwrite the notes and bonds of the city, pushing it to the brink of bankruptcy.

Mayor Abe Beame, a product of the Brooklyn Democratic organization, was an accountant who was viewed as a budget expert and fiscal watchdog, no small irony for the man who would preside over the city's financial collapse.

My appointment as chairman of the Metropolitan Transportaion Authority came about in an unlikely way. I was meeting with Governor Carey about another matter when he announced that he wanted me to be the chairman. After a pause—just long enough for me to figure out that he was truly and actually serious—I told him he was crazy and that he didn't ride the city subways; I did. "No one in his right mind would want to manage a system in the MTA's condition."

We negotiated the design and manufacture of 325 cars with Kawasaki Heavy Industries of Japan, paying a premium to make the cars of stainless steel, which could be washed clean of graffiti.

Running the MTA offered more than its fair share of challenges, including a subway derailment, a strike, and crazed gunmen.

Cheryl Tiegs ripped off for 75G Story Page Seven

NEW YORK POST METRO SPORTS FINAL

25 CENTS AMERICA'S FASTEST-GROWING NEWSPAPER

WEDNESDAY, APRIL 22, 1981

AVERAGE DAILY SALES RECORD 730,000

TV listings: P. 71

ASSASSIN ON THE LOOSE

Hunt gunman who tried to kill Ravitch

KOCH WARNS OFFICIALS: BE CAREFUL

FULL STORY PLUS LATEST ON THE SHOT COP: PAGES 4, 5

Mayor Ed Koch once characterized the transit workers as loungers and loafers. I responded that his comments were unfair and counterproductive, especially coming from a mayor who had just cut the city's contribution to the MTA. A few days later, he was "offering Ravitch the olive branch—in fact, the whole tree." I can't remember a moment of tension between us since then.

I was a lousy candidate for mayor of New York City and ended up with a stunning 3 percent of the Democratic primary vote in 1989. But the campaign was an experience I never regretted for one second, and I found it an exhilarating affirmation of my conviction about the wonder of the democratic process.

I've loved baseball all my life and jumped at the chance to become head of the Major League Baseball owners' Player Relations Committee.

I met Joe Califano in 1960 during the Kennedy presidential campaign when he was a young lawyer practicing in New York who hoped for a job in Washington if Kennedy was elected. Joe was with me fifty years later celebrating my birthday at a steakhouse in Brooklyn when I was quickly sworn in as lieutenant governor of New York.

After I became lieutenant governor in 2010, I searched for a substantive issue I could sink my teeth into and found it when Governor David Paterson asked me to make independent recommendations regarding the state budget. The issues I found have been of growing concern ever since.

When I left public office, I prevailed on my friend Paul Volcker to join in creating the State Budget Crisis Task Force and a three-year study to explain many of the reasons for the chronic fiscal dysfunction in New York and other states. Credit: Mary F. Calvert/*New York Times*/Redux Pictures.

AFTER DEALING WITH Co-op City, I knew I would be devoting a large part of my professional life to public affairs, but I did not think I would be back in government. True, with a new administration coming to Washington after the 1976 election, I would have loved to be appointed secretary of the Department of Housing and Urban Development. In December I asked Pat Moynihan and Lane Kirkland to recommend me to the president-elect. They did so, but President Carter picked someone with no experience in the field to be secretary, and the administration offered me the job of deputy. The costs of going to Washington were high. I would have had to divest myself of my interest in Waterside, and there was no one readily available who could take over the business of HRH Construction. These difficulties might have been worth it for a real chance to shape housing policy, but not for something less. I turned down the job.

Instead, in the summer of 1977, for the first time in years, I took a long vacation with my family. It gradually became clear that as long as I was actively running my business, there would be no time for the public activities that increasingly occupied me. For example, I mentioned to Michael Sovern, then dean of Columbia Law School, that very few lawyers in public service in New York were familiar with the securities or bankruptcy laws; that was why New York City was so dependent on private law firms during the 1975 fiscal crisis. In response, Sovern asked me to teach a seminar at the law school on public finance. I did so and, always having had an academic bent, enjoyed it. But I saw that teaching responsibly takes a lot of work, in amounts for which active business involvement simply does not leave enough time.

So I began to explore the idea of selling HRH. It would not be easy to do. The corporation was a service business with no hard assets; its most substantial asset was goodwill. It would be difficult to find someone to buy the business without my agreeing to continue to operate it for five years or more. I felt obligated to protect the jobs of the firm's employees, and there was the problem of covering the firm's overhead if it stopped undertaking new construction contracts.

But I finally made a deal with a competing company. They agreed to give jobs to all of HRH's employees except me and complete all of HRH's existing contracts, allocating the benefits and burdens of those contracts to me. Completing the contracts took a year. But the process ended as I had hoped, with HRH's assets consisting of cash and a group of happy former employees and colleagues. My only continuing active business involvement was as the general partner of the partnerships that owned Waterside and Manhattan Plaza.

∿

MY FIRST POST-SALE project began in 1977 with, as usual, a call from Governor Carey. He and Mayor Beame had decided to try to have New York City chosen as the site of the 1984 summer Olympics. Would I head up the campaign? It sounded a lot better than dealing with tenants and bond lawyers, and I happily agreed to meet with them the next day. We agreed that hosting the Olympics would be a dramatic way to show that the city's fiscal troubles were behind us. But the two men told me I would have to raise the money to cover the cost of the architects, planners, and staff we needed to design a plan to accommodate all the Olympic events in New York.

Raising the money was the least of it. We set up a nonprofit organization to manage the campaign. With great excitement in the business community about the challenge, we soon had the funds to cover our costs. The US Olympic Committee provided us with a list of all the Olympic events and the physical specifications for each venue, and told us we would also need a place for the athletes to live and a logistical plan for getting them to and from their events. We would be competing with Los Angeles to be chosen by the US Olympic Committee, which would then become the advocate of the selected US city at the meeting of the International Olympic Committee.

Over the summer, we met with people from each of the specialized sports federations to get an understanding of their sports' physical requirements. We examined all of the region's stadiums, swimming pools, and gymnasiums. Roosevelt Island was the ideal

location for the Olympic Village: from there, the athletes could travel
by water to most of the events. We scouted venues from New Jersey
to Connecticut and tried to think through the logistics of the two
Olympic weeks that we would have to manage if New York's bid
were successful.

The toughest problem was the question of where the central
Olympic Stadium should be. The space had to run a gauntlet of
requirements. It had to have capacity for enough people; it had to
be elliptical, so that it could accommodate the 800-meter race. New
York could not afford to build a facility that met all the requirements,
so we started exploring other ideas. The best one was to open up
the bleacher end of Shea Stadium in Queens and rebuild it to the
required shape. True, this meant that the Mets would have to play in
Yankee Stadium for two summers. But we figured that in return, the
city could amend the Yankees' lease to give the Yankees the benefit
of all the extra parking and concession revenues.

We finished our plans. The governor and the mayor approved
them, including the part about Shea Stadium. I recommended they
should now call George Steinbrenner, owner of the Yankees, to tell
him about our intentions for his future. Carey said I should call
Steinbrenner instead. I didn't know him, but Carey assured me that
he would know who I was and would take my call.

I went back to my office, placed the call, and was put on hold for
ten minutes. When Steinbrenner finally picked up, I went through
the whole explanation: the Mets at Yankee Stadium, the amended
lease, and the expanded parking and concession revenues. Steinbrenner then told me in classic language just what physically impossible
act I should perform on myself. I dutifully reported the conversation
to the governor, who laughed and said that was why it was a good
thing I had made the call, not him.

Steinbrenner aside, there was a genuine and growing enthusiasm
in New York about the prospect of getting the Olympics, particularly
after the press showed pictures of the plan and all the locations. But
by the time we were ready to leave for Colorado Springs, where the

US Olympic Committee was meeting, the 1977 mayoral primary had taken place. After the primary, the feeling among New York's public officials was less brotherly than it had been when they first launched the city's Olympic bid.

Mayor Beame had been determined to run for reelection that year, but very few businessmen, civic leaders, or other politicians backed him. Of the many other candidates in the field, Ed Koch had begun his political career by beating Carmine De Sapio in a Democratic leadership fight and then serving as a member of the City Council from Greenwich Village. Beginning in 1961, Koch represented New York's 17th Congressional District. In the House, Koch became friendly with fellow congressman Hugh Carey. Throughout the 1975 city fiscal crisis, when critical meetings took place in the governor's office, Carey would ask me to invite Koch to be there. But in 1977, when Koch ran in the Democratic mayoral primary, he did so without Carey's backing.

At that time, the *Daily News* was the city's largest-circulation newspaper, read by precisely the people who were likely to vote in a Democratic primary for a local office. The paper's editor, Mike O'Neil—writer of the memorable headline, "Ford to City: Drop Dead"—was a great journalist and a man widely respected for his devotion to the city. He urged Carey to back Mario Cuomo in the mayoral primary. Rupert Murdoch, who had just bought the *New York Post*, also asked Carey to support Cuomo. Carey obliged the two men and endorsed Cuomo for mayor.

During the primary campaign, however, Koch spoke out forcefully about eliminating the city's budget deficit and curtailing the role of the municipal unions. His positions changed the editorial minds of the *Daily News* and the *Post*. By the end of the campaign, both had strongly endorsed Koch, who won the primary election.

Koch was angry with Carey, who was humiliated by the episode. The bad feelings compromised the two men's ability to communicate with each other during the later stages of the city crisis. And, of course, Beame was furious with Carey. To round out the ironies, Carey's support for Mario Cuomo in the mayoral primary did not manage to earn him a decent relationship with Cuomo.

So, when it was time for the New York delegation to travel to Colorado Springs, Beame, now a lame-duck mayor, refused to fly with Carey in the state plane. Carey asked me to accompany him. Beame asked me to fly with him commercially instead. I flew with Carey but felt sorry for Beame and the whole mayoral mess.

Despite the internal drama, the atmosphere was festive at the famous Broadmoor hotel in Colorado Springs. Governor Jerry Brown of California and Mayor Tom Bradley of Los Angeles led off the Los Angeles presentation. Then Peter Ueberroth, who later became commissioner of Major League Baseball, supplied the details. Los Angeles had a slick but impressive story to tell. They were willing to invest more in new facilities than we were, and their existing Coliseum was an ideal Olympic stadium. But Los Angeles's most important asset in the competition was the chairman of the US Olympic Committee, former Treasury Secretary William Simon, who probably still harbored a good deal of disdain for what he believed was New York City's fiscal profligacy. Los Angeles won the competition, perhaps deservedly, and we returned home disappointed.

Mayor Beame did not nurse a grudge. Soon afterward, he asked me to chair a committee to pick a location for a major convention center in New York, yet another effort to bring business to the city and inject some excitement into the atmosphere surrounding its future growth potential. The hotel industry was pushing hard for the project. We heard proposals for sites in Brooklyn and Queens and on Long Island, but we all thought that a location on the West Side of Manhattan, near the rail yards and close to the Lincoln Tunnel and Penn Station, made the most sense and would have the most public support. Some twenty-five years later, it looks like we made a mistake: the convention center should have been larger, it should not have been put on such valuable land, and it should have been located outside Manhattan and used as a rationale for expanding public transportation. But those second thoughts came, as always, much later.

⌘

ED KOCH, AFTER winning the mayoral primary, went on to win the general election. Not many people in his political circle were skilled in financial management, but he reached out, brought many talented individuals into city government, and focused intently on the problem of restoring the city's fiscal health. He promised to balance the city budget in accordance with generally accepted accounting principles within four years, and he accomplished the task in three. He was honest, outspoken, and a marvelous cheerleader at a time when the city badly needed one.

Koch was also helped by the inflation that began to boost incomes and revenues in the 1970s; more than that, New York City's revival reflected fundamental strengths. But my experiences with the state and city's Mitchell-Lama troubles, and even with the Olympic bid, counseled a less sanguine attitude than the one I saw in many people around me.

Co-op City was an object lesson in how quickly good public policy intentions could fail in their execution and how very difficult it was, when this happened, to reverse the immense costs and pain of such failures. With the Olympics bid, we saw that while it was easy enough for us to announce that New York City had emerged from its troubles and was ready to stand astride the world once more, it was another matter to persuade non–New Yorkers to agree. For many people like US Olympic Committee chairman William Simon, New York still carried the burden of the fiscal trauma it had experienced and the limits the crisis had placed on the city's resources. When we made our Olympic bid, Los Angeles was not so constrained. In the future, the tables of urban fortune would turn. Los Angeles, like the State of California, would have its own dramatic financial reversals.

But New York's failed Olympics effort should have been a reminder of the lasting consequences of a city's fiscal decisions.

Meanwhile, UDC, under Ed Cohen's presidency, was winding down. It was successfully completing all its existing projects and managing their new financing. Because there was no available credit, there would be no new projects undertaken. I had a long talk with the governor, and we agreed that I would step down as UDC chairman and join the board of the Municipal Assistance Corporation. I still participated in discussions in Washington about the city's financial situation. Mayor Koch asked me to be deputy mayor for Economic Development, but I decided that I was largely done with the problems associated with public office.

Things did not turn out that way.

6

Guns, Wolves, and Stainless Steel:
Rebuilding the MTA

ONE HOT, SUNNY MORNING IN JUNE 1982, I was standing at an outdoor podium, holding forth before a sea of new Fordham Law School graduates on my favorite subject: public service. I told them that their legal education was the best possible training for public service and public service the best possible use of their legal education. At that moment, however, I wasn't so sure—about either the sentiment or my ability to get through the speech. The day was already oppressively humid. My cap and gown were black. The academic hood was heavy. And then there was the twenty-five-pound police-issue bulletproof vest I was wearing underneath.

The academic honor and the police protection were both courtesy of Governor Carey, who in September 1979 had appointed me chairman of New York's Metropolitan Transportation Authority.

In an almost literal sense, the MTA carries the lifeblood of New York City. For a nation to succeed, it needs the energy and creativity that cities generate. For a city to provide this energy and creativity, it needs to provide the means for people to circulate and interact. Private automobiles alone cannot do this job; a great city depends on public transportation. The prime example is New York, interconnected by the nation's most extensive public transit system. If New York is the world's most vibrant city, it is in large part because of the mobility and communication that the MTA makes possible.

But public transportation is governed by some stubborn facts. First, it costs more than what private markets can provide; it exists only if the public decides it should exist. All of the transit systems now run by the MTA were once owned and operated by private companies, but they all went broke. The immediate cause was that government regulators wouldn't let transit fares increase enough to cover the systems' costs, but the problem was deeper: if the fares had been high enough to cover the systems' costs of operations and capital, they would have been too high for riders to afford. Rather than letting them shut down, the transit lines were taken over by government. In 1968, under Governor Rockefeller, the state created the MTA to consolidate public ownership and operation of the systems. It was a bold but necessary step. Anyone who has lived in New York City through a blackout, 9/11, or Hurricane Sandy has some inkling of what life is like without a functioning public transit system.

The second stubborn fact of public transportation is that "public" means politics. The statute creating the MTA gave the governor authority to appoint most of the MTA board; other board members were appointed by New York City's mayor and the executives of the surrounding counties, in recognition of the central place of public transportation in the life of the New York region. The MTA was—as it still is—dependent on federal, state, and local political support for its solvency. Part of its operating revenues came from rider fares, but every fare increase occasioned a political ritual of posturing and protest, despite the fact that the funds were needed to keep the system running safely and prudently. And the rest of the system's operating and capital funds came directly from local, state, and federal governments.

By the time I took office in 1979, the governments responsible for the MTA were no longer providing anything close to the support the system needed. It was rapidly disintegrating, with the prospect of operating deficits of several hundred million dollars a year and a physical infrastructure that was falling apart.

My appointment as chairman of this crumbling enterprise came about in an unlikely way. I was on the board of Channel 13, New York City's public television station. Channel 13's president, Jay Iselin, learned that the Carey administration was planning to reduce subsidies to public television stations throughout the state. He asked me to arrange an appointment for him with Carey so he could plead the stations' case. Two weeks later, Jay and I sat in the state's New York City offices waiting for the governor who, as usual, was running late.

When Carey saw us in the waiting room, he motioned me into his office. He clearly had something planned for me. I had barely sat down before he announced that he wanted me to become chairman of the MTA. After a pause—just long enough for me to figure out that he was truly and actually serious—I told him he was crazy. He didn't ride the city subways, I said; I did. No one in his right mind would want to manage a system in the MTA's condition.

Carey answered—smiling—that he would not meet with Jay Iselin unless I agreed to do the job. I said I would consider it seriously. Carey met with Jay and later helped restore some of public television's state funding. By then, I was in government again.

After consulting with family and friends, and encouraged by Mayor Ed Koch, I agreed to take the MTA job on the same terms on which I had served at the Urban Development Corporation: I would work without salary and be free to pick my subordinates and counselors. I did not know much about the MTA. The learning curve was going to be steep.

પ

THE SHEER SIZE of the MTA is not easy to grasp. If it were a private corporation, it would rank near the top of the Fortune 500. It runs most of the transportation systems in the New York City region, including the New York City Transit Authority bus and subway lines, the Long Island Railroad, and the Staten Island Rapid Transit

System. It owns the roadbeds and tracks under the Harlem, Hudson, and New Haven commuter lines, now part of Metro North. The MTA board is also the board of the Triborough Bridge and Tunnel Authority, the TBTA, which owns and operates the Verrazano, Triborough, Throgs Neck, Whitestone, Henry Hudson, Marine Parkway, and Cross Bay bridges and the Queens Midtown and Brooklyn Battery tunnels.

The MTA operates more passenger railcars than all of the country's other transit systems put together. In 1979 it operated in seven counties, employed more than 50,000 workers, and owned over 1,700 miles of track, 700 stations, 8,000 railcars, and 5,000 buses. Its buses and subways accounted for more than three million rides every weekday; by 2013 the number exceeded five million. The New York City Transit Police Department was the sixth largest in the nation before it was merged into the city's police force.

Before my confirmation, John Simpson, the MTA's able executive director, helped organize my education about the system. I met with each MTA board member and the key people in each MTA operating organization. I started to learn just how desperate the MTA was for money and how big a backlog of deferred maintenance it had—maintenance that should have taken place yesterday, last month, or last year.

I also met with the state legislators and staffers on whom the MTA depended most. I knew some from my UDC days, including Stanley Fink, then the Democratic Assembly Speaker, and Warren Anderson, the Republican Senate Majority Leader. Anderson, valuable as always, said I had to get to know the chairman of the Senate Transportation Committee, John Caemerrer of Long Island, who had strong opinions and carried weight with his legislative colleagues. Caemerrer made it unavoidably clear that the Long Island Railroad was his highest priority. The MTA would get no further state subsidies unless Long Island was treated "fairly," by which he meant that the New York City subway would have to increase its fare above 50 cents before he would agree to any more subsidies. John was a decent man. But he was tough, and there was no doubting his seriousness.

However, Governor Carey, in exchange for Mayor Koch's support for Westway, the perennially proposed but never-built highway on the West Side of Manhattan, had publicly declared that there would be no subway fare increase until 1981.

I was getting a sense of the MTA's basic political dilemma. The elected officials with power over its subsidies were never of a single mind, but they were united in their aversion to fare increases for their constituents. They saw anything the MTA needed and asked for as an invitation to political suicide. By the time I walked into my confirmation hearing, I knew that whatever I said was going to get me into trouble with somebody, and I sensed that I would be ground down by the conflicting pressures unless I could develop another, more public constituency for the MTA.

I knew one of the state senators at the hearing, Manny Gold from Queens. I asked him to pose a question: were there any circumstances under which I would raise the subway fare? Manny told me I must be unhinged. "You're going to be confirmed," he said. "Why should you ask for trouble?" But I insisted, and during the hearing he asked the question. I answered that I hoped a fare increase wouldn't be necessary, but if there was no other source of funds to operate the subway system safely, there would be no choice but to raise the fare.

That, of course, was the news story that came out of the confirmation hearing. The governor's staff was furious, and I heard about it.

I no longer had close ties with Carey's staff. After he was reelected in 1978, the people with whom I had worked most closely during his first term moved on. Judah Gribetz and David Burke went into the private sector. Peter Goldmark became head of the Port Authority of New York and New Jersey. I never had much chance to develop relationships with their successors.

Carey himself, I learned later, didn't mind what I had said in the confirmation hearing. He knew he shouldn't have promised that there wouldn't be a fare increase, and he thought my statement could help him avoid the consequences of the commitment he had made to Koch. At the time, however, all I saw was the steam rising from the direction of the governor's office.

I knew I could avoid antagonism from the staff by taking direction from them instead of acting as a fiduciary for the people who rode and worked for the transit system. I chose to go my own way. At a press conference in November, I said that the MTA's deferred maintenance practices had to end. That meant the MTA would have to increase fares or get more subsidies from Albany—which, in turn, meant more taxes.

There was more anger from the upper echelons of the state executive branch. State Commissioner of Transportation William Hennessy thought the MTA should report to him and so called to tell me the governor would not support either new taxes or a fare increase. Relying on my prior relationship with Carey, I wrote the governor a letter saying that the continued safety of the MTA system could not be assured without the reinstitution of major maintenance programs, which would require new revenues.

Carey agreed to seek new revenue from the legislature, but only on the condition that I would not try to raise the subway fare. The legislative leaders, for their part, said they would not approve any new taxes unless there was a subway fare increase at the same time. Restoring the MTA would require assembling a puzzle of thousands of pieces of funding, engineering, organization, and politics—and each piece had extremely sharp edges.

It took several years to do the job: to get a plan through the state legislature providing subsidies and authorizing the MTA to raise more capital, to raise the authorized capital, and to begin the actual restoration. But before any of it could begin, the MTA and I had to lurch through a string of crises needing immediate attention.

⁂

MOST IMMEDIATELY, Koch and Carey's opposition notwithstanding, there had to be a fare increase; and the MTA board had to vote to enact it. Orchestrating that vote was not easy. New York State has an open meetings law that requires public bodies like the MTA board to make decisions in sessions open to the public. The goal is worthy; but before the board met publicly on the fare increase, I had to know there were enough votes to pass it. To finesse the open meeting requirement, I invited all the board members to dinner at the Century Association, a private club, the night before the public vote.

At that time, in 1980, the Century admitted women as guests but not as members. When Carol Bellamy, president of the New York City Council and an MTA board member, got my invitation, she phoned me and told me in strikingly colorful language that she wasn't about to attend a dinner at a gender-segregated club. MTA counsel warned that if the dinner took place, Carol might tell the press, and the press might make the dinner look like a private meeting. If that happened, the open meetings law would throw the legal legitimacy of the next day's vote on the fare increase into doubt.

Further ingenuity was needed. I booked a room at the Yale Club, two blocks away from the Century Association, and sent half the board members there for dinner. With no quorum present in either place, there was no illegal meeting. I literally ran back and forth between the two places, puffing for four hours, until I was sure of the votes for the next morning.

While that problem had its comic aspects, other immediate issues were not so funny. The MTA's contracts with workers for the Long Island Railroad and the New York City Transit system were expiring. Just three weeks after I took office, the seventeen unions of the LIRR went on strike. The LIRR was owned and heavily subsidized by the MTA. But because it was a railroad, its unions were not subject to the state's Taylor Law, enacted after the 1966 New York City subway strike, a law that bans strikes by state public employees. Instead, labor relations on the LIRR were governed by federal law, which sent the dispute into mediation. It ended in a settlement that preserved some of the LIRR's worst labor inefficiencies. The MTA challenged the position that federal law preempted the Taylor Law, taking the issue all the way to the US Supreme Court. We lost.

In contrast, the MTA's dispute with Local 100 of the Transit Workers Union was governed by state law, including the Taylor Law prohibition on strikes by public employees. But the TWU had a still older tradition: if there was no new contract by midnight of the day when an existing contract expired, the union would—legally or illegally—strike. Their contract would expire on March 31, 1980. The union had not had a wage increase in five years and was seething with resentment.

When it became clear that there would be no easy resolution to the contract issues, I made it my business to get closer to the president of Local 100, John Lawe. He had driven a bus for the Fifth Avenue Coach line when it was a private company. He spoke with a thick Irish brogue, as did his equally shrewd and experienced counsel, John O'Donnell. Local 100 was divided. Lawe had been elected in 1975 without a majority of the votes cast. A loudly militant element in the union was eager to get rid of him and his old guard. The union stated it would take nothing less than a 30 percent wage increase.

On the management side, the MTA's contract with the TWU would expire on March 31, just before the expiration of a number of New York City's collective bargaining agreements. What happened in the transit negotiations would, arguably, set a precedent for the city labor negotiations to follow. Mayor Koch announced that the city, still emerging from fiscal crisis, could not afford more than a couple of percentage points in wage increases. The newspapers exhorted me to be resolute and tough. I said the MTA would give no more than 3 percent a year.

As the calendar edged toward the contract expiration date, Lawe and I knew we had some things in common. We knew the final settlement would end up somewhere between 7 and 9 percent over two years. We knew we had sharply divided constituencies. And we knew we did not know exactly how we would get our respective boards to approve the inevitable settlement numbers.

Former Mayor Wagner had become a friend, and he armed me with some advice: when you're a public official negotiating a labor contract, remember that what's most important to the union leader is to come out looking like a winner; let him do that, and you'll save the public a lot of money. On the night of March 30, the day before the contract expiration, Lawe and I met with our counsels and my vice chairman and friend Dan Scannell and developed a strategy.

I would meet with Lawe's executive board at about 10:00 P.M. on March 31 and make what I would say was my last and final offer. Lawe would throw me out of the room. He would put my offer up for a vote. The offer would lose. Lawe would then tell his board that the union should put its own final offer on the table before going out on strike. He would outline an offer and tell his board he was sure I would reject it, though he knew otherwise. Once his board voted to put the union's offer on the table, I would be invited back into the room and presented with the ultimatum. I would reluctantly bow my head and accept.

Another tradition was that all of the many people involved in transit talks would stay at the Sheraton hotel on Seventh Avenue so they could be negotiating nonstop, or at least appear to be doing so. By the morning of March 31, the hotel was a media circus, and Passover was beginning that evening. I wouldn't be at my family's Seder this year; my older son was going to preside. But the governor called in the morning to say he wanted to leave no stone unturned in ensuring that he, the mayor, and I had a common position in the transit negotiations. So he was inviting Koch and me to a Seder with him at the St. Regis hotel, where his son Chris was the banquet manager.

Koch and I arrived at the hotel at 6:00 that evening. There was a spread of gefilte fish, horseradish, and matzoh ball soup. There was a Haggadah. There was an abbreviated telling of the story of the Exodus. But, like much else that night, the governor's plan for a meeting of the minds did not work. If I had told Carey and Koch about the plan that Lawe and I had cooked up the night before, Koch would have been furious and Carey wouldn't have supported me against him. So the conversation went nowhere. I finally excused myself. I went back to the Sheraton to await Lawe's phone call.

At 10:00 I got the call. I went to the conference room where the union's executive committee was meeting. I made my offer. It was rejected. I left the room. Then something went wrong: I was never invited back. The transit strike began at midnight. The next morning, John told me that half the executive committee had been drunk at the meeting the night before. They had shouted down his effort to put together a counteroffer.

The strike lasted eleven days. Millions of New Yorkers, in those days before telecommuting, were unable to get to work. Mayor Koch stood on the Brooklyn Bridge, rallying citizens who were walking into Manhattan and exhorting them to resist the union. Under the Taylor Law, the striking workers were losing two days' pay for every day of the strike. The union, which was violating the law's antistrike injunction, was subject to heavy fines.

With the strike in full swing, Koch invited me to Gracie Mansion. He told me he was going to file a motion with the State Supreme Court in Brooklyn to impose a fine on the TWU—a fine big enough to throw the union into bankruptcy. He wanted my support.

I resisted telling him that if the TWU went bankrupt, the Teamsters were ready to step in to represent the city transit system's forty thousand hourly-wage workers. The Teamsters had much deeper pockets than the TWU's. If they took over, the strike would last much longer.

Our discussion became heated. Voices were raised. One of the people in the room, a Koch appointee to the MTA board and a friend of mine, was Bobby Wagner, son of the former mayor and the grandson of the US senator who had sponsored the federal law that legitimized collective bargaining. I told him his grandfather would roll over in his grave if he could hear what the mayor was proposing. Koch was unmoved; he was going to file his motion.

I was so worried that Koch would turn a bad strike into a worse one that I did something I can report now only because of the passage of time. The Brooklyn trial court judge who had the city's motion before him hailed from the Brooklyn Democratic organization—as did the presiding judge of the Brooklyn appeals court, Milton Mollen, a friend whom I knew from the days when I was building Waterside and he was head of New York City's housing agency. I had an MTA police car take me to Brooklyn to pay Milt a visit. I explained what would happen to the strike and the city if the TWU went broke. The next morning, the trial judge heard the city's motion for a very large fine. He imposed a smaller, wiser one.

The strike was finally settled with a wage increase in the range Lawe and I had foreseen. No one, including me, was happy with it. Koch, trying to bolster his bargaining position in the city's approaching contract talks, lashed out: "The city won the battle in the streets; the Metropolitan Transportation Authority lost it at the bargaining table." History would show that he was wrong, but that was the kind of zero-sum frustration that the city's fiscal crisis had produced.

In the meantime, after the TWU settlement, riders' complaints about MTA service seemed to accelerate by the week. The system's personnel were demoralized by years of hearing from MTA senior management that they simply had to do more with less. And I had only been in the job for six months.

⌀

EVEN BEFORE STARTING to find the money for the MTA's rehabilitation, I had to determine just how far the physical decline of the system had progressed. I spent the better part of the following months talking with the engineers and operating personnel, visiting almost all of the stations, and examining bus garages and railcar maintenance facilities. The deterioration of the physical plant was even more extreme than I had anticipated. Increasing delays, breakdowns, and accidents were inevitable.

We needed unarguable, credibly presented facts about the gravity of the situation to persuade local, state, and federal elected officials to give the MTA the vast amounts needed to stem the decline—or to give us the authority to raise the money. I asked MTA personnel for the replacement cost and useful life of every component of the system; this was the only rational basis for determining how much the MTA should spend on capital investment every year. Having never before been asked for this type of information in this level of detail, they were more than happy to produce it. I was making progress.

Then someone tried to shoot me.

I normally arrived at the MTA office on lower Madison Avenue at 7:00 in the morning to read memos from the system's chief operating officers before the endless phone calls started at 8:00. But on this particular day, I was scheduled to give a mid-morning speech uptown and was enjoying the luxury of a couple of extra hours at home when the phone rang. It was a police captain who told me to lock the doors, stay away from the windows, and wait for the arrival of a police detail. I heard the sirens almost immediately.

When the police arrived, they said the off-duty plainclothes police officer who worked as a security guard at the MTA office had been shot by a man who called out my name and said he was going to kill me. They asked where my wife and children were so that they could send protection. I left for the hospital where the officer was in surgery.

He recovered, but they never found the shooter. From then on, I had to wear a bulletproof vest in public. I was accompanied by a security detail at all times. And this was not the last attack. On another occasion, a different man walked into the MTA offices and announced that he had a personal gift to deliver to me and me alone. The police security officer wouldn't let him pass. The man pulled a knife, stabbed the officer, ran down the stairs, and escaped. Fortunately, the policeman was carrying a thick wallet that stopped the knife. But I continued to function, despite the lack of privacy and the occasional bad dream.

Around the time of the shooting, I came under a less life-threatening but intensely annoying attack from Mayor Koch. One of the unattractive qualities of the subways in those days, perhaps the most visible evidence of a system out of control, was the graffiti continually painted inside and outside the cars, usually by kids who enjoyed making trouble and had no other outlet for their so-called artistic impulses. Koch publicly called on me to put wolves—yes, actual wolves—in all the subway yards to protect the cars when they were out of service. I told him someone could get hurt, not to mention the cost of the wolves. The mayor, unpersuaded, redoubled his efforts to publicize his idea. Mutual friends reported that calling me soft on graffiti had become one of his favorite dinnertime activities.

It finally got under my skin. At my urging, the transit police stepped up their patrols and successfully arrested a couple of offenders for trespass and defacing public property. After a week, when there was still no word of their fate, I called Mario Merola, the Bronx district attorney, and asked whether he was going to prosecute. I remember his answer: was I nuts? Did I know he didn't have enough staff to type up indictments for homicides, let alone graffiti? I had a lot of nerve.

Merola eventually did prosecute, all the while muttering that I didn't always have to follow the mayor's orders. The cases went to court, and the kids went free. I phoned Leo Milonas, a great public servant who was then chief administrative judge of the State of New York, and asked why. Leo asked whether I'd ever been to the New York City Department of Corrections facility on Rikers Island. I hadn't, so one morning he escorted me there. The conditions were appalling. The place seemed designed to turn minor offenders into long-term criminals. Without words being exchanged, I understood why Leo didn't want to send kids to that jail.

࿐

OTHER WOLVES APPEARED at the door as we analyzed the MTA's capital needs. One day Governor Carey called to say he wanted the Triborough Bridge and Tunnel Authority to finance a new West Side convention center on the site I had recommended to Mayor Beame three years earlier. The hotel and tourism industries were pressing for the convention center, which they thought would be a huge moneymaker. And they needed a creditworthy entity to issue the bonds—like the TBTA, which had been issuing bonds for years, backed by the toll revenues from its bridges and tunnels.

I protested to Carey: the MTA needed those TBTA revenues to finance the acquisition of subway cars. In Carey's inimitable style, he didn't argue or issue orders. He just said, "If you won't do it, figure out another way." I did find another way, although, in retrospect, not one I'm very proud of. The TBTA did issue the debt for the convention center's construction, but the TBTA's obligations on the convention center debt were subordinated to its obligations on bonds it might issue in the future for transportation purposes, for example, financing MTA capital needs.

The means I suggested to Carey for achieving this involved establishing a state public authority, the Convention Center Development Corporation, which would own the convention center and issue debt to build it. The debt would be secured by rent paid to the authority by its lessee, the state itself. The state would then sublease the center to another public authority, the Convention Center Operating Corporation, which would pay rent to the state out of the promised profits from all the promised convention activity.

The rent to be paid by the state to the Convention Center Development Corporation was subject to annual appropriation by the state legislature; if the appropriation wasn't made, a bondholder had no recourse against the state. If the convention center profits never materialized, the debt service would still be paid through state appropriations; the MTA would be protected. Wall Street did not object to this subordination of the convention center bonds it was selling. It just wanted the TBTA's name on the securities.

The convention center never did turn a profit, the TBTA never ever used its toll revenues to pay a dime on the bonds, and state appropriations service the debt to this day.

ANOTHER "WOLF" FIRST appeared in federal clothing. In the 1980 presidential primary, Mayor Koch supported Ted Kennedy's failed challenge to President Carter, a move that did not endear New York City to the White House. I had developed a good relationship with Carter's secretary of Transportation, Neal Goldschmidt, who helped the city in various ways, but not this one. In the fall of 1980, the MTA received a letter from the Department of Transportation announcing that because the city's subway stations were not fully handicapped-accessible, the system would no longer be eligible for the $300 to $400 million it received each year in federal aid.

Making the city's four hundred subway stations accessible was not going to be part of the MTA capital plan, because it would have cost a billion dollars the authority didn't have. At a public meeting of the MTA board, I proposed that we invoke the spirit of Henry David Thoreau and engage in an act of civil disobedience, regretfully announcing that we could not comply with the law and daring the federal government to cut off funding. The board agreed. The action was widely reported.

The next day was unseasonably hot. Early in the morning, people in wheelchairs started arriving at the MTA office. I once again received a visit from a police captain, this one identifying himself as the officer responsible for demonstrations by the handicapped. He advised me to authorize the police to evict the demonstrators immediately, before the media arrived in full force.

Outside the building, the number of demonstrators was increasing—people with partial paralysis, missing limbs, and a large variety of other infirmities whose nature could only be guessed. I didn't want to be responsible for their getting hurt. I told the captain to wait.

Within an hour, every elevator on the premises was stalled. The building had stopped functioning. Demonstrators were chanting, "Hey, hey, ho, ho, Ravitch must go." Crews had arrived from every television station in New York to film the protestors, who were accusing me of being a hard-hearted bureaucrat insensitive to the needs of the disabled. Finally, I had to meet with the press. A reporter asked me what I had to say for myself. I answered, "They are here because you are here. When you leave, they'll leave." A TV camera operator I knew said, "Dick, throw them out now so we can get our film and get out of here. It's too damn hot to stick around." I told him what the members of the press could do to themselves. But finally I had to ask the police to forcibly evict the demonstrators, an event documented in detail by the TV cameras. That night, I was at a dinner and called home to ask how my teenage kids were. My wife said they were watching the eleven o'clock news. They were upset with their father, who was being characterized as insensitive to the needs of the handicapped.

The Reagan administration later took a more measured view of what federal law required, but the stalemate continued under state law. It was not settled, and the renovation of subway stations could not proceed until 1984, after I had left the MTA. But several years later, when I ran for mayor of New York, the head of the Eastern Paralyzed Veterans Association, which had organized the MTA demonstration, endorsed me and wrote to explain why. "Every other politician gave us double talk," he said. "You were straight, and we admire you for that." You never know.

ധ

FINALLY, ON NOVEMBER 25, 1980, we released the two hundred–page MTA capital plan. It concluded that the replacement cost of the MTA's assets was around $55 billion. On the basis of the useful lives of these assets, we should have been spending more than $1 billion a year on their upkeep. Instead, we were spending just $200 million. It would take $14 billion over the next ten years to begin to restore the region's transportation system to a state of good repair.

The report was short on moral exhortation. Its aim was simply to show, with the engineers' detailed numbers, that the system's physical infrastructure was on an unsustainable downward course. But it wasn't just a well-documented wish list; it included ideas about how to provide the needed resources. It urged that the law be changed to authorize the MTA to raise money by issuing bonds to be serviced by MTA revenues, including fares. This meant that fares would go up, but the only alternative was an increasingly and dangerously dysfunctional system.

The report also recommended authorizing the Triborough Bridge and Tunnel Authority, whose surplus revenues subsidized MTA operations, to sell another $500 million in bonds for MTA capital needs. It recommended changing federal law to allow public authorities like the MTA to benefit from the same investment tax credits that were available to private companies when they bought capital assets like buses or trains. It recommended—taking a cue from public policy in the construction of low-income and moderate-income housing—that the federal government not just appropriate mass transit funds but enter into long-term contracts to provide these funds to public transportation agencies, so the agencies could gain access to capital by selling bonds that would be serviced by the assured stream of funds.

At first, the papers ran the capital plan story on their back pages as just another MTA plea for handouts. And if the newspapers didn't treat the report seriously, it was unlikely that the politicians would. I explained the problem to Max Frankel of the *Times* and Mike O'Neil of the *Daily News*. They responded with strong editorials that got Albany's attention.

But the next step, actually pushing the expensive and complicated MTA capital plan through the state legislature, would require very different skills from those it took to prepare the report. The mayor was up for reelection in 1981, the governor in 1982. Political ambition, inflation, partisan politics, differences between city and suburban interests, and my lack of strong personal ties to some of the players made most people pessimistic about the capital plan's fate. But the objective situation was so bad—the system falling apart, a summer fare increase inevitable—that there had to be a resolution.

Mayor Koch said he would support the plan if fares didn't increase faster than the consumer price index. State legislative leaders said the report had good ideas, but the initiative lay with the

governor. Carey had no initial response. In itself, that was not bother-
some; it wasn't Carey's style to commit to an idea until he had a sense
of other people's positions. More disturbing was another phone call
from Bill Hennessy, the state transportation commissioner, who said
the MTA should wait a year before pressing its case. Maybe it was a
message from Carey himself; I couldn't be sure. I wrote the governor
another personal letter, saying that without the MTA program, the
transportation system would be in serious trouble and, potentially, a
political liability.

In early March, the governor convened a meeting of the legislative leaders to discuss a plan to address the MTA's capital crisis. But
a personal dispute erupted at the meeting between him and Warren
Anderson. The argument escalated, with everyone accusing everyone else of obstruction and bad faith. The meeting turned into a
donnybrook.

The governor then took another tack, appointing a blue ribbon
panel of business leaders to study the MTA's future. When the panel
reported, it did not question our numbers. But it recommended less
borrowing and a new financial control board to supervise the MTA,
with no politicians as members. This was bad advice, but I knew
Carey would pay attention to it. The business community was ap-
plying pressure in other places as well. Felix Rohatyn visited Mike
O'Neil at the *Daily News* and asked him to write an editorial criticizing the proposed MTA borrowing on grounds that it would compete with the city's sale of MAC bonds.

For the first time, I was discouraged.

But the panel's heavy-handedness turned out to be a blessing.
O'Neil called to tell me about Felix's visit and asked me why the
MTA borrowing authority was so important. I explained, and he
wrote an editorial that strongly supported us. When in doubt, he later
said, he tended to go with the guy who had the real responsibility.

The businessmen's effort to deny the MTA borrowing authority
and exclude politicians from its oversight also moved the legislative
leaders to take matters into their own hands. Stanley Fink phoned

me to say the legislators did not need a bunch of businessmen to tell them what was in the best interests of the State of New York.

Fink was as close to an ideal politician as any official I have ever met. He never forgot his roots in Brooklyn but never wore his liberal politics on his sleeve. He was a strong leader of the Assembly's Democratic conference. He had a first-rate staff, and they worshiped him. We became good friends. With the friendship, came a substantial amount of trust, the most important determinant of political success.

Stanley was extremely friendly with Warren Anderson, despite the latter's Brooks Brothers style and comfort with denizens of the financial world. If the two of them agreed on a piece of legislation, the legislature would follow. Fink invited me to meet "very privately" with him and Anderson in Albany. The message was clear: I should not call the governor's office to arrange to fly on the state plane.

We met in Anderson's office. The two men were prepared to negotiate a bill along the lines of the MTA report, including $3.5 billion in bonding authority. Under the bill, the MTA would submit a five-year capital plan to a new board made up of the governor, the New York City mayor, and state legislators, who would ensure a politically equitable distribution of funds. Fink and Anderson asked me not to tell the governor's office.

I felt a small pang of disloyalty to Carey, but the bill passed in June. Carey later told me he understood why I did what I did, and by then it didn't matter, because history was giving him deserved credit for his role in rebuilding the state's transportation system. Elected officials who know they must ultimately support an unpopular action sometimes devise ways of just not preventing it from happening, even vocally opposing it while waiting to see how things turn out. Some people take such behavior as evidence that politics is corrupt and politicians are two-faced. But in this instance, as in others, it led to the kind of results that were the reason I went into government.

Bill or no bill, the subway fare, then fifty cents, was projected to rise to seventy-five cents in July 1982; without additional state revenues, it would have to be raised to a dollar. But there was no consensus on how to raise new tax revenues to mitigate a fare hike. Everyone wanted the other guy to pay. Some people didn't care if the fare went up to a dollar and beyond—for someone else's constituents. And the legislature was due to recess for the summer on July 10.

Under a very private agreement I reached with Anderson and Fink, the MTA board voted two fare increases. One, to seventy-five cents, was effective immediately; the other, to a dollar, would take effect on July 10, after the legislature had recessed. I told them that the second increase would be repealed if the legislature passed new transit taxes before it recessed. There was an outcry in Albany. As agreed, Fink publicly lambasted me for blackmailing the legislature; but I knew he and Anderson were behind us. The real problem was to find the votes for a transit tax increase. There were not enough Republican votes in the Senate. Anderson asked me to help produce them.

I phoned David Rockefeller and made what I said was an audacious request. Would he get up at 5:00 in the morning and let me take him on a tour of the subway system? Once he said yes, I asked him to invite Dick Shinn of Metropolitan Life and Bill Ellinghaus of AT&T. None of them, I suspected, had ridden a New York City subway recently.

On the appointed morning, the transit police collected the three men and we began our tour. I showed them the empty inventory shelves in the maintenance facilities, the dreadful conditions in which the employees worked, the bus garages built in the nineteenth century. I have no firsthand knowledge of what they said to Anderson, but Warren called the next day to say he had the votes to pass what the Assembly had approved.

The legislature enacted five separate taxes before it recessed in July, and I kept my promise to Fink: the MTA board met and repealed the second fare increase. The taxes produced only $600 million, not the predicted $850 million, but the legislature later enacted enough additional taxes to keep the fare at seventy-five cents through 1982.

As in the UDC and city crises, the merits of the case—combined with a little luck, a lot of theatrics, and the support of the press and key business leaders—produced a package of laws that constructively addressed a critical public problem. Once again, elected officials voted for things that they had sworn over prior months never to support. The system had worked to forge another link in the chain of events that had to take place if the MTA's decline were to be reversed

The next step was to submit a five-year plan to the new MTA Capital Review Board, with the felicitous acronym METCRAP. The plan called for the purchase of almost two thousand subway cars and 1,600 buses, as well as spending billions more to rehabilitate bus garages and railcar maintenance facilities and modernize power substations and subway signal and communications systems. There would be comparable expenditures for the Long Island Railroad and the Westchester commuter system, including the purchase of almost five hundred new railcars. On December 22, the MTA got a large Christmas present: the review board approved our $7.9 billion capital plan. Few in the MTA outposts had thought they would ever have the resources to restore the system to a state of good repair. Now morale was high. The staff dug in to begin the process.

MTA management had to be reorganized to provide the capacity to execute the plan effectively. The existing LIRR president, Francis Gabreski, would have to be replaced. The railroad needed a chief who had the management skills to implement the capital program. In addition, because of the LIRR's poor service, the roiling anger of its commuters, and the MTA's critical need for support from elected Long Island officials, a new chief needed experience in customer relations. The headhunters came up with an eminently suitable candidate: Robin Wilson, then working for Trans World Airlines. The problem was that he wanted to be paid more than $100,000 a year.

That amount was not large enough to be of material consequence to the MTA, but no one in state government in 1982 earned a salary even close to $100,000. The number would produce headlines and irritate political sensitivities. The better part of wisdom was to call the governor and give him advance notice. Carey's first response was that it was more than he was making. There was an awkward pause. But, he continued, echoing Babe Ruth, maybe Robin Wilson had had a better year than Hugh Carey had. I hung up with relief. This was Carey's way of agreeing to the salary while maintaining the freedom to reverse himself if the press made a big issue of it. Robin turned out to be a terrific manager who deserved much of the credit for the improvement that the LIRR began to experience.

And, finally, there was peace with Mayor Koch. Probably in anticipation of the MTA's next contract negotiations, he was quoted one morning on the front page of the *New York Times* characterizing the transit workers as loungers and loafers. At a speech I gave that day to the New York City Partnership, an organization that had recently been established to represent the business community on policy issues, a reporter asked me what I thought of Koch's comments. I said they were inaccurate, unfair, and counterproductive, especially from a mayor who had just reduced the city's contribution to the MTA.

The newspapers landed hard on Koch, saying that the MTA now had the financial and management resources to improve the public transportation system and he should be constructive for a change. Koch realized he had made a mistake. A few days later, he walked into the City Hall press room and said he was "offering Ravitch the olive branch—in fact, the whole tree."

Eating crow, as the press described it, was unusual for Ed Koch. So I invited him to our home that Sunday night for the urban ritual of Chinese takeout. He came, and we had a congenial time. I can't remember a moment of tension between us since then.

♪

THE FEDERAL GOVERNMENT was another target in the MTA's quest for funds. When Ronald Reagan became president in 1981, he said Americans should rely less on the federal government and more on states and localities. We couldn't tell whether that meant reduced federal aid to public transportation. More optimistically, we wondered whether Reagan's Economic Recovery Act of 1981 would include some provisions that were helpful to us. We weren't going to stop campaigning for federal help; we would just work on adjusting our pitch.

I paid a call on Reagan's new secretary of Transportation, Drew Lewis, who showed an impressive degree of interest and business acumen. He pointed out that big city mayors were not among a Republican president's chief constituents, but that might mean transportation money would be distributed more in accordance with need than with politics. I got the message. In the allocation of federal transit money, New York had suffered for Ed Koch's support of Ted Kennedy; the big city mayors who had supported President Carter had done much better. New York might benefit from a new administration.

I presented Lewis with some proposals, including the use of the investment tax credit by public authorities and multiyear federal commitments that could serve as a basis for financing. I also met with David Stockman, the new director of the Office of Management and Budget. He wondered why, if we were so desperate for public transportation money, we didn't take advantage of the federal law allowing states to trade federal highway funds—like the money currently allocated to the Westway highway project—for mass transit funds. I told Stockman that New York's governor, New York City's mayor, and President Reagan favored Westway. But if the Reagan administration changed its mind, I was ready to collaborate.

Stockman talked to Lewis. We came up with a trade-in proposal for them to present to the president. I wasn't sure how I would deal with the governor and the mayor, whose appreciation for my single-minded pursuit of money for the MTA would have been substantially outweighed by their annoyance at my undermining Westway.

That worry turned out to be academic. Lewis and Stockman gave Reagan a memo urging the trade-in. The president put it in his briefcase and took it with him on a trip to New York. His first stop was the *Daily News*, where O'Neil and the paper's publisher, Tex

James, were leading Westway advocates. The first question they asked was whether Reagan would make sure Westway got built. "Yes," he answered without qualification. It became a banner headline in the next day's paper, set in the largest possible type. I asked Drew Lewis what had happened. He said the president probably hadn't read the memo.

It was years later, after I left the MTA, when Westway was finally dropped and its federal funds were traded for mass transit money.

Dealing with the federal government also meant dealing with Alfonse D'Amato, who became US Senator from New York in 1981 after beating Jack Javits in the Republican primary. Javits was a good man. He was sick with Lou Gehrig's disease when he decided to seek reelection; perhaps he shouldn't have run. D'Amato, then an unknown, won with the support of the Conservative and Right to Life Parties. Soon after he was elected, he phoned and asked me to meet him for breakfast at a diner in Garden City, Long Island.

At breakfast, D'Amato said he thought mass transit was going to be a hot issue and he wanted to get a lot of money for the MTA. He asked whether I could help him get appointed to the Senate Appropriations and Banking Committees, which had jurisdiction over transportation. I told him I would like to be of help but had none to give, having been a Democrat all my life.

D'Amato then asked whether I had voted for him. I said that in all my voting history I had never pulled a lever for a Right to Life candidate. It was okay, he said; he didn't really believe all that stuff. He knew I had been president of the Jewish Community Relations Council. He asked, why did I think he had received so few Jewish votes? I said his having defeated Javits was probably not viewed by the Jewish community as a friendly act. He was persistent. Did I know the heads of the national Jewish organizations? I did. Would I arrange a dinner with them for him, so that he could show his bona fides on the issue of Israel? Yes, I would.

The conversation returned to the MTA. D'Amato wanted to know about its history, its funding, and what it needed. Suddenly, the discussion turned substantive. It was three hours later when we left the diner, having struck up a relationship we both thought would be useful.

A few weeks later, just before the dinner at our home that I had organized for D'Amato with Jewish leaders, he called to say he had gotten appointed to the committees he wanted. He was exultant: "I am going to get more fucking money for the MTA than you could possibly spend!" And he did turn out to be a big supporter of mass transit. With a swing vote on the Senate Appropriations subcommittee that handled the MTA, he helped secure the federal funding we received during the Reagan years.

His style, however, left something to be desired. Drew Lewis phoned me one day: "I am never going to cut a check to the MTA again if you don't get that foul-mouthed son-of-a-bitch D'Amato off my back." I told D'Amato he had to make amends to Lewis, then flew to Washington to make sure it happened. Lewis and I arranged to meet in the vice president's office, off the Senate floor. I asked Nicholas Brady, at the time a US Senator from New Jersey, to pull Al off the floor to meet with Lewis. D'Amato walked into the room where we were waiting with his broadest smile and his trademark greeting: "Drew, baby!" He could not have been more propitiating. The checks continued to be cut.

The MTA had another important congressional ally in Jack Kemp, whom I met through Pat Moynihan. Kemp, once a football star with the Buffalo Bills and now a Republican congressman from western New York, was what was called at the time a "supply-sider," who believed Republicans should not just cut deficits but promote growth through tax cuts. Like Ronald Reagan, Kemp had the personality of a happy warrior: he saw his agenda as promoting prosperity for rich and poor alike. His views were very influential in the Reagan White House.

I gave Jack, as I had given Drew Lewis, my spiel about making the investment tax credit available to public entities like the MTA. The issue was this: since the early 1960s, the federal government had provided tax benefits like the investment tax credit to businesses that invested in certain types of capital assets, on the theory that the tax incentive would spur more investment. But the tax credit was not available to governments, because, the reasoning went, governments did not respond to tax incentives in the way businesses did. A government would never buy more police cars or fire engines because of the investment tax credit than it would have bought otherwise. But that general reasoning about governments did not apply to public transportation. New York and other governments would, in fact, buy more transportation infrastructure if they had the tax credit.

Kemp was sympathetic. He took me to meet the Treasury Department officials who were preparing a tax law change designed to stimulate the economy through what came to be known as "safe harbor leasing," a successor to the investment tax credit. Under the proposed legislation, safe harbor leasing was not going to be available to government agencies like the MTA. We set out to change that.

Moynihan was a key supporter of the MTA's effort. So was Representative Charles Rangel, a Democratic congressman from Harlem. With additional help from New York Republican Congressman Bill Green, we succeeded in changing the 1981 bill to allow public authorities like the MTA to take advantage of safe harbor leasing. When the MTA bought equipment, it would be able to take advantage of tax benefits equal to around 20 percent of the purchase price. That meant we would be able to get five of whatever we were buying for the price of four. We retained Citibank as a financial adviser to sell these tax benefits to the highest bidder. They turned out to be worth around $600 million in extra revenue to the MTA, funds we could invest in new railcars and buses.

✺

THE FEDERAL TAX law change, however, was only the beginning of the story of the MTA's new rolling stock.

There are three separate New York City subway lines: the BMT, the IRT, and the IND. The IRT, now the numbered lines running from the Bronx to Brooklyn, was built first and had the greatest need for new cars. It also used different-sized cars from those used by the other two lines, complicating the design process. We began discussing the design and manufacture of 325 cars with Kawasaki Heavy Industries of Japan. We were going to pay a premium to make the cars of stainless steel, which could be washed clean of the Magic Markers used by the graffiti artists.

Under state law, the normal procedure, meant to prevent corruption, would have been to solicit sealed bids from companies that wanted to build the railcars. But there were many variables involved, including not just price but design and reliability. And because interest rates were at an all-time high, the financing that a seller offered was an important part of the deal. We could get better financial terms if we negotiated the purchases instead of taking sealed bids.

We drafted state legislation to allow the MTA to acquire several thousand railcars through negotiation rather than bidding and sent it to Stanley Fink and Warren Anderson. A week later they asked me to come to Albany.

Meeting with Fink, he said the Assembly's minority caucus bitterly opposed the bill because there was no mandate to hire minority contractors. He asked me to meet with him. He brought Arthur Eve, chairman of the Assembly's minority caucus, to the meeting. When we sat down, Stanley turned to me and, with Eve as audience, chewed me out. Was I so fucking stupid, he asked, that I didn't understand the entitlement of minority contractors to a piece of the MTA's business? Stanley then pivoted and began to scream at Arthur. Did Eve think that dividing the pie by race was more important than getting a good deal for the millions of people of every race who rode the subways every day?

Fink then said he was going to leave us alone to resolve our differences. He walked out of his office and slammed the door. Arthur and I immediately broke out laughing. Within minutes, we had agreed on the language that was the minimum required to satisfy his caucus.

Anderson had a deeper problem: many of his caucus members did not know me. Some were worried that if I had the discretion to negotiate the subway car purchases, I might use it to raise a lot of money to reelect Hugh Carey, who was thought to be running for a third term that year.

Anderson asked me to meet with the members of the Republican conference. I replied that if it would help, I would give them the confidential financial disclosure documents I had submitted when I was appointed MTA chairman. He said I didn't have to do it, but I was willing. Before the meeting I called John Marchi, Republican chairman of the state's Senate Finance Committee, and asked him to distribute the disclosure. When I got to the meeting, the members were still poring over the documents, which showed that I had given nothing to the Carey campaign in 1974 and a grand total of $500 in 1978. Senator Douglas Barclay, a Republican from upstate New York, looked up from his copy of the papers and said, "Ravitch, all this proves is that you're a really cheap bastard." The bill was passed that afternoon.

ঞ

THE MTA USED its negotiating authority to conclude the Kawasaki deal. More than a third of the cars' physical elements would be manufactured in the United States. Japan's export bank would finance the purchase with a loan at substantially lower than market rates. We knew we had purchased the best available cars at the best available price.

Kawasaki did not want to take a bigger order for cars but agreed to let other manufacturers license its design. Our largest order for additional cars went to another non-US manufacturer, the Canadian firm Bombardier, which had been in the snowmobile business and had just begun to expand into railcar production. In May I shook hands with Bombardier's chairman, Laurent Beaudoin, and Ed Lumley, CEO of Canada's export bank, on a huge purchase of 825 cars.

Prime Minister Pierre Trudeau announced the deal in Canada. The MTA did the same in New York.

But the subway car purchases stirred up firestorms small and large. At the small end, we celebrated the Bombardier deal with a fancy dinner at a New York restaurant right after we signed the contracts. Steve Polan, the MTA's chief counsel, and Dan Scanell joined me. There were people from Bombardier and the Canadian government. At the end of the meal, the Canadians asked for the dinner check. Steve quietly reminded me that I had issued a policy memo prohibiting MTA employees from accepting meals from people with whom they did business. I couldn't see asking for separate checks— it seemed out of keeping with the occasion—so I said New York would buy. Several weeks later, the charge for the dinner, more than $1,000, appeared on my credit card.

I figured that between the safe harbor tax deal and the export financing from Canada, I had saved New Yorkers more than $600 million. I submitted an expense voucher, the only time I did so while I was MTA chairman. A few weeks later, a big headline in the *Daily News* trumpeted "Ravitch's 1,000-Token Dinner" at taxpayer expense. There were denunciations from assorted elected officials. I never found out who told the press. I loudly refused to return the money.

But the subway car purchases also stirred up larger controversies. In buying the cars, the MTA took full advantage of the generous credit terms that foreign export banks were offering in order to promote their nations' products. Some people in US government argued that the size of these subsidies violated the General Agreement on Tariffs and Trade, GATT. A GATT meeting was scheduled for Brussels in May.

The MTA was in danger of being portrayed as a poster child for the practices that the US government opposed. After the Bombardier deal, one congressman asked whether "you people up there in New York are Americans." US Trade Representative Bill Brock said the deal would undermine the coming economic summit in Brussels. A newspaper story reported that Washington might impose counter-vailing duties on the importation of the Canadian subway cars. At a press conference, I said that if we had to raise the fare to pay for the countervailing duties, we would produce a new subway token with President Reagan's face on it. The next day, the New York tabloids ran front-page photos of a token bearing the president's image. James Baker, then Reagan's chief of staff, later told me the White House was truly enraged.

At the same time, the bus and subway car deals drew attention from Kansas Senator Robert Dole, chairman of the Senate Finance Committee and one of the Senate's most powerful and respected members. Dole believed the safe harbor leasing provisions in the 1981 tax bill were excessive. I came to have enormous admiration for Dole. But when I picked up the *New York Times* one day and saw him quoted as saying that the MTA's bus leasing deal was a rip-off and that Congress should eliminate safe harbor leasing from the Internal Revenue Code, I called a press conference and asked why a tax rule that was good enough for a railroad moving cattle in Kansas wasn't good enough for subways moving three million people a day in New York City.

The comment got a lot of coverage, but I was reminded that Dole was the elected chairman of the most important committee in the Senate, while I was just a temporary local office holder. More than that, I came to understand that the safe harbor tax law was being mis-used by major American companies to avoid paying tens of billions of dollars in taxes without making the increased investment that the tax benefit was meant to promote. I felt guilty. Sooner than expected, I got an opportunity to make amends.

In late May 1982, I received a subpoena to appear before a Sen-ate Finance Committee hearing on the Bombardier deal. It took place in the same Senate hearing room outside of which I had stood in line to watch the Army-McCarthy Hearings thirty years earlier. Now the room was filled with media from all over the world and representatives of the many interest groups involved in international trade. The atmosphere was nerve-racking.

The hearing began with the secretaries of the Treasury and Labor and the US trade representative denouncing the Bombardier transaction and saying Congress should stop it. I sat and listened to one witness after another condemning an action that I had planned and executed and of which I was very proud. Finally, around 1:00 P.M., I was called to testify. Adrenalin surged: I ignored my written testimony and spoke to Dole directly, telling him how bad the transit system was in the nation's largest city, how we had taken to heart President Reagan's counsel that we not wait for federal money but take our own initiatives to solve local problems, and why this purchase was in the best interests of the citizens of New York.

After my peroration, the first question came from Senator John Heinz of Pennsylvania—home to a competitor of Bombardier, the Budd Company—who asked whether I cared about my country. I told Senator Heinz that I had served twice in the military and spent the better part of the last few years trying to help the place in which I grew up but would leave to others the characterization of how much I cared. There followed several hours of questions, almost all, with the exception of those from Pat Moynihan and Senator Bill Bradley of New Jersey, hostile to the Bombardier transaction. In an act of friendship I will never forget, Charlie Rangel came over from the House to weigh in with a passionately effective plea for New York.

Finally, around 5:00 P.M., Dole banged his gavel to close the hearing. The committee would reconvene at 8:00 the next morning to decide on its advice to Congress about what action it should take on the Bombardier transaction. Then he said from the rostrum that if he had my job, he would have done exactly what I did. It was an act of stunning generosity.

On the train back to New York that evening, I wrote to Dole expressing my thanks. I told him my first job had been on the Hill, and my respect for the legislative process had only been deepened by the day's events. A few days later, Dole invited me to Washington and asked whether I would help him get his tax reform bill through Congress if he maintained the MTA's access to safe harbor leasing.

Dole's bill was going to curtail safe harbor leasing drastically. He wanted support from Moynihan and Bradley, who were deeply committed to mass transit. He also thought I might have influence with other mass transit executives around the country, whom we had organized to support safe harbor leasing in 1981.

But lobbyists from industries that benefited from the current rules, like the airline industry, were fighting Dole vigorously. They said that if the MTA got Moynihan and Bradley to support them, they would ensure that the resulting legislation protected our interests. But if Moynihan and Bradley voted with Dole and he lost, the lobbyists would see to it that mass transit lost its safe harbor leasing.

Moynihan and Bradley said they would vote in whatever way would most help mass transit. I heard my long-ago Hill experience kicking in: "When in doubt, go with the chairman." They did. The airline lobbyists were incensed. Dole got his reform package through Congress with safe harbor leasing provisions that were good to the MTA. In general, the safe harbor benefits would last for just one more year. But for mass transit, the benefits were extended for five years, through 1987—the year we expected the Bombardier cars to be delivered.

We still faced intense opposition. The Budd Company, actually owned by German interests, asked Treasury to rule that Bombardier had gotten its MTA contract only because of Canadian government export subsidies. If so, Budd would be entitled to borrow money from the US Export-Import Bank on the same terms as those the Canadian government had given Bombardier. We spent weeks rebutting Budd's claim, explaining why we would not have bought the subway cars from Budd in any event.

Treasury ruled against Budd, but Budd didn't give up. At the company's urging, the Commerce Department began considering the imposition of $90 million in countervailing duties on our new subway cars. We spent still more time in Washington defending the

Bombardier transaction, while we quietly negotiated another deal, this one with Westinghouse and the French manufacturer Francorail, to assemble 225 cars at the Brooklyn Army Terminal. As we did so, the Budd Company gave up. It announced that it had won the "principle" of its battle and would take no further legal action.

One group of opponents was tougher and more implacable than any US manufacturer: organized labor. When the MTA was first given authority to negotiate the purchase of subway cars, the AFL-CIO filed a lawsuit, later dismissed, asserting that we had violated state procurement statutes. Throughout the controversy, labor was a major factor behind the political pressure on the federal government. I had several meetings with Lane Kirkland, who had become president of the AFL-CIO, but the unions continued lobbying until we promised that we would not purchase any more foreign-made cars until after the end of 1985.

Our original purchases, however, had survived intact.

ॐ

As these efforts were under way, we were also working to establish the marketability of the debt we hoped to issue to raise the money we needed over and above what the export banks of Japan, France, and Canada were providing.

The credit of the Triborough Bridge and Tunnel Authority was clearly established in the markets on the basis of the stream of toll revenues it had collected for years, but no one had ever sold a note or bond issued by a mass transit carrier whose revenue was made up of both fares paid by the public and subsidies voted annually by governments. Thus, we said at the outset that we would give our bondholders a first lien against the MTA's revenues. When collected, the revenues would be used to make debt service payments before they could be used to pay the MTA's day-to-day operating expenses, including wages. The unions were not happy with this concession to the markets but ultimately understood that there was no other choice.

The leading public finance firms—Goldman Sachs, Salomon Brothers, Merrill Lynch—were so skeptical about our financing plan that they would not spend the time and money to explore its feasibility. But at a lunch I had with Dillon Read's Bob Gerard—the Ford administration's assistant secretary of the Treasury for domestic finance, with whom I had negotiated New York City's federal loan guarantees in 1975—he expressed interest in the plan. He brought Nick Brady, by then the firm's CEO, into the discussions. Brady heard us out and approved getting the effort under way.

First, we had the eminently reputable firm of Charles River Associates confirm our assumptions about the amount of revenue we could raise through fares. Next, we needed a credit rating high enough to market the bonds. But Standard & Poor's raised some unpleasant questions. Would debt service be paid even if the politicians stopped appropriating operating subsidies? Would some future generation of politicians simply let the MTA go bankrupt? In response, the MTA agreed contractually never to file for bankruptcy.

S&P's rating of the MTA's debt was BBB+, the lowest investment grade, but the agency called the MTA's capital plan "essential to the future well being of New York City" and deemed the program "well designed and one that the MTA is capable of achieving." Moody's was even tougher in its analysis but, like S&P, finally gave us an investment grade rating. In October the bonds sold at a better price than predicted. I threw a party for the engineers who had designed the capital plan. Dillon Read went on to be the largest underwriter of transportation securities in the business. Nick Brady became my friend.

⁂

AMID THE MTA's march to sustainability, an unsought opportunity occasionally came our way. One day at lunch in New York, Drew Lewis told me that President Reagan was committed to privatizing Conrail, which then operated the New Haven and New York Central commuter lines on roadbeds owned by the MTA. Lewis knew he wouldn't be able to sell Conrail as long as it had to operate the commuter lines. Would the MTA be interested in taking them over?

My answer was a fast yes: the only question was the price we would get for doing so. Thus, MTA's Metro-North was created to operate the commuter lines. The MTA got substantial federal funding, which covered the costs of the takeover and helped defray the first year's operating expenses. I named a talented New Jersey Transit executive, Peter Stangl, as president. The commuters were thrilled, at least for a while, at the prospect that service would improve.

By then I had learned something about labor relations. When the time came for the MTA to negotiate a new contract with the transit workers, we made sure the agreement would not expire until after the next expiration of the city's contracts with its municipal unions. The last time around, our negotiations had come first and, it was said, set a precedent for the city's talks. That was why we had drawn fire from Mayor Koch. It wasn't going to happen again. The next time the MTA negotiated with the transit workers, the city would already have finished its negotiations with the municipal unions—and we would know what the city had paid.

But at Metro-North the labor inefficiencies far exceeded those of the subways. We called for changes that would let us set our own manning schedules: it was absurd, for instance, to have two conductors on two-car or three-car trains during off-peak hours. What we got was a strike that lasted for weeks. We had little support from the politicians. To this day, the inefficiencies in the commuter railroads' labor rules remain.

In Washington, however, Drew Lewis was succeeding in his effort to get more funding for transportation infrastructure. The Carter administration had proposed raising the gas tax, but it never got out of committee on the Hill. After Reagan took office, he proposed a four-cent increase, with one penny going to mass transit. It sailed through Congress. In the aggregate, it was the largest public transportation subsidy ever from Uncle Sam. As MTA chairman, I was invited to the bill signing at the White House. I watched a reporter

ask the president how he could have pushed for this tax when he had
been elected on a platform of "no new taxes." It wasn't a tax, Reagan
answered equably. It was a "user charge."

⁂

AND THEN, AFTER the shooting and the knifing and the "wolves" and
the accusations of un-American activity, I learned that a new New
York governor had a very different view from mine about the role
an MTA chairman should play.

In 1978 the incumbent New York lieutenant governor, Mary
Anne Krupsak, challenged Hugh Carey in the gubernatorial primary and, predictably, failed. Carey needed a new running mate and
picked Mario Cuomo: honest, a great speaker, a brilliant lawyer with
a talent for mediating disputes. He had no apparent flaws and, at the
time, no enemies.

I had few dealings with him. As I was to learn, a lieutenant governor has little to do in actually running the state unless the governor
assigns him or her specific responsibilities, which Carey rarely did
with Cuomo. But Mario and I occasionally had lunch and flew back
and forth to Albany together. In December 1981, he invited me to
breakfast; he wanted to run for governor in 1982. I mentioned that
as MTA chairman I had to deal with all parties and officeholders,
regardless of whether Carey sought another term. I wasn't going to
get involved in the campaign.

Carey didn't run again. Cuomo beat Ed Koch in the Democratic gubernatorial primary and easily won the November election.
During the campaign, he called for the abolition of the MTA. This
was no surprise. Almost everyone who ran for elective office cam-
paigned against the MTA. It was too inviting a target not to attack.
More surprising, Cuomo announced in his first State of the State
address that his administration would undertake a major investigation of the MTA.

For the next three months, he never took a phone call from me,
and there began to be speculation in the press that he wanted to

replace me as chairman. But I didn't take the talk seriously. I was preoccupied with the birth of the labor-troubled Metro-North and our plan to introduce monthly passes and replace subway tokens with magnetic cards.

Then, at the beginning of June in 1983, I got a call from Cuomo's chief of staff, Michael Del Giudice, whom I had known and respected since the early 1970s. Mike asked me to come to the governor's New York City office, then in the World Trade Center. There he told me that the governor's MTA study was done. Cuomo was going to hold a press conference at Grand Central Terminal the next day and announce his recommendations, which would include a bill to add three more gubernatorial appointees to the MTA board and require the MTA chairman to serve at the pleasure of the governor rather than for a fixed term. Mike said Cuomo believed that the governor should take more responsibility for the transit system and be politically accountable for it. If I supported his proposals, Cuomo would reappoint me under the new regime.

I asked to see the governor. Mike walked into Cuomo's office a few feet away, then came back to tell me that Cuomo wouldn't see me until I agreed to support his plan. After a few choice words, I walked out of the office, not knowing what would happen next.

Del Giudice phoned me several times that night, trying, unsuccessfully, to change my mind. The next morning, I went to Cuomo's press conference and listened to his proposals. There was only one change from the message of the day before: when Cuomo's proposals were legislated, he would appoint me under the new system.

Michael Oreskes of the *New York Times* saw me there and asked whether I would serve as MTA chairman if the law were changed. Yes, I said, I would serve—for exactly as long as I would serve if the law were *not* changed. Oreskes was too smart to let me get away with that. Would I vote for Cuomo's plan if I were in the legislature? I didn't relish picking a fight with Cuomo, but it was a moment of truth. No, I said. The MTA got its resources from local governments as well as the state. It had to deal with local executives as well as the governor. It also had fiduciary responsibilities to its riders and, after its bond sale, the bondholders. An MTA chairman could not fulfill these responsibilities if he was merely an agent of the governor.

Every newspaper in the region criticized Cuomo's proposal. So did Mayor Koch. Two days later, I got a joint call from Fink and Anderson. They had just had breakfast with Cuomo, and he had asked them to pass his MTA bill immediately. They had told him that not a single member of the legislature would vote for it. He had been politically humiliated.

The subject never came up again. To this day, I don't understand why Mario went as far as he did. I resigned from the MTA six months later, at the end of 1983, exhausted after four years of intense job pressure and inadequate time with my family. I would like to think the exhaustion had nothing to do with Cuomo, but there was no doubt that the fun quotient of the job had been diminished by the governor's inexplicable hostility.

Governors and mayors have different governing styles. Carey and Koch shared a style: they put a high priority on staffing their administrations with the highest-quality people they could get. Once they had appointed them, they didn't try to micromanage them and didn't begrudge them credit. If they didn't like what their appointees had done, they simply let them go. Control was not uppermost in their minds. This was not and is not the Cuomo style, and the difference raises the broader question of which style is calculated to bring better people into government and keep them there.

My four years at the MTA were the most exhilarating of my life. Once again, I had been able to address a major public problem. Once again, by chance or luck, I had been able to draw on many of the friendships and relationships I had developed over the years. But the exercise gave me an acute sense of the tension between political connections and political independence in trying to make a mark on public policy.

Politics is a species of human relations. You don't stand a chance of having a significant policy impact unless you participate in the political process and establish relationships, which may include a degree of manipulation but, to a surprising extent, consist primarily of treating people with the decency you would wish for yourself.

Yet a willingness to participate in the political process is not enough; the process also has to be bent to useful public ends. When a public service is inadequate or a bridge, subway, or highway is in danger of collapse, elected officials will have an almost irresistible temptation to criticize, blame their opponents or the bureaucracy for the problem, and avoid voting for expenditures that require more taxes. There is no way to overcome this feature of democratic politics unless people possess professional skills, as well as a sufficient sense of self not to become financially or emotionally dependent on the political process. They must use the tools available to them—like the press, their relationships with the business, labor, and civic communities, and the goodwill of fellow professionals—to change the odds in the contest.

7

On the Public-Private Seesaw

WHEN I FINALLY LEFT THE MTA in November 1983, I was thanked and feted—more than I deserved, as I had just ended the four most exciting years of my life and felt I should be thanking others for the experience. Chief among them were the government employees of the MTA. Thirty years later, the country would be astonished at the speed with which they brought New York City back to life after Hurricane Sandy. Having seen their skill and dedication at close range, I was wholly unsurprised.

But I still thought of myself as a businessman on loan to the government. Indeed, for the next couple of decades, I bounced back and forth between the public and private sectors—embarking on business ventures that I thought were going to be the primary focus of my energies, then being pulled back into public life. Along the way, I got a multifaceted view of the changes taking place in New York's and America's institutions.

∽

AFTER I LEFT the MTA, Nick Brady asked me to join Dillon Read, but I couldn't see myself as an investment banker. Several law firms also offered me partnerships; but for all their talk about their interest in my skills, they were clearly more interested in my contacts. I was

looking for something more unusual, but something that would replenish the coffers.

It came along in a phone call from Bud Gravette, chairman of
the Bowery Savings Bank. Gravette was one of the last people I'd
expected to hear from, because in my previous contacts with the
Bowery I had played what was becoming my habitual role with respect to public institutions: Cassandra. The bank had not appreciated
me or my dire predictions.

The Bowery, founded in 1834, was one of New York's oldest savings banks. From the Depression until the late 1970s, savings banks
played a distinctive role in American finance. They were prohibited
from offering commercial banking services, and federal regulations
set the rates of interest they could pay their depositors. The savings
banks used their depositors' funds primarily to make mortgage loans,
performing the very useful function of employing some people's life
savings to finance other people's homes.

As nonprofit institutions owned by their depositors—they were
also known as mutual banks—savings banks developed a tradition of
being civic-minded. Their executives populated the leadership ranks
of do-good community organizations. George Bailey, the small-town
savings bank president in Frank Capra's 1946 film, *It's a Wonderful Life*,
was an idealized version of these executives but one that was widely
recognizable to an American audience. When I was asked to join the
Bowery's board of trustees in 1977, I readily accepted.

But by 1979 the distinction between savings banks and commercial banks was collapsing. Inflation was soaring. Commercial banks
found ways around the interest-rate regulations and were paying
higher interest rates on their deposits. As a consequence, money was
moving out of the savings banks. The government responded by allowing the savings banks to pay higher rates as well. But that was
not enough help for the savings banks, because they had already
invested their deposit funds in long-term assets, like mortgages and
government bonds, which paid interest to the banks at relatively low
interest rates that were fixed in earlier times. The government could

permit savings banks to pay higher interest rates to their depositors, but the low rates the banks were earning on their own investments did not allow them to do so.

The savings banks began to lose money. Their depositors were protected against the possibility of bank failure by the Federal Deposit Insurance Corporation, but FDIC protection was limited to $100,000 per account. Many Bowery depositors, including large nonprofit organizations, had accounts far larger than the FDIC-insured amount.

At one 1979 Bowery board meeting, I asked whether the bank should send a letter to these large depositors to warn them that the bank's surplus was being wiped out and there was a limit to their deposit insurance. Most of the board disagreed, on grounds that a warning letter would produce a flood of withdrawals and could push the bank into bankruptcy. I resigned from the board.

That was why it was hard to imagine what Gravette had in mind when he called me in 1984. But it turned out that he wanted me to replace him as chairman. He said the bank was now in serious financial trouble. He was looking for an institution to buy the Bowery, but he hadn't been able to find one that was acceptable to the FDIC, which would have to approve the takeover.

Because one of my primary objectives at the time was to make some money, there wasn't much appeal in the idea of becoming chairman of a semi-insolvent mutual savings bank. But might it be possible to convert the Bowery to a regular for-profit bank owned by stockholders? The combination of the Bowery's importance as a New York institution and the chance at a lucrative financial deal was my kind of challenge.

Don Rice, a lawyer who had worked with me at the Urban Development Corporation, was the first person I asked about the idea. He said it was possible, in theory. But because the Bowery's financial assets were earning interest at rates lower than the rates the bank was paying to its depositors, there was no reason for private investors to put money into the bank, unless the FDIC was ready to absorb the cost of the existing gap between the bank's earnings and its obligations.

The negotiations with the FDIC would be complicated, filled with novel and nonmeasurable risks. But unless private investors could be found for the Bowery, the FDIC would itself have to take over the bank, at a still greater cost to taxpayers. With Dillon Read as financial adviser, I began almost a year of negotiations with the FDIC's professionals.

The FDIC was interested in making a deal if it would cost the government less than a takeover—and if the private investors in the deal contributed $100 million in equity. Dillon Read thought it could, again in theory, raise the money on terms that would leave me with a significant piece of the equity in the bank.

First, however, I had to review the creditworthiness of the assets the bank owned, examine all fourteen of its branches, and determine whether its personnel were capable of running an institution whose nature was about to undergo a fundamental change. As the talks proceeded, the FDIC personnel grew nervous. They had never done a deal like this. The transaction would be highly visible. If the buyers made a fast profit, the government would be criticized for having given away the store. Therefore, the FDIC made clear that any quick returns were off the table. But as the FDIC became more demanding, the job of raising the $100 million became harder.

The discussions went on until March 1985, when the FDIC suddenly indicated possible termination of negotiations because the transaction was going to be too expensive. Bill Isaacs was then the FDIC's chairman. He agreed to let us pay him a final visit before we folded our tent, to try to explain to him why the FDIC's costs were not going to be as high as he feared.

It worked. We persuaded him that the private investors were going to assume more of the risk than the government would. Besides, if interest rates went down, as we thought they would, the deal would cost the public very little indeed.

Then came another kind of crisis. Dillon Read prepared a private placement memo for potential investors. It outlined the transaction's risks and potential benefits. A prominent part of the document was a description of me and how I was said to have saved other major institutions. It made me as uncomfortable as I had been when Ed Logue offered HRH a large amount of money to build something that could not be successfully built. I wasn't going to set out to raise money on the basis of an implied representation that I was a kind of Rumpelstiltskin with an ability to turn straw into gold.

Instead, I called Laurence Tisch to see whether he might be interested in investing the required equity. Larry Tisch was a kind of financial wunderkind. He had earned an MBA from the Wharton School when he was twenty years old and made his first real estate investment at the age of twenty-three. By 1980 he was a billionaire and one of New York's major philanthropists. He was also a friend. It took him just a few hours to understand the transaction and say he was in.

Tisch could not invest more than $25 million in the transaction. Otherwise, his company, Loews, would own more than 25 percent of the private equity in the bank and, thus, become a bank holding company subject to detailed regulation. So Tisch called *his* friend, Warren Buffett, and introduced the two of us. We had a brief meeting, and Buffett agreed to invest $25 million. With those two commitments in hand, it was not hard to get the rest. Nick Brady and the investment banker Lionel Pincus committed $25 million each. The transaction closed.

I moved into what were then the Bowery's splendid headquarters on 42nd Street with Tess Ankis, my secretary since the 1970s, Don Rice as my counsel, and my first major new hire, Ed Grebow. Ed worked for the Morgan Bank, but I knew him as head of the Waterside Tenants' Association. He and I had negotiated many rent increase packages. I was well aware of his brains and energy.

I had promised the investors that I would stay at the Bowery for five years, substantially reduce overhead, and close branches that couldn't make money. The only thing I wasn't going to do was fire

Joe DiMaggio, the bank's spokesman and its biggest advertising expenditure. At the first opportunity, I took him to dinner. The ostensible reason was to offer to extend his contract. The real reason was to tell him about all the times I had gone to see him play at Yankee Stadium. He turned out to be a fairly boring fellow. When you're Joe DiMaggio, I figured, you're entitled.

The Bowery continued to support civic causes, but our major goal was to turn it into a profitable operation. That was tougher than anticipated. Our competitors were offering higher and higher interest rates to depositors in order to accumulate the largest possible pools of deposits. They were accumulating these deposits so they could invest them in assets that provided even greater returns. The high-return assets were often junk bonds and highly leveraged real estate loans. We were unwilling to take those risks. But if the bank had to offer competitively high interest rates to attract depositors without earning the profits provided by the risky investments, it couldn't produce the returns on equity that the investors wanted.

True, the Bowery had depositors to whom it still paid low interest rates, the passbook depositors left over from the bank's time as a mutual savings bank. Periodically, we sent these depositors notices informing them that they could change their passbook accounts to accounts that earned higher interest rates. Many of them did not change their accounts. The reasons, I gradually realized, were inattention and ignorance. The bank was making money off a lot of poor people who didn't know better. This was not a particularly appealing enterprise.

Moreover, even with depositor ignorance, we were not going to be able to increase the value of the bank without taking on risks that we all thought imprudent. Buffett and Tisch were eager to sell. Less eagerly, I went along. We retained Goldman Sachs to find a buyer. In short order, they brought us the Home Savings Bank of California, which wanted the Bowery's depositor base so that it could increase its junk bond acquisitions.

Thus, in 1988, after three years of ownership, we sold the bank for a respectable profit. Cassandra as always, I (along with the FDIC's professionals) predicted that the bubble in which many savings banks were investing was going to burst and that the industry would be in chaos within a few years. The Home Savings Bank of California was later sold to Washington Mutual Savings Bank, which filed for bankruptcy some years after that. The magnificent bank building on 42nd street is now a fancy catering hall.

൴

As I was getting this profitable education in the banking business, New York City was heading toward yet another crisis, this one not fiscal but fundamentally political. Under the city charter in effect since the five boroughs became the City of Greater New York in 1898, the city had an executive branch, a legislative branch, and something in between, a hybrid called the Board of Estimate, which approved the budget and city contracts and had the final say on land use decisions. The board was made up of the mayor, the president of the City Council, and the city comptroller, each with four votes, and the presidents of the five boroughs, each with two votes. The equal voting power held by each borough reflected the view that no borough should be treated prejudicially in the allocation of city funds and facilities.

In 1981, though, certain Brooklyn activists challenged the structure of the Board of Estimate on grounds that Brooklyn, the city's most populous borough, had no more votes on the board than Staten Island, the least populous. In their view, Brooklyn residents were being denied equal protection of the law under the Constitution, in violation of the one-person-one-vote rule. In 1987 the US Court of Appeals for the Second Circuit ruled for the activists and against the Board of Estimate.

Mayor Koch responded by appointing a Charter Revision Commission to propose changes to the structure of city government. He asked me to chair the commission. From the prior public lives I had led, I knew almost all of the other appointees. Luckily, one of them was Judah Gribetz.

We received city funds and hired a staff director, Eric Lane, an impressive lawyer with whom I had worked in Albany when he was employed by the state Senate's Democratic minority. First, we considered some threshold questions. Should we do the least that was necessary: maintaining the Board of Estimate and trying to cure its constitutional defect through some expedient like weighted voting? Should we abolish the board altogether? Should we examine the whole city charter?

As Mayor Koch recommended, the commission decided to undertake a wholesale review of the way the city governed itself. I added one item to the agenda: public financing of city election campaigns. Scholars like Herbert Alexander of the Citizens' Research Foundation were making headway in convincing the public that something had to be done about the excessive influence of campaign money on city politics. On the basis of my government experiences, I emphatically agreed.

We held hearings all around the city, mostly at night and on weekends, as the commission members had day jobs. Anyone could express an opinion or advocate a charter provision. Along the way, our ambitions grew still broader. At the time, tales of corruption seemed to be on the front pages every day. People were concerned about not just campaign ethics but public ethics in general. The commission eventually voted to add a new code of ethics to the city charter.

In the center ring, however, was the Board of Estimate issue. There were impassioned appeals to figure out some way of continuing the board. In February 1988, the board's members hired their own counsel and began using every piece of political muscle they could to put pressure on the commission. The borough presidents argued that if the city moved to the simpler executive-legislative model used in most US cities, there would be no authority to ensure interborough equity in land-use decisions (and, not incidentally, nothing much for the borough presidents to do). Even members of the state legislature tried to intervene to protect the board.

But the commission was convinced to the contrary. Scholars said that if we tried to preserve the board we would almost certainly face protracted litigation under the Voting Rights Act; the validity of city decisions would be in question. Indeed, civil rights advocates were starting to press for not just expanding the powers of the elected City Council but also choosing its members from smaller constituencies in which minority groups stood a better chance of being represented.

The debate was expected to culminate in the coming November election. But in early April, to almost everyone's surprise, the US Supreme Court agreed to hear an appeal from the Second Circuit's decision against the Board of Estimate. We could not include any proposition dealing with the board on the November ballot.

We put the rest of the commission's recommendations to the voters that November, and they passed overwhelmingly. The city's old Board of Ethics became a Conflict of Interest Board with independent members. A model system of public funding for city elections was imposed. I got particular satisfaction from the passage of a provision—something I had implemented at the MTA—requiring the city to publish the useful life and replacement costs of its infrastructure assets.

⁂

EVER SINCE OUR reconciliation during the MTA years, Koch and I had remained good friends. He made his decisions on the merits and listened to arguments even about issues on which some people thought his mind was closed. Like Hugh Carey, Koch had a real zest for politics. Combined with his extensive substantive knowledge, it made him an extremely effective leader. He regretted having run for governor in 1982; he loved the city and the dramas that bubbled around City Hall far more than the broader policy and budget issues that occupied Albany. He was as narcissistic as any politician; but unlike most others, he could laugh at himself. Once when he got under my skin, I sent him a black box that when opened played thunderous applause. I wrote on the box, "What to listen to when you get into bed at night." Far from being offended, he used to play the box for the people who came to dinner at Gracie Mansion.

Koch was going to be finishing his third term in 1989. Racial tensions had grown, and there were scandals plaguing his administration. Koch's popularity, like that of everyone in politics, was time-limited. If he decided to seek reelection, any number of people thought about running against him.

A mutual friend of ours told me Koch was unlikely to run again. That was when I started thinking seriously about running for mayor myself. Over lunch, I told Koch I was considering the race and was going to resign from the Charter Revision Commission. He quickly replaced me with Fritz Schwartz, the city's corporation counsel because the Supreme Court was expected to decide the Board of Estimate appeal fairly soon. If the Court affirmed the Second Circuit, the commission had to be ready to put a measure to replace the Board of Estimate on the 1989 ballot.

The Court did affirm, and in 1989 the voters approved a new system. The Board of Estimate was abolished. Legislative and executive powers would be traditionally divided between an expanded City Council and the mayor. A Districting Commission was created to draw the boundaries of the new Council districts.

But the new charter contained one provision that was offensive: the Districting Commission that set the boundaries of the City Council districts was to be made up of members of different ethnic groups "in proportion, as close as practical, to their population in the city." I had supported enlarging the City Council to increase the chances that minority group members would be elected; but dictating the proportions of minority groups on the Districting Commission was a blatant, plainly insupportable quota.

I therefore brought suit against the city in federal court over a part of the new charter, which I had helped design. I won on a motion for summary judgment, and the quotas on the Districting

Commission were gone. It was a good day's work. In the years since then, no one has suggested that the absence of quotas led to discrimination by the Districting Commission or that the city's varied ethnic groups aren't represented in city government.

⁂

PEOPLE HAD BEEN urging me to run for mayor since the summer of 1988. Vernon Jordan and Frank Thomas, Victor Gotbaum and Al Shanker, Felix Rohatyn and Walter Wriston were among them, all seeking someone who would continue Koch's fiscally responsible policies without stirring up racial tensions. I had reason to believe that the Queens Democratic Party organization would collect enough signatures to put me on the ballot. Robert Rubin, then chairman of Goldman Sachs, and attorney Lawrence Buttenweiser, both longtime friends of mine, offered to lead the fund-raising effort.

With the new, Ravitch-authored public finance provisions of the city charter in place, I could not spend more than $3,000 of my own money on my campaign without giving up all public financing. Some people said I was hoisted by my own petard. Others said I had engineered the public financing provisions on purpose, to keep from having to spend my own money. A few people knew that when the public financing provisions were written, I didn't have a clue that I would be a candidate a year later.

Early in the campaign, I had substantial labor and civil rights backing. But in December, at the urging of several prominent city and national leaders, including Jesse Jackson, David Dinkins, the borough president of Manhattan, entered the race. There was no point in my trying to maintain the support of those labor leaders and civil rights activists whose constituencies were excited at the prospect of a black man becoming mayor of New York. Furthermore, David Dinkins was—and is—a hell of a nice guy, toward whom it was impossible to feel anger or resentment. I thought about quitting the race, but by that time a corps of volunteers was telling me to stick it out. And if Koch decided not to run, I might appeal to a large segment of his constituency.

But those who knew Koch best predicted that Dinkins's candidacy would push the mayor into a reelection run, and it did. When the city comptroller, Jay Goldin, joined the race, there were four of us running for the Democratic nomination.

It wasn't just the fractured field that doomed my election bid; I was a lousy candidate. I ended up with a stunning 3 percent of the Democratic primary vote. But the campaign was an experience I never regretted for one second. I got up every morning at 5:30 and went to a different subway station to greet voters. I visited coffee klatches, churches, community groups, and social service organizations. I talked with thousands of people, who almost without exception were courteous, curious, and caring about their city. Most of my friends assumed that it was a painful, difficult exercise. But the truth is that I found it an exhilarating affirmation of my conviction about the wonder of the democratic process.

And I had dinner with Ed Koch on the night after David Dinkins beat us both, pleased to know that the mayor and I were still friends.

I WAS EARNING my living as the general partner of partnerships owning 3,200 New York City apartments, including Waterside and Manhattan Plaza. I also stayed active in housing policy at the national level. In 1988 I served on the congressionally authorized National Housing Task Force. A decade later, Congressman Barney Frank and Senator John Kerry asked me to be the Democratic cochair of another congressional effort, the Millennium Task Force on Housing. Like the National Commission on Urban Problems of the late 1960s, these later commissions produced plenty of good ideas, some of them the same as the ideas proposed forty years before. Once again, few of the ideas saw the light of legislative day. Except for the very poor, Americans were reasonably well housed. For most people in politics, the issue had become secondary.

But it was not secondary to the AFL-CIO, which saw better housing as a way not just to provide decent living places at affordable rents but also to produce jobs for union members and investment opportunities for union pension funds. AFL-CIO president Lane Kirkland and I had remained friends since Al Shanker introduced us thirty years before, partly because of our shared politics: we were anticommunist, pro-growth, involved in civil rights, and committed to the security of Israel (Kirkland's elegant wife, Irena, being a Holocaust survivor). In 1991, at Kirkland's request, I became chairman of the AFL-CIO Housing Investment Trust, established to create new housing built by union members and financed by construction union pension funds. We hired a talented guy from Boston, Steve Coyle, to run the organization, and we built up a fund of almost $5 billion. It is one of the highest-return fixed income funds in the country.

I also stayed involved with the AFL-CIO through its insurance company, the Union Labor Life Insurance Company, which sold life and other insurance to unions and union members and managed a multibillion-dollar real estate investment fund that was the company's biggest profit center. When ULLICO was on the verge of bankruptcy and mired in scandals, John Sweeney, who had succeeded Kirkland as AFL-CIO president, asked me to help save the company. I became chairman of the finance committee and recommended Ed Grebow, who had worked for me at the Bowery, to be CEO. With some difficulty, we refinanced ULLICO, and Ed oversaw the company's recovery.

Around the time I started to chair the AFL-CIO Housing Investment Trust, Mike Sviridoff of the Ford Foundation, author of many of the antipoverty programs of the 1960s, introduced me to Julie Sandorf, with whom he had been working on a plan to deal more effectively with the homeless people who were sleeping in city streets and armories and getting little sympathy from their fellow citizens. Sandorf and Sviridoff's idea was to work with major foundations and local nonprofits to create permanent housing for the homeless and provide them with medical and social services. They asked me to chair the new enterprise, build a board, and coordinate with the foundations that were going to fund the effort. It became the Coalition for Supportive Housing, which now operates in a dozen states.

I joined the boards of Mount Sinai Hospital, the American Stock Exchange, and some companies in which I had made small investments. I was elected chairman of the Citizens Budget Commission, a business-funded civic organization that tries to put pressure on politicians to be fiscally responsible. But these pursuits did not answer the fundamental question. Once again, not yet sixty years old, I had to figure out what my main work would be, public or private.

☙

FORMER SECRETARY of Commerce Pete Peterson and financier Steve Schwartzman had recently formed the Blackstone Group, an investment banking firm, and asked me to join. They were enthusiastic and welcoming. Absent conflicts of interest, there would be no restrictions on my serving on organization boards. This time, though still uncertain about whether I was cut out to be an investment banker, I took a chance, and knew within a year that I had made a mistake. Finding and financing new investments was not the exciting enterprise it had seemed in prospect.

Once again, serendipity intervened—twice. Nick Brady, who had become Ronald Reagan's secretary of the Treasury in 1988 and continued under George H. W. Bush, told me the federal government was creating a new institution, the Resolution Trust Company, to reduce the government's losses from the collapse of many of the country's savings banks. The junk bond bubble had burst, the exposure of the FDIC and other regulatory institutions was enormous, and Nick knew I had predicted much of what had taken place. He asked whether I would consider becoming head of the RTC.

I was thrilled; my next exit had materialized. I arranged to go to Washington the next day to meet with the FDIC chairman, Bill Seidman.

But the next morning Russ Reynolds, a respected headhunter, called to inform me that the owners of the thirty major league baseball teams were looking for a way to change the economics of the sport so that teams in smaller markets could compete more successfully. They wanted someone who could make the transition happen. The day after returning from Washington, I met with three of the league's most active owners: Bud Selig of the Milwaukee Brewers, Jerry Reinsdorf of the Chicago White Sox, and Stan Kasten of the Atlanta Braves. Suddenly there were not one but two exciting opportunities.

I had dinner with my sons the next night. One of them had become a lawyer; the other wrote fiction. A few years earlier, I had been divorced. In the time since then, the kids had been protective. They were not just my family but also my board of advisers and best friends. I asked them which job I should take.

My sons were not ambivalent. If I went to Washington, they said, government conflict-of-interest rules would make me divest most of my commercial assets, including Waterside, and resign from almost all my boards in return for the privilege of working seven days a week.

In the baseball job, by contrast, I would have no conflicts of interest, many perks, a substantial salary, and plenty of time to enjoy an active social life. Besides, I had loved baseball all my life. I had stood in line most of the night to get a ticket the first time Jackie Robinson ever played in New York, in a 1947 exhibition game against the Yankees at Ebbets Field. I was at the Yankee-Dodger World Series in 1941, when Mickey Owen dropped the third strike on the Yankees' right fielder, letting the Yankees come from behind and win. I hadn't missed a Yankees World Series since then.

I was more than willing to follow the kids' advice.

As soon as I took the job, I began visiting as many of the owners as I could. One stop on my tour was Gene Autry's home in Studio City, California. Autry had become an icon as America's singing cowboy, complete with guitar and famous horse. In retirement, he bought a baseball team, the Los Angeles Angels. Autry welcomed me into his living room. A life-sized stuffed horse was standing in the middle of it. I searched my brain for a conversational connection. "Trigger?"

I asked gamely. There was silence. "That was Roy Rogers," Autry finally answered. He was resigned. This had clearly happened to him before. "My horse was Champion."

Autry turned out to be a fine and decent man, as did some of the other owners I met—like Ewing Kauffman, owner of the Kansas City Royals, who willed the team to the Greater Kansas City Community Foundation upon his death. For owners like Kauffman, team ownership was a matter of civic pride and a contribution to the community. For others, a team was a moneymaking proposition, either on its own or combined with related businesses like television stations.

Because the owners were divided in their reasons for being in the baseball business, they were divided in their views about how the business should work. Baseball was not subject to the antitrust laws, and owners had considerable freedom to make joint decisions about economic matters. Through most of the sport's history, the owners had paid the players whatever the players could negotiate individually. Reserve clauses bound the players to their teams for as long as the owners wanted them.

However, under Marvin Miller, an economist who became executive director of the Major League Baseball Players Association in 1966, the old system began to break down. The players' union gained enormous leverage. Player salaries skyrocketed. Teams in bigger cities, with bigger TV audiences, had more revenue at their disposal and could offer bigger salaries to star players. The discrepancies among the teams grew, and the quality of the game suffered.

Most owners wanted to change the system by negotiating a revenue-sharing agreement among themselves and a contract with the players' union reflecting that agreement. One of those in favor of a new system was George W. Bush, then the general partner of the Texas Rangers. Bush also seemed sanguine about the prospects for my success. As he told the *New York Times*, "I imagine trying to handle the subway situation there in New York has got a lot of parallels with trying to figure out how to try to make baseball come together."

He was wrong. Baseball was a lot tougher.

It took over a year to get the baseball owners to agree to a sensible revenue-sharing plan, along the lines of the arrangements that had been adopted in football and basketball. It was not a pretty process. At one owners' meeting, Yankees' owner George Steinbrenner, who had shown me the door telephonically when New York City asked him to help with the city's Olympic bid, ranted against the idea of sharing revenues with teams like the Los Angeles Angels. He said they were in trouble only because they were so badly managed. As I got up to take a bathroom break, I noticed Gene Autry, the Angels' owner standing at the back of the room with tears in his eyes. His wife was with him, and I asked her whether Gene was well. Health wasn't the problem, she said. In 1974 Steinbrenner had pled guilty to making an illegal contribution to President Richard Nixon's reelection campaign and to a felony charge of obstruction of justice. He paid personal and company fines and was suspended from baseball for fifteen months. Steinbrenner desperately wanted a presidential pardon. After Ronald Reagan's election in 1980, Steinbrenner asked his baseball buddy Gene Autry, a close friend of Reagan's, to secure a pardon for him. Autry obliged. Now Autry was experiencing Steinbrenner's gratitude.

The owners finally agreed to changes, including a cap on the total compensation each team could pay to its players. In order to put the cap into effect, the owners needed a new contract with the players' union. We approached the union with an offer that included the largest salary and benefits package in the sport's history. But we couldn't overcome the history of bad blood between the owners and the players' union—or the fact that some of the owners, having agreed to revenue-sharing in public, took private steps to ensure that they wouldn't suffer any competitive disadvantage from it.

There was an impasse. The result was the baseball strike of 1994, which led to the cancellation of the 1994 World Series and extended into 1995. What had seemed like one of the country's most glamorous businesses turned out to be conducted with a degree of dysfunction that made John Lawe and the executive board of the Transit Workers Union look like the Roman senate. I was a negotiator by experience and temperament, but this was an arena in which nothing constructive could be achieved through negotiation. All that could happen was that the parties would eventually wear themselves out.

Thus, my professional baseball career came to an end. Life went on. Don Rice and I formed a partnership that engaged in a variety of legal and commercial endeavors for fun and profit. I thought my vulnerability to the siren song of public service was finally abating. After the Dayton Accords ended the Bosnian conflict, the White House called to ask whether I would go to Bosnia for a year and take charge of the economic rebuilding process; but that prospect stretched my feelings about public service too far.

More important, in 1996 I met Kathleen Doyle, a beautiful woman full of warmth and generosity, a widow with three extraordinary daughters. Kathy and I married a few years later. We have been together every day since then, and my happiness with her is a constant reminder that personal contentment is a much more valuable commodity than professional success.

By 2008, I was again convinced that my public life was over.

❧

BUT IN THE summer of that year an economic crisis had begun for the country, and so had a new crisis for the MTA. The system needed a new five-year capital plan to continue its job of restoring the system to a state of good repair, but it had no obvious means of funding the plan. The MTA's labor contracts had expired and were being arbitrated under the Taylor Law; the outcome would determine the largest part of the system's operating expenses. There was going to have to be a fare increase, but neither raising fares nor cutting services would be enough to meet the system's continuing restoration needs or fund expansion projects already under way, like the Second Avenue subway.

By then, David Paterson had become governor upon the resigna-
tion of his predecessor, Eliot Spitzer. In hopes of generating some consensus about who was going to pay to meet the MTA's needs, Paterson
appointed a citizens' commission. Knowing that I would be a sympathetic audience for concerns about the state's infrastructure, he made
me chairman. As is usual with such commissions, most of the members
would be engaged in their customary business and professional activities. The work of the commission would be the chairman's work.

The commission included the city and state budget directors,
prominent business executives, the president of the state AFL-CIO,
and several individuals I had recommended because of their previous
involvement with MTA issues. The cast of characters was a familiar one, which was a significant advantage. We held our hearings
throughout the MTA region—the mood cordial this time because
the players were so familiar with one another. Marc Shaw, a former
MTA executive director who was now a senior adviser to the governor, was immensely helpful. So was the MTA's chief financial officer,
Gary Dellaverson, who made his staff available to provide data and
ideas about possible sources of money.

The issues were politically toxic and intensively covered by the
press. Every rumor of a new tax or user fee provoked a press story
featuring some elected official who attacked the commission, or me,
for even thinking about it. Others were lobbying just as hard against
any service cuts. It was critically important to maintain confidential-
ity until a consensus could be forged among the commission members, many of whom had constituencies that thought they knew the
right answers.

It was—Yogi Berra's phrase is familiar, but nobody has said it
better—déjà vu all over again. At least they were not baseball owners.

The commission issued a unanimous report recommending a
new payroll tax for all employers in the MTA region, inbound tolls
on all the Manhattan bridges that weren't owned by the Port Authority or the Triborough Bridge and Tunnel Authority, and future

fare increases based on inflation so as to reduce the political circus that occurred every time it was necessary to raise the fare. I had been in touch with the mayor and the governor, who were supportive. But there was going to be serious opposition from state legislators, who would find it very difficult to vote to impose new charges on their constituents.

On the basis of many years of experience, I knew that part of my job was to visit the editorial boards of the major newspapers and persuade them to put pressure on these legislators. I got the newspapers' support, as well as backing from the organized business community and the labor unions. But that was not enough. In the legislature, all of the players were accessible and respectful. The speaker of the Assembly, Sheldon Silver, whom I had known for twenty-five years, said he would support the commission's recommendations if the bridge tolls were reduced, especially the tolls on the bridges over the Harlem River. The Senate, however, was another matter. The Republicans opposed every one of the commission's recommendations. The Democrats nominally controlled the Senate, but only by one vote, and their leadership was not strong enough to get unanimity.

The legislature finally passed most of the commission's recommendations, but not the critical institution of bridge tolls. Coincidentally, each of the three state senators who led the fight against the bridge tolls has since been convicted of a crime and is serving time in prison.

The only consolation was that this time I was taken more seriously than when I had last recommended increased bridge tolls thirty years before, as chairman of the MTA. I was back in Albany, working with the legislature and the press. It was an unplanned training exercise for what was about to come.

8

Becoming Lieutenant Governor

O N JULY 3, 2009, I WAS on vacation on Long Island with my family, preoccupied with nothing more momentous than the question of whether to go sailing or play golf, when I got a call from Charles O'Byrne. He had been David Paterson's chief of staff and remained the governor's closest political confidant. It was O'Byrne, at Paterson's behest, who had asked me to head the citizens' commission on the MTA in 2008. O'Byrne arrived soon after the call and, without preliminaries, told me what the great urgency was: if Governor Paterson asked, would I take the job of lieutenant governor of the State of New York?

I was both flattered and flabbergasted; I hadn't held a major state government post in more than twenty-five years. During that time, Mario Cuomo had finished twelve years as governor. In 1994 he lost the governorship to a Republican, George Pataki, who served another twelve years. In the 2006 election, Democrats Eliot Spitzer and David Paterson were elected governor and lieutenant governor in the usual way, on the same ticket.

Spitzer had been the state's aggressive attorney general; with his election as governor, he began to be talked about as a contender for the Democratic presidential nomination. Paterson had been a state senator for twenty years, occupying the seat once held by his father, the legendary Harlem politician Basil Paterson. New York political observers looked forward to another long stretch of years marked by a governor who was a strong political force and a lieutenant governor who was marginal to the business of running the state.

But this more or less orderly pattern of New York gubernatorial politics was interrupted not much more than a year after Spitzer took office on March 17, 2007, when the governor resigned in disgrace after having been identified by federal investigators as a client of a prostitution ring. David Paterson succeeded to the governorship. The post of New York lieutenant governor became vacant.

But that didn't explain why O'Byrne was asking whether I was willing to be appointed to the job. The New York lieutenant governor was an elected official. Normally, if the post was vacant, the majority leader of the state Senate would take over the lieutenant governor's duties until the position was filled by election again. But these weren't normal times in New York. For one thing, the state was in a fiscal meltdown stemming from a national economic downturn and years of imprudent budget practices. Even more explosively, since June 8 the state Senate had been deadlocked, evenly divided between Democrats and Republicans—which would have been bad enough—and paralyzed by lawsuits, lockouts, and mutual accusations of double-dealing and corruption. The crisis was precipitated when four Democratic state senators temporarily defected to the Republican side. Three of them would later end up in jail, convicted of offenses ranging from assault to embezzlement.

One result of the crisis was that Governor Paterson was unable to travel outside New York State, because if he did so the president pro tem of the Senate was supposed to serve as acting governor. But the competing factions in the Senate were making different claims about just who the president pro tem was. The possible disasters in legislation and governance were limited only by the imagination.

O'Byrne said the governor's lawyers had concluded that while it wasn't a sure bet, Paterson probably had the authority to appoint someone to the lieutenant governor's post for the remaining year-and-a-half of his term. Moreover, there were reasons why Paterson wanted me to be that someone. First, people knew I didn't aspire to elective office, so I wasn't likely to be seen as a threat to any elected official beyond Paterson's term. Next, I was a Democrat but had a reputation for not being a down-the-line partisan. Finally, I had played a role in overcoming a succession of New York financial crises, and there was no doubt that the state was now facing one of them. Paterson said he needed my fiscal expertise.

I was intrigued, but some questions had to be answered. Did I have any conflicts of interest on account of my business dealings and board memberships? What would my colleagues in these enterprises, for-profit and nonprofit, say about the added burdens that would fall on them if I took the job? What would my wife, Kathy, think of my spending substantial amounts of time in Albany, 140 miles and a cultural world away from New York City?

O'Byrne said the governor's counsel, Peter Kiernan, was standing by to help answer at least some of those questions. He explained the issues that had to be addressed, adding that if I was seriously considering the governor's offer, I should retain my own counsel.

Kathy knew what it would mean to me to be able to serve in this situation; she was totally supportive. I called my business and non-business colleagues. They, too, were encouraging. I asked my friend and neighbor Matthew Mallow, then a partner at Skadden Arps, to begin studying the conflict-of-interest issues. A few days later, Paterson himself called, and I told him that if I had no conflicts, I would take the job. With Matt and Peter's help, I concluded that there were none. On July 6, I told the governor I would accept.

The next evening, my birthday, Kathy and I were meeting Joe and Hillary Califano for dinner at Peter Luger, the famous Brooklyn steakhouse. Leaving Manhattan in the car, I heard that Paterson was on television announcing my appointment. I knew the press calls were about to start. But the first call wasn't from a journalist. Kiernan called to say he had learned that the Republicans were hunting for a state court judge who would grant an after-hours injunction against my taking office. Because of the deadlock in the Senate and the issues it raised about gubernatorial succession, the governor wanted me to be sworn in before the litigation began. Kiernan said I should sign the oath of office immediately. With any luck, the secretary of state in Albany could then certify it before a judge could act.

Matt arranged for a notary to get into a taxi to Brooklyn. By the time the notary arrived at Peter Luger, our dinner order was on the table. So I signed the oath amid the steak, tomatoes, and creamed spinach. The document was driven by taxi straight from the table to Albany, where it was duly certified and filed—just one hour before lawyers for the state Senate's Republican majority leader, joined by one of the defecting Democrats, found a Long Island judge and persuaded him to issue a temporary restraining order.

The governor got ready to appeal the court's order. Under normal circumstances, the state's attorney general would have argued the governor's case. But, as with so much else at this time, the circumstances were not normal. When the state's attorney general, Andrew Cuomo, son of the former governor, heard that Paterson might appoint his own lieutenant governor, Cuomo opined that the appointment would be unconstitutional, a "political ploy that would wind through the courts for many months."

Cuomo, it turned out, miscalculated the impact that the depth of New York's political and fiscal crises would have on the state's courts. With the attorney general unwilling to make the governor's argument, Paterson retained Kathleen Sullivan, a prominent constitutional litigator, to represent him. On the one hand, New York law generally permits the governor to fill vacancies by appointment. On the other hand, a section of the state constitution provides that the president pro tem of the Senate is to "perform all the duties of lieutenant governor" during a vacancy in the lieutenant governor's office. If the president of the Senate was to "perform all the duties" of the lieutenant governor, did this mean there was no vacancy that the governor could fill? Or did it just mean that the president pro tem was supposed to pinch-hit until the governor filled the vacancy in the same way he filled many other state vacancies?

There was also a broader question: if a governor appointed a lieutenant governor to serve until the next election, would the appointment violate the general principle that the lieutenant governor should be an elected official?

The issues were abstract, almost metaphysical; but the consequences of the courts' decision would be very concrete. The lower courts ruled against the governor but called the issue "one of great import" that "ought to be resolved finally and expeditiously" and allowed the governor to appeal directly to the state's highest court, the Court of Appeals. On September 22, in a 4–3 decision, the Court of Appeals upheld my appointment. The majority cited the need to "assure the structural integrity and efficacy of the executive branch." I could finally take the oath of office in person. By that time, though, I had learned enough about New York's fiscal problems so that they cast a pall over the fun of winning.

❧

THE JOB OF lieutenant governor has its share of perks. I had offices in Albany and New York City, with a highly competent administrative assistant in each. The New York State Police provided me with security and drove me, at speeds not available to civilians, between New York and Albany, New York and Washington, or wherever I had to go.

My New York City offices were nondescript, part of the quarters that the state owned in a big office building on Third Avenue near Grand Central, the southern terminus of the Albany–New York rail route. My Albany offices, in contrast, came—literally—from another century. They were in the State Capitol, a strange and magnificent structure that housed both the state's legislative branch and the highest reaches of the executive branch. The Capitol had taken more than thirty years to build. It was finished just before the turn of the twentieth century and was the most expensive government building of its time.

Because the lieutenant governor presides over the state Senate, my Albany offices adjoined the Senate floor. They featured extremely high ceilings, extremely elaborate carved-wood paneling, and extremely copious gold leaf. Over time, the rooms came to seem like a metaphor for the job I held, elaborate and empty. True, my sole official function, presiding over the Senate, included the power to cast tie-breaking votes. One might have thought that the power to break ties would have made me at least a potentially important part of the legislative process, but it didn't really amount to much. For one thing, the state constitution had been interpreted to permit the lieutenant governor to break ties only on procedural matters, not substantive ones. Also, I had decided that even where I did have a tie-breaking vote, the better course would be not to cast the vote but to convene the leaders of both parties and try to work out a compromise.

As things turned out, even the hypothetical tie-breaking situations soon became, in practical terms, nonexistent. At virtually the same time when I was appointed lieutenant governor, and perhaps because of the appointment, the last holdout among the defecting Democratic state senators who had brought the Senate to a standstill switched his allegiance again and returned to the Democratic fold. The Democrats regained a 32–30 margin of control and held it for the rest of 2009 and 2010.

The partisanship in the Senate remained bitter. Both sides were preoccupied with the coming 2010 legislative elections, because the party that held the majority in 2011 would control the legislative redistricting that was set to take place in 2012. The 2012 redistricting, in turn, would determine the future balance of power in the state Senate for a decade. But there was no way for me to have much effect on these issues.

I did what I could. I tried to reacquaint myself with the state legislators I already knew and make the acquaintance of those I hadn't met. I got to know people in the executive branch. I offered to help the governor's staffers in any way I could, while making clear that I wasn't going to interfere with their prerogatives. Not infrequently, state legislators or state commissioners in the executive branch faced policy issues that I knew something about. When they asked for my opinion or help, I gave it. I visited Washington often and stayed in regular touch with the staff of New York State's Washington office, which had the big and often thankless job of making sure that the New York congressional delegation understood the impact of federal legislation, enacted and proposed, on the interests of the state. I lobbied to the extent I could on behalf of federal funds for the state's education and Medicaid programs.

Still, I had no political relationship with any elected official and no political clout that would have flowed from such a relationship. I was allowed to hire only one staffer of my own, the talented Suzanne Garment, whom I had met more than thirty years before when she worked with Pat Moynihan at the United Nations and who became my special counsel. One more staffer was assigned to me by the governor's office. I was lucky that it turned out to be Michael Evans, an extraordinary young man who is now president of the Moynihan Station Development Corporation. I had help from Nora Fitzpatrick, an employee of the Federal Reserve Bank of New York, which was rightly concerned about the effect that the fiscal plight of states and their cities could have on the nation's municipal securities markets. Nora was assigned to me for a full year. Later on, when I got support for my work from several New York foundations, their funds paid for additional staff.

But I had no portfolio, no duties, no one in state government to whom I had to report or who had to report to me. In that sense, the eighteen months I spent in the lieutenant governor's office were the most professionally frustrating period of my life.

ↂ

IN THE ALBANY of 2009, compared with Albany four decades earlier, the power of organized political parties had diminished, but political partisanship had increased. This was not as paradoxical as it might seem.

Much has been written about the decline of political parties and its effects on national politics, but the decline has affected state politics as well. As parties have mattered less to the outcome of elections, political contributions that candidates raise for themselves have come to matter more. A legislator's ability to raise this kind of money has increasingly become the measure of his or her success, and the contributions increasingly come from groups with concrete interests in the actions that state legislatures take.

In fact, the change has been even more marked in state politics than at the federal level, because holding an elected state office doesn't confer anywhere near the prestige, or the salary, of holding federal office. Raising money for state election campaigns is even harder than at the federal level, and there is less of the regular public attention that would otherwise set bounds on the influence that political money wields through campaign contributions and lobbying.

For these reasons, running for state legislature, when compared with all the other kinds of rewards that a prosperous society like ours offers to well-educated young people, is not a pursuit calculated to attract the best and brightest. Over time this problem has gotten worse, as the concrete rewards available to state legislators fall further behind those they could gain in the private sector.

So it was no surprise to me that when I became lieutenant governor I found the state's political arrangements not to be working as well as I remembered from thirty and forty years before. In fact, what was more remarkable, given the circumstances, was the number of outstanding individuals who still populated state government and made it possible for the system to work very well when it absolutely had to. Still, too many people now in state government have an interest in obfuscating issues or, even when they have exemplary motives, are unable to explain their positions well.

The decline in state parties has also changed elected officials' relationship with the press. Politicians are more dependent on the press, not just to win elections but also to communicate their day-to-day activities to the electorate. Elected officials, well aware of the map of hot-button issues among their constituents, try to be quoted on these issues as often as possible. Thus, journalists have become accustomed to seeing elected officials as supplicants who constantly seek them out to get coverage.

The inevitable result is that journalists become skeptical or even cynical, quick to impute manipulative motives to the politicians who court them. Journalists also manipulate officials, of course, in order to be able to write the news stories they wish to write. But this moral symmetry doesn't generally make the press more tolerant of politicians' actions; indeed, many journalists seem unaware of it.

Again, what is true on the national level is even more pronounced in the states. State politics is not a particularly attractive beat for a reporter to cover. The officials are not as glamorous as their counterparts in Washington. The issues discussed do not have the cachet of matters of war and peace. Equally unattractive, state capitals, by design, are often located in out-of-the-way parts of the state, which are considered to be close to the virtuous heartland and far from the corrupting influence of big cities. Thus, state governments are geographically isolated from the places in which ideas germinate and writers, including journalists, naturally congregate. This means a lack of cross-fertilization between the world of politics and the world of ideas. Most journalists simply don't want to go to places like Albany; and, as media economics shrink the scope and resources of the press, editors feel less and less compelled to send them there. The inadequacy of coverage increases. The lack of transparency persists.

There isn't a great interest in most of the issues state politicians deal with; many of them are very parochial or very local thus contributing to the disdain or cynicism with which they are covered. This formula pulls news desks toward stories of corruption and wrongdoing, financial or sexual. The search for low motives has become a substitute for seeking real transparency in the formation of public policy.

The hunt for corruption has, perversely, made government less rather than more effective in the ways that advocates of good government would like it to be. To understand how, we should begin with the point that state politics and government do not work the way most people think they do. Yes, the distinction between political parties determines who controls the legislative bodies and the patronage and fund-raising capacity that follow. But in other ways, party differences matter less than differences among individual politicians and their constituencies. More often than not, it is the personalities, abilities, and, sometimes, pathologies of individual politicians that determine outcomes.

Moreover, as tax laws, federal mandates, and health-care and education issues become more complicated, legislators—the intellectually sophisticated ones as well as those with more limited comprehension—increasingly depend on their individual and committee staffs. On the whole, these staffers are able and honorable. They have enormous influence and responsibility, especially as they become more experienced, and they exercise a great deal of control over the substance of state decisions in both the legislative and executive branches. While I was lieutenant governor, the most critical discussions about the state budget took place among key staffers to the governor, the speaker of the Assembly, and the majority and minority leaders of the state Senate.

Legislators also depend heavily on their leaders, the individuals elected as speaker of the Assembly and majority leader of the Senate, who pick the committee staffs. Legislative leaders, especially at the state level, occupy an almost unique position in our political system. They are elected because their members believe they have the capacity to negotiate consensus among a diverse group with varying constituencies and differing, genuinely held points of view, as well as to help raise money to help individual members get reelected.

The dependence on staffs and leaders is not generally unhealthy, but it collides with certain journalistic ideals of transparency in government. In Albany, the drive for transparency has created a phenomenon called "leaders' meetings," in which the governor, the Assembly speaker, and the majority and minority Senate leaders discuss issues in public. I attended many of these meetings. Not surprisingly, they do not accomplish much.

Meeting out of the direct glare of press attention would accomplish much more. But secrecy, like politics, has become a pejorative word. Many press outlets have become politicized; others play to the public's frustration with the unsatisfactory outcomes that politics produces and the suspicion that such outcomes must reflect conspiracies against the public interest. Some in the media would rather seek out cases of what they consider illegitimate secrecy than deal with the complex legal and economic facts that governments have to address.

What press there is assiduously follows the politicians around the Capitol in Albany, and no politician wants to take the chance that journalists will find out about a private meeting and run a story picturing it as an act of conspiracy. Therefore, if a problem has to be solved through private communication, it will usually be a one-on-one conversation, the kind whose existence and substance are relatively difficult for the press to pin down. Sometimes a key staff person is present, sometimes not. If no staffers are there, there is an added risk that the principals will misunderstand each other and there will be delay while the confusion is cleared up.

Thus, the cycle of sub-optimal government is perpetuated. Journalists portray legislatures as dysfunctional, even when their behavior reflects legitimate disagreements and conflicts among different constituencies. The press concentrates its coverage on malefactors, who are a distinct minority. A lot of bright young people are discouraged from entering public life. Citizens, reinforced in their view that politics is all about corruption, are allowed to avoid focusing on issues that are potentially more lethal, like state budgets.

This was the system within which I had to work.

⁂

But it was also a system in which I had some advantages. My absence of official responsibilities gave me a considerable amount of freedom, and my experience had given me a sense of the uses to which I could put this freedom. I thought a lot about how I could apply the lessons I had learned from the years when I had real functions and responsibilities. And over those years I had acquired relationships with journalists; the press had always been my sword and shield in public life.

At no time in my public career did I ever employ a press agent or public relations firm—not out of an excess of modesty but because I quickly understood that if you are seen as seeking self-interested publicity, the press will lump you together with all those politicians whom journalists view as manipulative supplicants. Instead, I was usually able to gain my objectives by establishing a different kind of relationship with the reporters who covered matters in which I was involved.

One night in 1975, when I was new to government, I was schmoozing in an Albany bar when a reporter asked me what I thought of Governor Rockefeller's legacy. Nelson Rockefeller, I began my answer, was a cross between Ponzi and Robin Hood. The next morning, I was mortified to see my remark on the front page of the local newspaper. So by the time I became lieutenant governor, I had learned, when in doubt, to say "off the record."

More important, I did not find it difficult to establish relationships of trust with reporters, because I shared many of the values with which most reporters approached public issues. A good number of these reporters were my friends. When I wasn't in government, I saw them socially. We came to have a fair amount of mutual confidence. As long as I never tried to mislead a journalist in order to get a favorable story published, I had an excellent chance of getting accurate, fair reporting.

Serious journalists also liked the opportunity to intellectualize the political events they were covering; I enjoyed the same process. I spoke to them with a candor that satisfied them and me. I would talk to them frankly about events in which I was involved, help them develop a story, and make sure they knew I had no interest in having my name mentioned.

By the time I arrived in Albany as lieutenant governor, I had also learned something about the role of editorials in politics, especially state politics. Many people in politics take positions on the basis of editorials because they don't have a strong internal compass that dictates their own opinions. If an editorial is written with some intelligence and expresses a clear point of view, it carries a surprising amount of political weight and can have a profound influence on political decisions.

More particularly, I had learned about the *New York Times*. Politicians who run for office pay close attention to any and all media outlets. But in New York, especially when I first entered public life and even now, there is no question that the *Times* was the dominant factor in the way the press mirrored government and politics. In the political culture in which I grew up, an event never really happened unless it was reported in the *Times*. Television news desks often got their stories from early editions of the *Times*. Getting praise from that newspaper or looking good in its pages was a valuable political asset. Candor requires me to acknowledge that a call from the *Times* never failed to get a rapid response. It often took a fair amount of time and effort to provide the information a reporter asked for and to explain, sometimes ad nauseam, the parts that he or she didn't have straight. But those efforts bore fruit in the way events were reported.

In the most general sense, my aims were usually congruent with those of the *Times* editors; it was not a stretch for me to make the arguments that I thought would get their support. But there is no denying that the values of those editors, actual and perceived, had the power to shape the positions of even public officials who might otherwise have acted differently. Once, during one of the many school-busing controversies that rattled the country, I remember being dumbfounded when Pat Moynihan, then a US senator, took a pro-busing stance that seemed to contradict decades of his past writings. I asked him why. He raised those famous eyebrows of his and said simply, "The *Times*, my boy, the *Times*."

⅋

SO, WHILE I was lieutenant governor, I had no real power but enjoyed the advantage of a sympathetic forum. Wanting to do something useful, I began to study and report on some of the fiscal issues I thought were particularly important to New York. They involved both the reasons why the state budget was in such crisis and the consequences of the crisis.

The chief reason for the crisis was Medicaid, which made up fully a third of the state's budget and, as I learned, was a case study in the costs of good intentions. Medicaid—not the same as Medicare, though the two overlap—provides joint federal-state health-care coverage to low-income Americans. The federal government reimburses state governments for part of what they spend on Medicaid and sets rules for state Medicaid programs.

I found that New York has two large structural problems with Medicaid. The first is that it simply does not get enough federal reimbursement. The federal government's Medicaid reimbursement rates to the states vary widely, from 74 percent down to 50 percent. The rate depends on a state's average income. New York has a high average income, so it gets a low reimbursement rate.

But two states with the same average income can have different Medicaid needs. One state may not have many rich people, but not many poor people either. Another state with the same average income may have more rich people, as well as more poor people, who put larger burdens on the state's Medicaid program. New York is the second kind of state, with large Medicaid needs. Its federal reimbursement rate does not reflect these needs.

The second structural problem with Medicaid is that federal reimbursement money is not free money; it is matching money. That is, a state has to spend its own funds in order to get the federal funds. From the beginning of the Medicaid program in 1965, New York, for generous reasons, designed its state program to attract the maximum number of matching federal dollars. For example, New York's is one of the few state Medicaid programs that cover low-income adults who have no children. New York thereby gets more federal money but spends more state money to do so.

A mountain of lesser problems is piled on top of these structural problems. Some of the added problems are nationwide. For instance, states spend disproportionate amounts of their Medicaid money on people who are "dual-eligible," eligible for Medicaid because they are poor and for Medicare because they are old or disabled. Because these people receive Medicare as well as Medicaid, Medicare's "freedom of choice" rules keep states from being able to serve them better and more economically through managed care.

Other problems are New York problems. In New York, payment rates to health-care providers are set by the state legislature rather than by administrators, making costs harder to control. New York is one of the few states that shares Medicaid administration and costs between the state and its counties; this, too, makes cost control more difficult. New York's medical malpractice system costs so much that it seriously distorts the allocation of health-care resources.

I prepared a report that recommended the enactment of a bill to reform the malpractice system, limiting awards so as to save the health-care system hundreds of millions of dollars. It urged a state takeover of Medicaid and eliminating the legislature's power to set reimbursement rates directly.

I had a lot of help from talented bureaucrats in the state's health-care agencies, health-care experts in the state Budget Division, think tanks like the Urban Institute, private foundations like the Kaiser Family Foundation, and, above all, from Jim Tallon, president of the United Hospital Fund and former chairman of the New York State Assembly's health committee. Though the report was never acknowledged by the governor or his chief of staff, Larry Schwartz, I was gratified by the reaction it received from the press. But the problem of Medicaid's high burden on state budgets continues. And since the

Affordable Care Act relies on Medicaid to provide health-care coverage to more Americans, the problem may get worse.

⁂

IF MEDICAID WAS Exhibit A in the causes of the state's budget crisis, the state's infrastructure, along with public higher education, was at the top of the list of victims of the crisis.

My interest in transportation infrastructure had its roots in personal history, and one of the jobs I undertook as lieutenant governor was to report on infrastructure and the budget crisis. When I began preparing the report, state inspectors had just discovered that the Crown Point Bridge, which connected New York to Vermont across Lake Champlain and served as a route to and from work for thousands of people, had deteriorated much more rapidly than anticipated. It was no longer safe, and it could no longer be repaired. It had to be closed and dynamited. While waiting for a new bridge, people had to make a hundred-mile detour to and from their jobs every day. There were even bigger disruptions to come: the Tappan Zee Bridge connecting Rockland and Westchester counties and the Kosciuszko Bridge on the Brooklyn-Queens Expressway were at the end of their useful lives. They would have to be replaced, at a total cost of more than $10 billion.

The problem extended far beyond bridges. Parts of the state's highways, roads, rail lines, public transit, airports, and seaports had deteriorated to a state in which they could pose a serious threat to the state's prosperity. And the state was going to have an extremely hard time paying to restore the system to a state of good repair, let alone expand or improve it. With vital help from the MTA and the state's Department of Transportation, I set out to explain the issue to a wider audience.

Part of the state's transportation infrastructure is under the jurisdiction of the MTA; part belongs to the Department of Transportation. In both cases, the principles are the same: operating expenses and maintenance of these systems, including normal replacement, should be paid for out of recurring revenues. Capital improvements, as laid out in multiyear capital plans, should be paid for out of dedicated funds or long-term borrowing. In both parts of the state transportation system, I found that the operation of these principles had been seriously distorted by a chronic lack of funds.

For example, the MTA was seriously short of money to fund its capital plans. Its decisions about allocating the funds it did have were distorted by its relationship with the federal government. Some MTA projects were heavily dependent on federal matching funds and grants. If the MTA failed to fulfill its own funding of these projects, Washington would demand repayment of its money in prohibitively large amounts. So the projects dependent on federal funding continued to get MTA money, while the MTA's core program of normal replacement was in danger of not being adequately funded, and its ability to maintain a state of good repair was placed in jeopardy.

The state itself was also seriously short of money to fund its capital plans, and it had mixed its recurring revenues, debt, and dedicated funds in byzantine ways that made it unable to fulfill its current and future obligations. The state was increasingly using state-supported debt to pay for maintenance expenses that should have been funded by recurring revenues. At the same time, the state's highway and bridge trust fund, which was meant to fund capital projects out of dedicated revenues from fuel taxes and automobile fees, was so depleted that it had to draw on the state's general operating funds to pay for these capital projects. More than that, both the state and the MTA had restructured their transportation infrastructure debt, in operations fittingly called "scoop and toss," to produce short-term savings at the cost of incurring more debt in the long run.

I recommended that the state begin prioritizing its transportation projects more rigorously and facing its need for more recurring revenues, raised through devices like special tolls and taxing districts. I only hoped that state policy makers would eventually listen.

BUT ANY INTEREST people may have had in the staggering growth of Medicaid, the deterioration of the state's transportation infrastructure, or the state's budget gaps in general was swamped by their fascination with the scandals engulfing the Paterson administration. The scandals reflected not just the governor's weaknesses but also a state political system that had lost its ethical gyroscope. It oscillated between insensitivity to major offenses and hot pursuit of minor or imagined ones.

Though I did not know it at the time, the complications began just a month after I was sworn in as lieutenant governor. At the end of October 2009, New York City police were called to the apartment of an aide to Governor Paterson, David Johnson, who had begun working for Paterson as an intern and chauffeur and was now one of his closest advisers. The complaint was that Johnson had assaulted his girlfriend. After the visit by the city police, who had jurisdiction over the case, the state police and other Paterson aides contacted the girlfriend repeatedly. In early February, a Paterson aide persuaded the woman to call Paterson, who later said he did not talk about the assault case but merely asked about her well-being and offered his help. The next day, the woman failed to attend a hearing on her case, and it was dropped.

A week later, the *New York Times* began a series of stories on Paterson and the assault case. Paterson denounced the *Times* and on February 20, 2010, began his campaign for election as governor in his own right in November. The *Times* later reported on the involvement of the state police in the Johnson assault case. Paterson asked Andrew Cuomo, as the state's attorney general, to investigate. But less than a week after launching his election campaign, Paterson ended it, citing the "accumulation of obstacles that has obfuscated me from bringing my message to the public." One of New York's US senators, Kirsten Gillebrand, called on Paterson to resign.

For about a week there was real speculation that the governor would in fact resign. I started getting a lot more attention. Some friends wrote memos recommending the actions I should take during my first few days as governor. One of them drafted a speech I could make on the occasion of the transition. Assembly Speaker Sheldon Silver suggested that I have coffee with Attorney General Cuomo, with whom I had not spoken since assuming the lieutenant governorship. Cuomo asked, if I became governor, whom I would appoint as my lieutenant governor. I assured him that as he was clearly going to be the next governor, I wouldn't make any appointment without consulting him.

There was more to come. Back in October, Paterson had accepted free tickets from the New York Yankees to the opening game of the World Series. The New York Public Interest Research Group filed a complaint with the state's Commission on Public Integrity, which began investigating. On March 3, the commission stated Paterson had lied under oath in maintaining that he had intended to pay for the tickets.

Attorney General Andrew Cuomo was by then the clear front-runner for the 2010 Democratic nomination for governor. He recused himself from the investigations of the assault case and the Yankee tickets, saying he wished to "avoid any possible appearance of any political interest or conflict whatsoever." Instead, he appointed the former chief judge of New York, Judith Kaye, to investigate the charges. At the end of July, Kaye said Paterson had shown a "remarkable lack of judgment" in the Johnson assault case but "violated no criminal laws." A month later, she reported that in the Yankee tickets case, Paterson gave "inaccurate and misleading testimony" that "warrants consideration of possible criminal charges." In December 2010, with less than a month to go in Paterson's term, the Commission on Public Integrity found it "reasonable to infer that the Governor lied" when he said he had intended to pay for the Yankee tickets. Paterson was fined $62,125.

These things were not, strictly speaking, my problem. But in New York City the lieutenant governor's offices share a suite with the offices of the state police, and we were connected by a stairway to the governor's office on the floor above. There was no ignoring the drumbeat of resignations by high state officials: the state police superintendent, the first deputy superintendent, the governor's deputy secretary for public safety, the director of communications.

It was around this time that Andrew Cuomo, now viewed as the inevitable victor in the 2010 gubernatorial election, began to make his presence felt within the Paterson administration. It was nothing formal. But Paterson, after the string of scandals that beset his administration, never recovered his authority; people on Paterson's staff, as well as senior civil servants, became increasingly responsive to public and private statements made by the governor-in-waiting. It was clear to most observers that Paterson's chief of staff, Larry Schwartz, was already taking direction from the attorney general. Cuomo had the good taste not to try to preempt Governor Paterson's authority explicitly, but everyone inside the apparatus had a clear sense that the transition of power was well on its way.

❧

MUCH OF THIS came later. But as early as the fall of 2009, there was a pervasive tension in the upper reaches of state government, the result of the clash between the parochial self-protectiveness of a system to which outsiders had not paid attention for years and the increasingly peremptory demands for disclosure; some of them came from the press and others embodied in the state's burgeoning system of ethics laws, ethics rules, and ethics enforcers. There probably weren't many senior state officials who didn't keep at least one eye on the need to cover themselves.

Governor Paterson had asked me to make independent recommendations about the state budget. To do that, I had to learn more about the state budget than the Budget Division had the time to teach me. I also had to be able to take a more comprehensive view than the one that day-to-day budget crises forced on the people inside government. There wasn't a lot of money available for this purpose, and even if the money had been there, no one would have had any incentive to turn it over to a lieutenant governor with no apparent power base. I would have to raise my own funds.

With those funds, I launched a study of the state budget with a view to recommending a system that would better guarantee that the state's expenditures were matched by its recurring revenues. The Rockefeller Institute of Government, part of the State University of New York, was our administrative home. New York foundations with differing missions and political views, including the Rockefeller Foundation, the IBM Foundation, the Revson Foundation, the Achelis and Bodman Foundations, and the New York Community Trust, agreed to contribute the funds to hire budget experts like Carol O'Cleireacain, former budget director of New York City and deputy treasurer of New Jersey, and Donald Boyd, senior fellow of the Rockefeller Institute, who had the knowledge to analyze the state's fiscal situation in the comprehensive manner we needed. This was, I thought, an exemplary instance of a public-private partnership in pursuit of the public interest.

But one day a story about our project appeared in the *Daily News*, and it was not a story of a public-private partnership in pursuit of the public interest. Instead, it was a story of corruption. Private foundations, the item stated, were contributing money to support a project that was going to influence decisions that by rights should be reserved solely to the people of New York, acting through their duly elected and appointed representatives. The paranoid nature of the logic did not make it any less disturbing. I explained the project to the editorial page editors of the *Daily News* and said that the contributing foundations had no control over its conduct or conclusions. The editors responded with an editorial that rejected the premise of the news story and endorsed the project. I thought the controversy was over.

But answering the story on the merits was one thing; dealing with its effect on the governor's staff was quite another. I was told that we had to ask for an opinion from the New York State Commission on Public Integrity.

There began an exchange of letters that only an underemployed lawyer could have found illuminating. The commission opined that under state ethics laws I was not allowed to raise money from foundations for our budget project. This was bizarre: as the chief lawyer for the State University of New York pointed out in his answer to the commission, I was going to be doing exactly what the presidents of all the colleges and universities in the state university system did every day, which was to raise nonstate money to support their projects and institutions.

The commission retreated, but not fully, noting that when state university presidents raise nonstate money, they did so under state university resolutions that permitted them to do so. Therefore, something like an executive order allowing me to do the same thing, "while perhaps not required by law, would serve the interests of all concerned because doing so would minimize the risk of a conflict or the appearance of a conflict of interest." In other words, the governor's having asked me to study the budget and make recommendations about it was not enough.

So we obtained an official statement from the governor saying that, yes, he did want me to study the budget and make recommendations about it and, yes, it was all right to raise the money needed to do so. We continued our fund-raising efforts.

As we proceeded with our project, this was the atmosphere that served as our background: nervous, legalistic, unable to distinguish between corruption and cooperation, fatally distracted from the real problems facing the state. There was not much we could do about this. But we could try to understand the state budget in all its complexities, determine whether the state's current budget practices and politics were sustainable, and bring our findings into the line of sight of nonspecialists. We thought we might be able to get some of Albany's attention.

9

The Great Shell Game:
Facing the New York State Budget

GOVERNOR PATERSON SAID HE wanted me to make recommendations about the teetering state budget, so I set about to do
just that. This is the story of what I found, what I recommended, and
what happened to the recommendations. The story does have some
politics and human drama in it, but it is—there's no getting around
it—a story about a budget; and any reader who is being asked to
wade through a story about the New York State budget deserves to
be told why the trip is necessary.

People generally know that underlying much of what they want
to accomplish in their personal or family lives is the reality of a budget. The best things in life may be free, but for everything else we
need financial resources. If we spend more than we take in, we won't
have those resources after a while. Most of us aren't happy about this
fact, but we cope.

People also cope with other bedrock financial facts. Some necessities, like a home, cost too much to be paid for out of day-to-day
income. Not accidentally, these costly items are often things we will
enjoy for years. So people spread the cost of these items by borrowing to pay for them and repaying the debt over time, sometimes a
very long time.

Another bedrock fact is that no one can reliably predict the future. No matter how intelligent your budget is, there will be events, good and bad, that go down contrary to expectations. You may require surgery or lose a job. You may, even less reliably, get a windfall in the form of a lucky bet on the stock market, an inheritance, or a winning lottery ticket. Two kinds of people react in two different ways to these uncertainties. Some try to anticipate the unfortunate events by laying aside a reserve of funds. Others deal with emergencies by still more borrowing.

Despite all the attempts at obfuscation, these principles also apply to state governments. As for state expenditures, these are determined by the public obligations the state has undertaken. Most of those obligations have become predictable over time. Some, like rent, contracts, and debt service, have been fixed by past public decisions. Some, like Medicaid, are partly fixed by federal statutory requirements. Unless there have been dramatic reversals in the economy, the changes in these obligations will be at the margins.

As for state revenues, the states' main underlying revenue sources are the fees they charge for services and the taxes they enact, along with grants from the federal government, which come from the same kinds of fees and taxes. States, like individuals, estimate their revenues for the coming year; some states are better than others at this exercise. States also borrow by issuing debt securities in the public markets in two ways: short-term, to close the gaps within a budget year between the times when payments come due and the times when revenues come in; and long-term, to fund capital expenditures for public goods, like roads and bridges, which will be enjoyed by successive generations. Some states lay aside reserves for bad times. Others deal with bad times by borrowing from the future in numerous and extremely inventive ways.

Almost invariably, making the budget is the most important job that state politicians do. These individuals represent a complicated array of competing constituencies, values, and interests. State budgets reflect those complications, beginning with the routine request by the

state's budget department that state agencies submit their budget requests, and ending with intense, sometimes frenzied last-minute lobbying and negotiation. This is, in concrete terms, democracy at work.

ઌ

MOST STATES HAVE fiscal years that begin on July 1. New York is
different; its fiscal year begins early, on April 1. This means budgeting has to begin in the fall. By the time I was definitively sworn
in as lieutenant governor in the fall of 2009, budgeting for New
York's 2010 fiscal year was well under way, and everyone knew the
numbers were alarming. In October the Budget Division released its
regular six-month review of the state's $135 billion budget for the
current year and the projections for following years, or "out-years."
The estimates—significantly worse than at the time of the original
budget—were for a $3 billion deficit for the remainder of the cur-
rent fiscal year, more than $10 billion for the following year, and still
larger deficits thereafter. The rates of increase in the state's Medicaid
expenditures and pension costs were far outstripping even the most
optimistic projections of the state's future revenues. And the amount
of state-related debt had climbed to $63 billion.

Governor Paterson was increasingly and appropriately worried.
He and I talked several times about how to address the widening gap.
Again he asked that I make recommendations—about not just short-
term fixes for the immediate problem but systematic steps we could
take to get control of the budget for the long term. He had given
me a clear mandate, I thought, for the remaining months of my job.

ઌ

GETTING TO KNOW the state budget meant, first and foremost, getting
to know the officials in the New York State Division of the Budget,
which, like budget departments in most states, sits at the heart of state
government. The Budget Division was one place where professional
standards and talent had not declined since the time when I first
knew it. The people I met there in 2009 were just as capable and just

as serious about their responsibility to protect the public treasury as their predecessors in the 1970s and 1980s. Indeed, the 2009 budget required even more intellectual bandwidth to master, given its vastly expanded size and its countless assumptions about things from the rate of growth in tax revenues and federal aid to future health-care costs, local needs, and infrastructure requirements.

But I couldn't understand the state budget through the Budget Division alone; there were many other federal and state institutions whose economic projections for the state bore on the Budget Division's calculations. These players included business organizations, labor unions, and civic groups. I talked to what seemed like all of them—and with the budget director of the City of New York, the Federal Reserve Bank of New York, and staffs of the state's large public authorities, including the Port Authority, the Thruway Authority, and the MTA. Then there was the state legislature, whose staffers had their own extensive experience in budget matters, and the Office of the State Comptroller, which was sounding some of the most vigorous alarms about the budget crisis.

There were differences of opinion. Some of them were politically inspired: as Richard Neustadt famously put it, where you stand depends on where you sit. But there were also substantial intellectual disagreements about the statistics, calculations, and trends that would determine what the future held. During these early stages of inquiry, almost everyone readily provided help when I asked. The resistance would come only later.

◌

ONE OF MY first questions was about a basic issue of causation: to what extent was the state's widening budget gap just a reflection of hard times? Every economic downturn increases state deficits, because tax revenues decline and demands on state social services simultaneously increase. The country had experienced one of those downturns beginning in late 2007 and accelerating in late 2008. Were we going to pull out of it in the way we had pulled out of previous downturns? In other words, was our problem merely cyclical?

There were certainly people making that argument, but it didn't take long for me to discover that the state's current budget troubles had been building for some twenty years. During those years, the state's recurring revenues—the revenues it could expect year-in and year-out—had rarely matched its recurring expenditures. In other words, the budget problem wasn't just cyclical; it was structural. In 2009, responding to the 2008 downturn, the federal government had pumped stimulus funds into state budgets, but these were temporary infusions, not meant to address, and not capable of addressing, the longer-term structural gaps.

These structural gaps had their origins in some uncomfortable facts about New York's economic position and prospects. New York still regards itself as the Empire State. When the rest of the country thinks of New York, it often pictures the spectacle of wealth that is Manhattan; and it is true that high incomes in New York City produce a high per capita income in the state as a whole. But this picture masks the facts of New York's relative decline. In 1950 New York held 10 percent of the country's population; now the figure is barely 6 percent. In the decade before the Great Recession, New York ranked just forty-first in state population growth and became the state with the country's highest rate of out-migration: A million-and-a-half New Yorkers left for other states. But New York had never really adjusted to these realities. Thus, in the previous ten years, state spending had increased 20 percent faster than state revenues.

This conclusion about the structural causes of New York's budget problems raised an even more fundamental question. New York's constitution and statutes, like those of almost all other states, required that the governor propose, and the legislature enact, a balanced budget. Unless the entire state government was engaged in a massive violation of law, how could the state keep running its deficits in the face of these legislative provisions?

When I asked this question, I started to learn just how skilled the budgeteers in the state's executive and legislative branches had become in evading the balanced-budget requirement in order to fulfill what they saw as their public responsibilities. In the same way that honorable people in the last generation had created New York City's 1975 fiscal crisis by trying to avoid unpleasant new taxes and unpopular cuts in public services, the same sorts of people in the present generation were doing the same things on the state level, with the same good motives and the same hope that they could defer tough decisions until future economic growth made the decisions unnecessary.

⸙

BUT THIS TIME around, the devices used to mask the state budget deficit and kick its problems down the road were far more numerous and sophisticated. The devices took advantage of some peculiar features of New York budgeting and state budgeting in general. While New York law required the governor to propose a balanced budget and the legislature to pass a balanced budget, it did not require the state to end the year with a balanced budget. In fact, New York courts had placed severe limits on a governor's ability to reduce spending in midyear. In other words, the law required the state budget to be in balance on the day it was enacted, but not after that.

New York shared another peculiarity with many other states: it does not have a single budget. It has something called a "general fund," but fully a third of the state's expenditures are not made from the general fund. Instead, they are made from one of the five hundred special funds that the state maintains, dedicated to specific programs or funded by specific types of revenues, for example, an environmental fund supported by taxes that were enacted specifically for environmental purposes. State laws require the general fund to be balanced, at least on the day the budget is passed, but they do not require the same kind of balance in the special funds. It doesn't take a budget expert to see what is likely to happen under this system: it provides both incentives and opportunities to transfer revenues from the special funds to the general fund and transfer costs from the general fund to the special funds, all to keep the general fund balanced. And that is just what happens, although this manipulation is only one of the various kinds of manipulation that take place within the system.

Finally, among the notable features of state budgeting, there was the magic of cash. Businesses generally keep their books under a system of accrual accounting, which means that when they incur a cost—when they receive supplies, or when a consultant has finished a project for them—they have to record the cost in their books, whether or not they have actually paid the supplier or consultant or even whether or not the supplier or consultant has sent the bill. In other words, businesses can't pretend they don't owe the money by just not opening their mail.

But New York, like many other states, uses cash accounting. Its costs don't count as costs until the cash goes out the door. In order to keep going, at least in the short run, the state doesn't have to accept the discipline of real budget balance; all it has to do is make sure it has sufficient cash to pay the bills that it absolutely must pay at any given moment.

This system provides many perfectly legal opportunities to make sure the state has enough cash to pay today's bills. For example, in March 2010 the state delayed making billions of dollars of school aid and local assistance payments until after the new fiscal year, 2011, began on April 1. That way, it could claim that its 2010 budget was balanced. But this system wreaks havoc on tomorrow. It enables the state to avoid giving the public the bad news that expenditures may be growing faster than recurring revenues.

⁂

GRADUALLY, I PUT together the picture of the ways in which the state was exploiting these opportunities. The methods were limited chiefly by the scope of the budgeteers' imaginations. But they had enough features in common so that there was a budgetary term of art for these techniques: "one-shots," expressing the reality that you couldn't count on their occurring again.

The one-shots fell into a few major categories. One category was fund transfers: the Budget Division would simply transfer cash from special funds, which did not have to balance, into the general fund, which did, in order to create general fund balance. There came to be a term of art for these maneuvers, too: "fund sweeps." Over time, the Budget Division expanded its authority to make these sweeps. They became routine.

But some of the one-shots were of a much larger order; they involved selling assets and borrowing money, devices that were possible because "revenues" was not a defined term in the constitutional and statutory language that required balanced budgets.

One asset sale that became famous within the limited confines of people who cared about the state budget was a "sale-leaseback" transaction involving Attica, a state prison that in 1971 was the site of what still stands as the nation's deadliest prison riot. In 1991, twenty years after the riot, the state sold the prison to one of its own public authorities, the Urban Development Corporation (of which I was no longer chairman). The sales price was $200 million, an amount that was used to balance that year's budget. UDC raised the money to buy the prison by issuing bonds; the security for the bonds was the stream of rent payments that the state would make to UDC in return for UDC's leasing the prison back to the state. By the time I became lieutenant governor, the state had spent $400 million on rent payments to UDC, twice the amount it had received for selling the asset.

But dwarfing even these devices was the state's use of its public authorities to issue debt. New York State has more than $60 billion of debt outstanding, but only $3 billion of it is general obligation debt, that is, debt actually backed by the state's full faith and credit. The reason there is so little general obligation debt is that New York cannot issue this kind of debt unless the voters approve it at the time of a general election. The approval requirement was deliberately designed to make it difficult for the state to issue general obligation debt, and it has succeeded. The public does not like to vote to incur debt, even when it approves of the use to which the funds would be put.

But for reasons good and not so good, the state has not simply accepted this limit on the debt it can issue. Instead, it has turned to borrowing through its public authorities, such as UDC, the TBTA, and the state's Dormitory Authority. This kind of borrowing by public authorities is not secured by the state's full faith and credit. Instead, it is secured by a particular stream of state revenues: the state's personal income tax receipts, its sales tax receipts, payments it receives under leases or contracts or, occasionally, user charges like park entrance fees or bridge tolls.

The issuance of this kind of debt must be approved by the state legislature, but it is rarely opposed, because the purpose for which the debt is being issued is usually attractive. The legislature must also appropriate the revenues that pay the debt service each year. If the legislature fails to do so, there is technically nothing the bondholders can do about it. But the legislature has never failed to make the debt service appropriations. If it did not act, and the bonds went into default as a result, the state and its authorities would lose their future access to the credit markets.

In fact, the financial institutions that underwrite this type of debt have always insisted, successfully, that the state legislature's first appropriation on the first day of the state's new fiscal year be the appropriation that covers all the outstanding debt service obligations on state-related debt.

There was a major problem with this debt. Large amounts of it—close to $10 billion, the state comptroller estimated—were being used not for long-term capital projects but to pay the state's operating expenses and provide it with budget relief. In other words, issuance of this type of debt had turned into another massive mechanism for kicking the budget can down the road.

IN 1998 THE nation's four largest tobacco companies agreed to pay $200 billion to settle a suit by the attorneys general of forty-six states based on the Medicaid costs that the states had incurred because of smoking-related illnesses. Some of the money was to be paid out over a number of years under a formula generally based on the numbers of cigarettes sold. New York, like other states, decided not just to wait for the payments from the tobacco companies but to securitize the stream of payments—in other words, to get cash immediately by issuing bonds that offered the future payments as security. In 2004 New York got more than $4 billion from issuing tobacco bonds. It did not apply this one-time injection of funds against a one-time expense or even use the funds to finance reforms that promised long-term savings. It simply used the money to balance the budget.

In 2009, as lieutenant governor, I attended my first leaders' meeting with the governor and legislative leaders. One of the issues, of course, was the state's huge and growing budget deficit. There was a solution to the deficit, said one official: New York could simply refinance its tobacco bonds. His argument was that interest rates were lower now than they were when the bonds were first issued. Therefore, the state could issue a larger amount of debt while paying no more in debt service. Even more attractive, under the plan that was being proposed there would be no amortization for the first five years. True, at the end of the five years a huge balloon payment would be due—but that would be then, and this was now.

The idea was appalling; it kicked the can down the road in the most blatantly irresponsible way. Even more appalling was the fact that so many state politicians were ready to embrace it. But the politicians were not the primary movers in this proposed transaction. The biggest proponents were the banks.

I learned that the banks were full of ideas about how to turn the state's future revenues into current cash, with a hefty discount, of course. Some banks had designed sale-leaseback transactions, like the Attica transaction, that involved state office buildings, courthouses, and bridges. Some presented proposals for securitizing lottery revenues; others explained how the states could permit privatization of managed-care plans and take a percentage of the profits. It was a long list, but the proposals had a common theme: solve today's cash shortage by making future generations pay for the things we are unwilling to pay for now.

The banks making these proposals were not fly-by-night institutions; they were the biggest names in the business. I knew the heads of some of these banks. They were often the same people who, filled with rectitude, regularly criticized state politicians for their irresponsibility in the face of New York's budget crisis. I asked bankers whether they would make their own contribution to the state's fiscal discipline by agreeing not to underwrite debt that was going to be used to plug the state's operating deficits. They expressed zero interest in the idea. They were making significant money from underwriting these securities, just like the banks that underwrote New York City securities in the 1970s. Moreover, in the ten years immediately before I became lieutenant governor, individuals and political committees from the state's five largest banks had contributed millions of dollars to state electoral contests.

Their refusal to connect their behavior with its consequences for the state was intensely frustrating, and I shared my frustration with some of the professional staff at the New York Federal Reserve Bank. They took the problem seriously enough to invite the CEOs of these financial institutions to breakfast with me at the Fed. Everyone was gracious but unmoved. They made it clear that they would not give up kicking the can down the road because, they explained to me patiently, as if I had not been a banker myself, if they didn't underwrite this debt, there would always be some competitor who wouldn't hesitate to do so.

⁊⁊

THE WORST OF IT was the use of all these devices to plug holes in the state's operating budget. Even in the midst of the prosperity of the 1990s, the state comptroller's office had issued a report noting that the state was consistently projecting budget imbalances in future years. The report allowed that recessions sometimes make one-shots necessary: revenue collections decrease, while expenditures related to unemployment increase. But the responsible way of dealing with these inevitable economic cycles was to put money into rainy-day funds during flush years and use the cushion during bad ones. In contrast, the report said, "What becomes a structural deficit is the use of these one shots simply because the political system is not willing to tax its citizens to pay for the benefits the system wishes to confer."

Things had not changed by the time I became lieutenant governor a decade later. While I was in office, the comptroller issued another report titled, fittingly, *New York's Deficit Shuffle*. It laid out in great detail the fiscal manipulations through which the state had used more than $20 billion in one-shots over the previous decade to balance its budgets and had hidden the facts of how unbalanced the budgets really were, so that New Yorkers were allowed to avoid the hard decisions needed to align the state's spending with its available revenues.

The comptroller's report, like my infrastructure report, laid out the problems in the state's highway and bridge trust fund, $33 billion from fuel taxes supposedly dedicated to providing capital for critical construction and repair. Only a third of the money was actually used for these purposes. The rest was swept into the general fund to pay the operating expenses of the Department of Transportation and Motor Vehicles. In the same way, the state had an environmental protection fund, supported by real estate transfer taxes and established, so the public was told, to fund environmental capital programs. But around $800 million had been transferred out of the fund and into the general fund. A public authority, the Environmental Facilities Corporation, had issued bonds—that is, borrowed—to replenish the fund. Only half of the transferred amount had been replaced.

When the comptroller's last report was released, not a single major newspaper covered it; to judge by relative coverage, the press was more interested in the story of the state senator who had cut up his girlfriend with a broken bottle. I asked staffers in the Budget Division whether the facts in the comptroller's report were accurate. They said the facts were accurate but the tone was unfair, because it failed to take account of the staggering difficulty the state was encountering in meeting its obligations in the midst of the Great Recession.

The problem with that argument, I came to see, was that the state's problem was more fundamental than the Great Recession. The gaps between revenues and expenditures had been significant for years, no matter the pace of economic growth. Just as important, the country was not in the process of recovering from a regular recession. There was no evidence that our economy was roaring back to what it had been before the housing bubble burst. On the contrary, there was significant evidence that the bubble had reflected not fundamental strengths in the US economy but, rather, cheap and poorly regulated credit. The world had changed; American economic dominance might never again be what it once was. All the more reason for the state not to keep relying on the fiction that its budgeting devices were just necessary ways to cope with the temporary exigencies of a recession.

ℐℓ

BUT THERE WAS every indication that the state intended to continue doing just that. When I saw the budget that was being prepared for the state's 2011 fiscal year, beginning April 1, I noticed an item called "pension smoothing." It was going to save the state $600 million. I asked the Budget Division about pension smoothing. The staff gave me the draft bill that was going to be submitted to the legislature along with the governor's budget. New York State and the cities that participate in the state's pension system are required to make minimum contributions to the system each year, in amounts that the actuaries determine. What the bill did was to allow the state and the participating cities to make their contributions to the pension fund not in cash but with ten-year promissory notes.

This was shocking. Just as shocking was that the state's public employee unions, whose members were going to be put at risk by this weakening of the pension system, were supporting the bill, so that the state would not have to enter the $600 million on the expenditure side of the budget and face more pressure for layoffs or new taxes.

I challenged people—in the Budget Division, the Comptroller's Office, the labor movement—to explain how this was justified. I never got a good answer, but the practice continues to this day. In fact, in 2013 Governor Cuomo proposed and the legislature passed a substantial extension of the pension borrowing scheme. As a result, more than two billion dollars of the assets of the New York State Employee Retirement System now consists of promissory notes, instead of the cash that governments should have been contributing to fund the system.

There was a series of these facts staring the state in the face. New York now has more than $60 billion in unfunded obligations to its retirees—OPEB, or "other post-employment benefits," mainly health-care coverage that the state pays to retirees until they are eligible for Medicare. This liability is growing as people live longer and health-care costs rise. New York owes $3 billion to the federal unemployment insurance fund, which lent the state money to pay unemployment benefits during the downturn. I pored over numbers and tried to talk to everyone in Albany who I thought was knowledgeable about budgets and likely to be forthcoming. Nothing I learned contradicted my growing sense that the state was on a very dangerous path. I asked the state's old-time budget hands how all of this could possibly be sustainable. They said it wasn't.

I wrote op-ed pieces and gave speeches, saying that New York was behaving like a farmer who eats his seed corn. When good farmers harvest a corn crop, the first thing they do, before consuming any of it, is to put aside enough to provide for the next year's planting. They know how foolish it is to gamble with this reserve. A sensible budget process would have restrained the state's average spending growth so that it could build reserves during boom years in anticipation of bad ones. But we had convinced ourselves that we did not need this kind of prudence.

People called me an alarmist, a preacher of the apocalypse. The press gave my concerns and predictions fair coverage, but none of the other major players in state politics, including the unions and the financial services industry, was interested in changing course. Even the Republicans were silent; they knew that no matter how irresponsible the current practices were, they had engaged in the same practices when they were in power. After previous recessions, economic growth had saved us. It was convenient for Albany to pretend that in the future, as in the past, "the dog would talk." Certainly all the political pressures encouraged that pretending.

∂∂

THE CONUNDRUM WAS this: most state elected officials don't go into politics to amass unbridled personal power. They are after a more complex kind of power that combines local influence, the feeling of being at the center of events, and the ability to work the levers of government to get things done. Those tasks usually involve benefits that cost the taxpayers money. Elected state officials do not expect to have their fingers on the nuclear button, but they do expect to be able to deliver benefits to their constituents.

This is a good thing; it is the definition of democratic responsiveness. But consider what happens when these politicians can no longer deliver the benefits, because the discretionary pot is no longer growing but shrinking. In this case, elected officials must allocate not benefits but pain. In some states, this situation does not produce shock; these are the states in which the dominant political culture values austerity and fiscal rectitude. But where these values are not dominant—which in New York they certainly are not—the political system struggles like a powerful fish on a line to avoid prudent, responsible actions that show concern for the future as well as the present.

To generate the political energy to change this pattern, you need a dramatic crisis, or at the least the sense of a crisis. The conundrum for me was that New York's political system was skillfully engineered to keep the crisis from occurring, even as the underlying problems grew worse.

As I came to these realizations, my own budget experts and I were getting closer to being ready to make the budget recommendations that Paterson had asked for. By now I knew that I couldn't just recommend a set of numbers; I had to figure out a way to reform the budget process itself. The new process had to be rigorous enough to counteract the massive political pressures that for years had prevented people from facing the decisions that had to be made. But it had to do this job without taking dispositive power away from the people whom the state's voters had elected—in other words, without abrogating democratic principles. It was going to be a real trick to pull off.

♫

ON MARCH 10, I reported to Governor Paterson on my recommendations for reforming the state's budget process. The report began by explaining that while the recession had tipped New York into budget crisis, the budget practices that had created the crisis had been maintained for at least twenty years. The state's structural budget gap, the gap that would remain even if economic times improved, was around $13 billion. New York had been able to avoid the consequences of the gap because of its cash budgeting and the manipulations that cash budgeting permitted, but increasing pressures on state spending— from aging infrastructure, the costs of existing labor contracts, rising pension and retiree health benefit costs, and increasing Medicaid costs—meant that the state would not be able to avoid the consequences indefinitely.

The state needed to link the annual budget process to a multiyear financial plan. The state's structural budget gap was so big that there was no way to close it in a single year without confiscatory levels of taxation or devastating cuts to essential services. But the state could plan to achieve structural balance within five years.

The first step was a change that might seem esoteric but was crucial: a change in the New York State fiscal year. With New York's fiscal year beginning on April 1, a new governor has no real time for consideration before the budget has to be finalized and presented to the legislature. It also means that the budget has to be crafted before tax returns are filed in April, so that the state does not have a clear picture of the previous year's revenues.

In addition to starting the fiscal year on July 1, the plan proposed that along with the budget, the governor would submit a five-year plan to the legislature. It would state its economic assumptions, project the state's recurring revenues and expenditures under those assumptions, identify the size of the gaps that existed, and lay out policy options for closing those gaps. The plan would not forbid one-shots, but they would be allowed only to meet temporary costs and only as part of the plan to bring the budget into balance within five years on the basis of recurring revenues. The requirement for balance would apply not just to the general fund but also to all state spending that was not federally funded. And "balance" would mean balance not on a cash basis but on the basis of Generally Accepted Accounting Principles—GAAP—as applied to governments, which would require the state to recognize revenues when they were actually earned and recognize expenditures when the liability for these expenditures was incurred.

GAAP is not a budget panacea; no budget system is immune to manipulation. But it is no accident that GAAP has become the standard for accurate financial auditing for governments as well as businesses. In 1975 the state required New York City to move to GAAP for budgeting purposes. The city achieved budget balance under GAAP within three years; and in the thirty years since then, the credibility of the city's budget balance has not been questioned. The state's doing the same, I said, would vastly improve the quality of financial data on which state budget decisions are based and would without a doubt enhance the state's creditworthiness. If moving to GAAP was within the capabilities of New York City almost forty years ago, it was certainly within the capabilities of the state's very sophisticated modern-day Division of the Budget, which already produces an audited financial statement each year in accordance with GAAP.

It was true that moving to GAAP would deprive the state of some of the ability it had under its current cash accounting system to put off paying its obligations. Therefore, when there were mismatches in timing between the payments the state received and the payments it had to make, the state would need to place more reliance on its reserves. I recommended that the state build, over time, reserves equal to at least 10 percent of its annual expenditures.

Just as important as recommending a new budgeting system was to figure out a way to ensure that the budget process would produce results that complied with the financial plan—and to do so without taking ultimate decision-making power away from elected officials. I recommended that the financial plan be updated each quarter and that each quarterly update, along with any actions the governor planned to take in order to close the structural gaps that the plan identified, go to an independent review board appointed by the governor, the legislature, and the state comptroller.

This would not be a control board; it would have no power to do anything except make findings. If the board found a current financial plan inadequate, it would inform the governor and the legislature— and, of course, the public. If the governor and the legislature did not agree on actions to close the gaps, the governor would have authority to make across-the-board spending cuts.

Thus, although the review board could not force the state to balance its budget, it could make elected officials face up to the need to do so and could provide cover if they had to cast unpopular votes. The Congressional Budget Office does this job at the federal level and, it is generally agreed, has strengthened the capacity of elected officials in Congress to govern responsibly. Other democracies are adopting similar mechanisms: Canada, Sweden, the United Kingdom, Chile, and Ireland have all adopted some version of an independent fiscal board to monitor government fiscal policies. Multiyear GAAP budgeting and an independent review mechanism have become the indicators that a political community has decided to impose budget discipline on itself, and it seemed to me time for New York to make that decision.

But the realities of New York's budget and political animosities also had to be given their due. Because the budget gap that had to be closed was so big, I recommended allowing the state to borrow a limited amount of money to close the current-year budget gap—if the borrowing was part of an overall plan projected to achieve structural budget balance within five years. And, to reconcile the state legislature to the new authority that the plan gave the governor to reduce spending during the year, I recommended a truce in what had become a bitter, long-running dispute between the executive and legislative branches about the power of the two branches in the budget process.

The budget bills that the New York governor submits to the state legislature are treated differently from other bills. The legislature has very little ability to amend the governor's budget bills; generally, it can just vote them up or down. The legislature has complained that the governor uses this power to insert provisions into the budget bills that really belong in regular legislation, which is subject to the regular legislative amendment process. So far, the courts have sided with the governor. I recommended an agreement between the two branches: in return for being given authority to make midyear spending cuts, the governor would agree not to insert language into his budget bills that was more than incidentally legislative. If language appearing in these bills was more than incidentally legislative, the state legislature could strike it.

The plan was a series of compromises, but it was far-reaching enough to do the job and workable enough for politics. Or so I thought.

જ્ઞ

WHEN I SUBMITTED my recommendations to the governor in early March, he and the legislature were at their usual impasse in budget discussions, with the usual deficit looming and the usual prospect that a budget would not be passed in time for the beginning of the fiscal year on April 1. I briefed the governor and his chief of staff, Larry Schwartz. They had no particular reaction. At first, this did not trouble me. Hugh Carey, after all, had often waited to take a position on an issue until he saw the reactions of other players, in and out of government. There was no reason Paterson and Schwartz should not do the same.

While I was waiting, I briefed the press, which provided generous coverage. The plan received nearly unanimous praise from major newspapers around the state. I also briefed the state legislature in groups—Assembly Democrats, Assembly Republicans, Senate Democrats, Senate Republicans. Here I had a surprise. There were a lot of questions from all these groups; but it was the Assembly Democrats, the politicians who were regularly excoriated by politicians on the right for their alleged budget heedlessness, who were the most interested. In fact, the speaker's unusually able budget staff actually drafted legislation aimed at putting my recommendations into concrete form. A process began that looked very much like real negotiations over a real bill.

Largely out of my view, however, other developments were taking place. The Albany correspondent for the Associated Press told me he had been advised that Attorney General Andrew Cuomo opposed my recommendations. I asked what reasons the attorney general had given for his opposition. The correspondent said no reasons were given, but he asked me to comment anyway. There was nothing I could say except to wonder what the objections were and why the attorney general didn't wish to share them with me or anyone else.

I could tell that Larry Schwartz did not support the plan. He, too, gave no reasons, but, as Paterson's chief of staff, he headed the meetings of top administration officials on the budget. Soon I began hearing about objections from other parts of the administration. People on the governor's staff mistrusted the motives of the Assembly's legislative drafters; the governor's staffers were saying that the Assembly's support of the plan was a Trojan horse, not really meant to promote budget balance but just a trick to strip the governor of his budget powers. I was reminded that I was a member of the executive branch; I was told that my discussing the plan with legislators was "outrageous" behavior. The Budget Division proposed its own version of a structural balance bill; in this one, the governor got more powers and the legislature got nothing. It was meant to be dead on arrival. Finally, the governor's office publicly announced its opposition to my plan on grounds that it would allow the state to incur debt. The state, after twenty years of running its budget into the ground, had donned the mantle of a budget hawk, at least retroactively.

JP

WITHOUT THE GOVERNOR'S strong support, my plan never had a chance. The unions, the banks, and the business community were not going to champion it. They were either content with the system as it was working or resigned to it and certain that it would never change. Right-wing ideologues objected to the plan on grounds that allowing any kind of borrowing, even to make the five-year plan work, was impermissible.

The most compelling conclusion I drew from my attempt, and the saddest, was that I had failed to energize the public enough to make the political system change its behavior.

10

One Country:
Recognizing the State Budget Crisis

I HAD NO INTENTION OF LETTING my disappointment keep me from trying to understand why there was so much resistance to my budget plan. The plan would have imposed immediate pain on a whole population of state politicians and officials who would have had to contemplate raising taxes or cutting services, precisely the actions they wanted to avoid. Some of them privately told me that the recommendations for change made rational sense but the incentives to stick with the old coping mechanisms were overwhelming. Imposing burdens on the generations of tomorrow was no impediment to reelection today.

But perhaps something still larger was at work. People in other states who heard about what I was doing had begun to contact me and the staff of my New York budget project. They, too, were worried about the unsustainability of their states' budget practices; they, too, were raising alarms and getting no political response. I realized that New York might not be fundamentally different from other states in the fiscal problems it was facing and the political obstacles to confronting them.

Almost all US states are required by their constitutions or laws to balance their budgets, so it was no surprise to me that they all did so, at least according to their official documents. And, like New York, other states were facing vastly increased budget pressures because of the economic collapse of 2008; that, after all, was the reason why the stimulus in the American Recovery and Reinvestment Act of 2009 distributed hundreds of billions of dollars to state governments, mostly for Medicaid and education. But from talking to people in other states I was learning that underneath the headlines announcing the stimulus grants were long-term structural problems that two years of federal generosity had not managed to eliminate.

What I did not know was whether other states had structural problems on a scale like New York's before the downturn, based on cost increases like those in Medicaid and public employee pensions. I did not know whether other states had budgets that were as opaque as New York's, making it so easy to avoid necessary choices. I did not know whether they used cash budgeting to cope with their budget gaps the way New York did. I did not know whether they used all of New York's devices to bring their budgets into balance, like counting their borrowings and proceeds of asset sales as revenues. And I did not know whether some states were coping with their budget constraints and inertia better than New York, so that we could learn from their example.

Having the temperament I have, I took these understandings and questions as a call to the next job I had to do.

⌘

EVERY STATE HAS its own highly particular constitution and statutes, its own demographics and tax structure, and its own political culture. Therefore, if I wanted to understand something about the fiscal stability of US states in general, I would need a study on a scale that far exceeded anything I could possibly do by myself.

My term as lieutenant governor was up on December 31, 2010. Soon afterward, I organized an effort that I called the State Budget Crisis Task Force, a project of the Research Foundation of the City University of New York, to undertake the study. Just as I had done in developing a budget plan for New York, I raised money from private foundations, $2 million this time, to cover an eighteen-month study. Paul Volcker, a friend in this as in many other things and a man uniquely attuned to potential threats to the nation's fiscal and financial stability, agreed to be my cochair.

As board members I gathered friends and acquaintances from years of prior public life and other people who would add scope and weight to the enterprise. George Shultz, Nick Brady, and Joe Califano agreed to join. So did Phillip Clay, a city planning expert and the former chancellor of the Massachusetts Institute of Technology; Peter Goldmark, a former New York State budget director, and Marc Shaw, a former New York City budget director; and David Crane, a former financial adviser to the governor of California. We were lucky to be able to add budget experts Alice Rivlin and Richard Nathan, two of the country's preeminent students of federal-state relations, to our group.

The project's staff was led by Donald Boyd of the Rockefeller Institute. Among the staff, Carol O'Cleireacain was joined by Don Kummerfeld, New York City's budget director and financial adviser during its 1975 fiscal crisis, and Edward DeSeve, who oversaw implementation of the federal stimulus. With these budget experts, the task force had the analytic firepower it needed. Peter Kiernan, counsel to Governor Paterson, joined the staff, as did Suzanne Garment, my special counsel when I served as lieutenant governor.

By the time the project got under way in early 2011, the nation was supposed to be recovering from what was still thought of as the 2008 recession. But there was a growing skepticism about whether this had been an ordinary recession or a credit crisis or something still more fundamental. There was an even deeper skepticism about whether we were in a bona fide recovery. A steady drumbeat of press stories reported on states and cities running into fiscal problems, including the problem of grossly underfunded pension obligations. All the stories were troublesome, and some raised the prospect of actual insolvency and loss of access to credit markets. Despite the stimulus, state and local employees were being laid off in substantial numbers.

States were reducing their spending on higher education and public infrastructure. Some observers said these things were just a reflection of the slow pace of national recovery. Others feared they were harbingers of worse to come. In either case, the reality was serious enough to call for more information and understanding.

But we quickly found out that the hole in the country's knowledge about state budgets was wider and deeper than we had expected. To my amazement, the Federal Reserve Bank of New York, which had encouraged me to undertake the study, readily admitted that it did not have much of the data needed to understand the states' growing fiscal problems. The professionals at the Department of the Treasury were equally supportive—and equally frank about their lack of knowledge of what was happening in the states. The municipal bond markets, which extended credit to states and localities, showed signs of anxiety. But for various reasons, chief among them the fact that no state would willingly risk losing access to the credit markets by defaulting on its debt, the markets were not going to be an early indicator of state and local fiscal troubles.

In short, no national institution saw itself as responsible for assembling the data that would make it possible to analyze the states' fiscal situation overall and in detail. I talked to many officials in Washington around that time. They were almost happy not to know what they didn't know, lest they be responsible for doing something about it.

The genius and frustration of American federalism lies in the number of its parts: there was no way we could closely examine the budgets of all fifty US states. Therefore, we decided to report what we could about the fiscal situation of the states in general, and then focus in detail on a half-dozen states. We would study New York, California, Illinois, New Jersey, and Texas, all of which were suffering varying degrees of fiscal distress. We would also look at Virginia, which we thought was handling its fiscal pressures in a way that might provide a positive example.

☙

POLITICAL ELITES LIKE to deal with issues and ideas that are large and elevating, not small and messy. As a result, we go to some lengths to try to avoid the fact that when it comes to government decisions that directly affect the day-to-day lives of Americans, the center of the action is not Washington but the capitals of the fifty states.

The federal government has around 2.5 million civilian employees. State and local governments, in contrast, have close to nineteen million employees, even after the recent layoffs. American states have a degree of sovereignty that is in many respects comparable to the sovereignty of national governments in other parts of the world. In America, the states bear primary responsibility for public safety, education, health care, and the public infrastructure. True, in the years since the Great Depression, the federal government has appropriated increasing numbers of dollars to aid the states in doing these jobs. The increased federal contributions have created their own pressures on state budgets, but they have not changed how the basic responsibility in these areas lies with the states.

Because of the degree of state autonomy, differences in the states' demographics, history, and politics make for significant differences in state fiscal situations. States with more poor citizens face larger pressures to enact programs to benefit these citizens. States with strong public employee unions face greater pressure to enact generous public pensions and other benefits. In states where opinion is heavily influenced by cosmopolitan elites, political fashions among these elites will heavily influence public policy. In states with a history of fiscal discipline, politicians develop assumptions conducive to discipline and transmit them to other politicians.

These differences in political cultures and institutions make big differences in states' abilities to deal with their fiscal pressures. But we found that in recent years the pressures common to the states, especially the most populous states, have grown powerful enough to threaten to overwhelm the capacities of even those states whose political systems are competent and resilient. And states are reacting to these pressures by avoiding them, using every available device to kick the can down the road.

Forty years ago, after we emerged from the New York City financial crisis, we told each other, "Never again." I never thought I would once more see the same fiscal gimmicks being used for the same purpose, obscuring the gap between recurring expenditures and recurring revenues. But here they were, multiplied.

♃

THE BIGGEST WEIGHT on the expenditure side is Medicaid, which in most state budgets has replaced education as the largest single expenditure. When Medicaid was begun in 1965, it was just a minor appendage to the poverty program. Today, sixty million Americans are on Medicaid. Overall, states spend 25 percent of their budgets on the program. It is growing faster than the economy and faster than state tax revenues.

Because the formula for federal reimbursement of state Medicaid expenditures is based on a state's average income, it puts a disproportionate burden on not just New York but all states that have large numbers of rich people and poor people, compared to states that have larger numbers of middle-income people. The first kind of state, because it has more poor people, has greater Medicaid needs. But the two types of states may have the same average income and, therefore, get the same rate of federal reimbursement. For years, Pat Moynihan, as US senator from New York, tried to change this formula. But he finally bowed to the bedrock political fact that New York doesn't have any more US senators than Mississippi does. He used to say that you can blame New York's Medicaid problem on James Madison.

Medicaid not only has a huge impact on state budgets today but may have more of an impact tomorrow. If the Affordable Care Act is implemented as enacted, Medicaid will provide health-care coverage to many more Americans. The federal government will pick up most of the states' costs in enrolling them, but only for a limited time. If the country has committed itself to ensuring health-care coverage for all Americans, it is still politically uncertain how much of the cost of this commitment will ultimately be borne by Washington—and how much will fall on the states.

The second major expenditure weight comes from state obligations to their retired employees. State statutes uniformly require that pensions paid to state and local retirees be funded in advance, through dedicated pension funds. Actuaries review the assets of the pension funds, make assumptions about the interest these assets will earn and the future liabilities the funds have incurred as a result of government commitments, and determine the amount of contributions governments must make to ensure that there are enough assets to meet the liabilities.

Actuaries now estimate that state and local pension funds are cumulatively underfunded by $1 trillion. Economists, using more conservative assumptions about the interest that pension assets will earn, say the underfunding could amount to as much as $3 trillion. To compound the problem, some states don't make even the lower level of contributions that the actuaries require. Over the last five years, state and local governments have underpaid their legally required contributions by more than $50 billion, and some states do not even have laws requiring that the actuarially required contributions be made. In 2010 the federal Securities and Exchange Commission went so far as to issue a cease-and-desist order against the State of New Jersey for failing to disclose in its official borrowing documents the extent to which it had underfunded its pension system.

People generally assume that a state's pension promises to its retirees are contracts that bind the state no matter how much fiscal distress it may cause to fulfill them. But pension benefit guarantees vary by state; and as the burdens of these promises increase, so will the challenges to the strength of the guarantees.

Not guaranteed are the "other post-employment benefits," mainly health care, that state and local governments have promised to their retirees. Unlike pension benefits, retiree health benefits are not prefunded but paid out of current state and local funds. As people live longer and health-care costs rise, these obligations will increase; but it is only recently that states have been required to reflect the obligations on their audited financial statements. A reasonable estimate would place state liabilities for these costs at around another $1 trillion.

Compounding the problem is the truth of the adage that fiscal stress rolls downhill. Every day we see press stories about the federal government's efforts to cut its deficit. Different kinds of plans have been proposed, some by rabid partisans and others by independent groups of experts with sterling reputations. But all of them would hurt state budgets, because states receive about a third of their revenues, more than $650 billion, from the federal government. A 10 percent across-the-board cut in federal grants to states, for instance, would cost California and New York more than $6 billion each.

And if fiscal stress rolls downhill from the federal to the state level, it rolls farther downhill from state to local governments. Though the levels vary from state to state, around a third of local government expenditures nationwide come out of state budgets. When states have serious budget problems, they tend to reduce their subsidies to the local governments within their jurisdictions. When states respond to their fiscal problems by raising taxes, counterpressures usually arise to put a cap on property taxes; but property taxes are the chief source of revenue for local governments, because cities and counties can't raise other kinds of taxes without state approval.

The problem is compounded in the states that were hit hardest by the recent downturn. There, property values declined. The decline is now showing up in reduced assessments of property value. The reduced assessments produce reduced property tax receipts.

Meanwhile, the expenditure pressures on localities continue to grow. Education is second to Medicaid on the roster of expenditures in most states, but states have far more discretion to reduce their education expenditures. When states cut their education aid to localities, the stress is felt at the level of city and local school boards. Moreover, cities that maintain their own employee pension funds face the same problems as the states in administering the funds. And states impose mandates on local governments that prevent localities from reducing their expenditures and so add considerably to the costs of running cities, counties, towns, and villages.

Some states monitor the fiscal health of their local governments carefully; most do not. A few states retain the right to approve any borrowing that their localities do; most do not. The fiscal pressures on localities are beginning to show up in credit downgrades and resulting increases in the amounts that localities must pay to borrow money. The localities' fiscal troubles will ultimately find their way back to state budgets. When Speaker of the House of Representatives Tip O'Neill delivered his famous dictum that "all politics is local," this is not the dynamic that he had in mind.

And on the revenue side, we found that volatility and an eroding tax base frequently add to a state's troubles in balancing its budget. State sales taxes have become less reliable as a revenue source because Internet sales are increasing. National politicians have not been able to reach agreement on how these sales can be equitably taxed to benefit the states, so the sales often escape taxation entirely.

As a result, states without oil or mineral wealth must increasingly rely on state income taxes for their revenue. Because income taxes are progressive, this means that states increasingly depend for revenue on the incomes of their wealthier residents and the financial markets that support them. These revenues are volatile, varying with national business cycles.

When recessions hit and state tax revenues decline, while state entitlement spending on programs such as Medicaid and unemployment compensation increases, states usually do not have adequate reserves to cushion the cycle; they react by cutting their budgets. Thus, at a time when the federal government is trying to stimulate the economy through government spending, state budget cuts run counter to the federal efforts. Despite all the federal money that was disbursed to the states through the stimulus in 2009 through 2011, state spending declined during those years.

Within the states, meanwhile, governments rely on cuts, nonrecurring revenues, and cash budgeting devices that push costs into the future. They rely on next year's revenues to pay this year's bills. As a result, even when times improve, states will emerge from each downturn in a weakened, more fragile condition.

ℐℓ

DESPITE ALL THE efforts to kick the can down the road, it is not being kicked far enough to keep the consequences of the state budget crisis at bay. Despite all the debates about what the country does and does not have to spend, the nation's political health depends on its continued prosperity, and its continued prosperity depends on its infrastructure, animate and inanimate. Its citizens must continue to get the education needed to make its economy succeed in a competitive world, and its physical infrastructure of roads, bridges, mass transit, water, air, sewage treatment must continue to be capable of supporting this human activity.

During the 2011–2012 school year, a Rutgers University study found, spending by the states on preschool education fell by 10 percent, or more than $548 million. In higher education, three young people get their college degrees from a public college or university for every student that graduates from a private institution. Yet even in many state institutions, traditionally the low-cost route to advancement, tuition has risen dramatically, so that it has become measurably harder for a poor kid to get a college degree. The field of education is rife with debate about what does or does not work and what level of expenditure is or is not cost-effective. But there is no plausible model of the connection between education and national economic health that would justify this kind of disinvestment. It is the emerging result of the state budget crisis.

Similarly, there is no exact way to measure how much the country must invest in its physical infrastructure in order to support sustained economic success; because the depreciation of government's physical assets is not counted as an expense under government accounting rules, we can't reliably estimate what we should be spending each year. But cumulative studies and the burden of expert opinion strongly suggest that the underfunding in this area runs into trillions of dollars.

We do know that China spends a percentage of its GDP on infrastructure that is seven times higher than what the United States spends. The American Society of Civil Engineers estimates that over the next six years our economy will lose almost $900 billion in GDP because of deteriorated surface transportation conditions. One of the few public policy positions agreed upon by the US Chamber of Commerce and the AFL-CIO is that we have an urgent need to increase our infrastructure replacement dramatically. But in another emerging result of the state budget crisis, what everyone agrees must be done is not being done and seems increasingly less likely to be done.

Other parts of the world are imitating what we did in earlier times by investing in infrastructure and education. But America's population is getting older, our health-care costs continue to grow faster than the economy as a whole, and the resulting drain on public resources creates powerful pressures to disinvest in the things that create and sustain economic growth.

୪

THERE IS AN almost irresistible impulse to pretend that these problems are only cyclical. A front-page newspaper headline recently announced that the budget of the State of California, recently plagued by deficits, is now in surplus. This fact should not provide much comfort. State revenues have increased, and the reasons include a temporary tax hike and decisions by wealthy taxpayers to sell capital assets now in anticipation of higher capital gains rates in the future. But the surplus also reflects the dramatic underfunding of state pensions, increased borrowings, deferred payments to schools and local governments, and other components of a vast amount of debt that the state shows little inclination to address.

The reality is that this country has made large promises to a number of different populations. The promises we hear most about were made at the federal level, including Social Security, Medicare, and Medicaid. But equally important promises were made to state and local public employees. At the current levels of revenue that our political systems are willing to extract from citizens, we cannot afford the costs of fulfilling these promises and, at the same time, invest in factors needed to sustain economic growth. And in the competition between promises made in the past and commitments to the future, the former enjoy more legal protections than the latter.

The imbalance between past and future is even more acute because of what the modern federal system has become. The federal government has the primary obligation to provide many of the entitlements the country has promised—Social Security, Medicare, a large part of Medicaid—and is acutely aware of this obligation. In contrast, the states have the primary obligation to invest in the human and material infrastructure underlying our future.

It is true that many dollars now flow from Washington to state capitals. But for a number of reasons—perhaps most important, the decline in the influence of political organizations that spanned federal, state, and local governments—there is a frightening disconnect between the politics of the states and the politics of Washington. People who are elected to Congress have surprisingly little incentive to concern themselves with state budgets. They may get political benefits from bringing home federal grants or contracts, but their reelection prospects have nothing much to do with their states' overall fiscal health. As a result, federal policy proceeds in almost total disregard of its effects on the nation's states.

I recall talking to state officials who were anxious about their huge unfunded state pension commitments but comforted by their certainty that if a crisis finally happened, the federal government would bail them out. One governor remarked that in the end, "the feds will make sure the benefits are paid."

These state officials are, to put it mildly, misplacing their confidence. There is very little inclination in Washington to bail the states out of anything. Indeed, federal policy makers seem to think they can address the federal deficit or reform federal taxes without taking the effects on state budgets into account at all. I recently asked Erskine Bowles, one of the authors of the Bowles-Simpson Commission report on federal deficit reduction, if his commissioners had considered the effects of their recommendations on state governments. No, he said, they had not. I asked the same question of Representative Paul Ryan, author of the House Republicans' deficit reduction plan. He said the effects of the plan on state governments were not part of his considerations either.

When policy makers propose reducing the federal deficit by raising the Medicare eligibility age to sixty-seven, they do not account for the effect on states that have contracted to pay health-care benefits to their retired employees until the retirees are eligible for Medicare. When federal tax reformers talk about limiting deductions and exemptions, they do not take account of the effect on the ability of states to raise capital funds.

This limited perspective may seriously impair the ability of the states to invest for the future. These policy blinders greatly increase the chances that as federal policy makers pursue deficit reduction, they will get not federal fiscal integrity but states whose incapacities will impose still greater burdens on Washington in the long run. American federalism is headed for major trouble if the federal government continues to behave as if state governments were not its concern. We can't properly address the imbalance between past promises and future commitments unless we address the impact of federal decisions on the fiscal health and governing capacity of states and localities.

An even more fundamental need is for policy makers to recognize that the fiscal difficulties in states and localities are not just a series of individual crises but also a national problem that reflects a national history of promises made and obligations undertaken, often for the best of reasons, without the present resources to support them. The consequences of the problem, both the underfunding of the physical and educational infrastructure on which future generations depend and the burdens placed on those generations by cutting or deferring so many expenditures, is a serious national issue.

Detroit, Michigan, is in bankruptcy as this book goes to press. But all bankruptcy means is that a federal judge will allocate Detroit's inadequate resources between citizens who lent the city money in good faith and employees who worked for the city in good faith. No matter how Solomonic the allocation, it will not rebuild the city's tax base. Does Michigan have a responsibility in rebuilding this base? Does it matter that Detroit's bankruptcy has raised borrowing costs for governments throughout the state? Does the federal government have an obligation to help in the rebuilding? If so, how could it possibly afford to do the same for all the other states and localities in trouble?

The same questions apply to hundreds of states and localities. As I've noted, Philadelphia's school district had to borrow to open its schools for the year. Colorado has announced that adequately funding its pension system would cost $15,000 for every taxpayer in the state. New York's upstate cities are squeezed between state-imposed caps on the property tax, one of a city's few sources of revenue, and the state and federal mandates that govern the services these cities must provide. Even New York City, for all its fiscal advantages, has $100 billion in unfunded retiree health-care obligations.

After the crisis that threatened to decimate the US financial system, federal legislation established the Financial Stability Oversight Council, tasked with examining and trying to mitigate the systemic risks to our financial system as a whole that arise because of flaws in our large financial institutions. Yet there is no risk to our institutions that is more systemic than multiplying and spreading fiscal troubles of the nation's states and localities. The federal government—in the end, a president—must assume some responsibility for the issue, not by writing a check but by using the resources of the federal government to provide the discipline and incentives that will force state and local governments to address their own fiscal future.

This may sound like a tall order, but there is really no acceptable alternative. I was born in the year when Franklin Roosevelt became president and have lived through a time marked by some of the country's greatest public achievements. We emerged from the Great Depression. We won a world war. We overcame racial segregation. We survived the threat of nuclear Armageddon and saw the demise of the Soviet system that produced it. In comparison, the issues we face today are a piece of cake—if people will participate in the democratic political process. Politics remains the only way problems like these can be solved in a democracy, but making the political process work better tomorrow than it does today depends on the willingness of good men and women to give a part of their lives to participating in it.

Postscript

I KNOW THAT I AM WITHOUT A DOUBT one of the luckiest people on the face of the earth. I have a beautiful, loving wife, two spectacular sons, three stepdaughters, four grandsons, and nine step-grandchildren, all of whom I adore. In my business ventures, I've made enough money to provide comfort and economic security for the people I love. I have a rich intellectual life, which is a source of professional strength and great personal pleasure.

I have been labeled a builder, a banker, a lawyer, a politician, and a guy who can't make up his mind about what he wants to do when he grows up. This diversity of experiences, along with the many kinds of people it has brought into my life, has added immeasurably to the good I've been able to do and the fun I've had. There have been moments when I've had pangs of envy toward people who knew exactly what they wanted to do, pursued their goal consistently, and achieved great recognition of a single talent.

Many of my friends—artists, lawyers, teachers, businessmen—say they are jealous of the many different lives I've led; and when I'm asked whether, looking back, I would have made any fundamentally different decisions about my career, the answer is an unequivocal no. There has been so much serendipity in so many of my choices that there is no way of knowing how things might have turned out otherwise. What has been constant is the gratification of having been able to try to match my good fortune with contributions to the community—although New York has been so generous to five generations of Ravitches that there's no way I could ever have given as much as I got.

ACKNOWLEDGMENTS

MONG THE MANY PEOPLE whose help I needed in gathering and shaping the material for this book, I would especially like to thank the following: Peter Osnos, for encouraging me to write it in the first place; Steve Strasser, for giving me a good start; Richard Marek, for educating me about the process of writing a book; Robert Kimzey, for being an invaluable editor with an acute sense of how to strengthen the narrative; the production and marketing team at PublicAffairs, who skillfully took me through the many complexities of preparing for publication; and Angela Baggetta of GoldbergMcDuffie, whose expertise in publicity was essential in bringing this book to the attention of the readers we sought to reach.

Above all, I am grateful to Susie Garment, whose friendship over many years, wisdom, and writing skills enabled me to see this project to completion.

INDEX

Richard Ravitch has been chairman of the New York State Urban Development Corporation, chairman of HRH Construction Corporation, chairman of the Metropolitan Transportation Authority, chairman of the Bowery Savings Bank, lieutenant governor of the State of New York, and co-chair, with Paul Volcker, of the task force on the state budget crisis. He lives in New York City.

PublicAffairs is a publishing house founded in 1997. It is a tribute to the standards, values, and flair of three persons who have served as mentors to countless reporters, writers, editors, and book people of all kinds, including me.

I. F. STONE, proprietor of *I. F. Stone's Weekly*, combined a commitment to the First Amendment with entrepreneurial zeal and reporting skill and became one of the great independent journalists in American history. At the age of eighty, Izzy published *The Trial of Socrates*, which was a national bestseller. He wrote the book after he taught himself ancient Greek.

BENJAMIN C. BRADLEE was for nearly thirty years the charismatic editorial leader of *The Washington Post*. It was Ben who gave the *Post* the range and courage to pursue such historic issues as Watergate. He supported his reporters with a tenacity that made them fearless and it is no accident that so many became authors of influential, best-selling books.

ROBERT L. BERNSTEIN, the chief executive of Random House for more than a quarter century, guided one of the nation's premier publishing houses. Bob was personally responsible for many books of political dissent and argument that challenged tyranny around the globe. He is also the founder and longtime chair of Human Rights Watch, one of the most respected human rights organizations in the world.

·   ·   ·

For fifty years, the banner of Public Affairs Press was carried by its owner Morris B. Schnapper, who published Gandhi, Nasser, Toynbee, Truman, and about 1,500 other authors. In 1983, Schnapper was described by *The Washington Post* as "a redoubtable gadfly." His legacy will endure in the books to come.

Peter Osnos, *Founder and Editor-at-Large*